RSITY O

· THE ·
INFORMATION
PARADOX

REALIZING THE BUSINESS BENEFITS
OF INFORMATION TECHNOLOGY
REVISED EDITION

JOHN THORP
and Fujitsu Consulting's Center for
Strategic Leadership

Toronto • Montréal • Boston • Burr Ridge, IL • Dubuque, IA • Madison, WI • New York
San Francisco • St. Louis • Bangkok • Bogotá • Caracas • Kuala Lumpur • Lisbon • London
Madrid • Mexico City • Milan • New Delhi • Santiago • Seoul • Singapore • Sydney • Taipei

ISBN: 0-07-092698-0

1234567890 TRI 09876543
Printed and bound in Canada.

National Library of Canada Cataloguing in Publication

Thorp, John, 1944–
    The information paradox : realizing the business benefits of information technology / John Thorp. – Rev. ed.

Includes bibliographical references and index.
ISBN 0-07-092698-0

1. Information technology – Management. 2. Information technology – Cost effectiveness. I. Title.

HD30.2.T46 2003   658.4'038   C2003-900263-2

Publisher: **Julia Woods**
Editorial Co-ordinator: **Catherine Leek**
Production Co-ordinator: **Andrée Davis**
Electronic Page Composition: **Heidy Lawrance Associates**

Dilbert Cartoons: Reprinted by permission of HarperCollins Publishers, Inc.; Copyright © 1996 by United Features Syndicate; Text Excerpt as submitted from Dogbert's Top Secret Management Handbook by Scott Adams.

FOREWORD

This book is dedicated to helping you understand how information technology (IT) can help your business. Specifically, it is about getting more value from the large investments all organizations are making in information technology — about improving the odds of success in managing IT-enabled change. It is designed to help your organization reap the benefits of Pareto's 80-20 law and find the 20 percent of technology dollars that will generate 80 percent of the business results you are looking for. In the pages that follow, we:

- Expose business managers to the critical issues in managing information technology that have a bottom-line impact on them and their ability to manage
- Expose IT experts to the key business implications of managing information technology
- Provide all managers with tested perspectives, methods and techniques for bringing "information" and "technology" together into winning IT-enabled change programs that deliver value to their organizations.

To achieve these aims, we present the Benefits Realization Approach, designed specifically to give managers the tools they need to get results from the business applications of information technology and to manage risk/reward relationships more effectively when developing those applications.

The Benefits Realization Approach is the product of a lengthy development process that has intimately involved Fujitsu Consulting practitioners and clients. Some eleven years ago, we embarked on a project to define and package Fujitsu Consulting processes into a set of integrated methods we refer to as the Macroscope®. As an IT services firm, we looked at strategy, architecture, and software development itself — the core of our business. But we felt there was something missing. In discussions with business and IT executives, it became clear that the paradigm under which we all operated — if the project is managed properly, the benefits will be there — was fundamentally wrong. In the real world, benefits do not materialize unless you understand and proactively manage the process to achieve them. The fundamental question in today's turbulent business environment is how does an enterprise select the right business and technology investments, and then turn those investments into tangible results? From this question was born a new way to look at the situation, a unique approach — the Benefits Realization Approach.

This book is organized into four parts. In Part I, we describe the symptoms of the Information Paradox, the problems associated with it, and its causes, and introduce the Benefits Realization Approach. In Part II, we go on to describe the three fundamentals of our approach in detail. In Part III, we provide more detail on the three necessary conditions for effective implementation of the approach. In Part IV we pull it all together in terms of how you can start implementing the approach.

Our approach is not theoretically perfect, and we make no claim to possess the one true management doctrine. But benefits realization as described in this book has one advantage over most other business theories — it is client tested. In developing the Benefits Realization Approach, we have been blessed with truly demanding customers when it comes to investing money in information technology.

Many of our clients have agreed to their stories being told throughout this book. Most of these client stories are grouped at the end of each chapter under the heading "Window on the Real World: Client Stories." At the beginning of each set of stories, we describe the basic problems that the organizations were facing, the key elements of the approach that were used, and the results that were achieved. While our approach is not mechanistic, and the reality is that no two organizations are the same, we identify the issues and elements of the approach that are common in these stories.

One organization, Nova Gas Transmission Ltd. (NGT), is featured in a number of stories throughout the book. NGT, which has since merged with TransCanadian Pipelines (TCPL), is one of North America's largest natural gas pipeline companies. Much of the initial work around the portfolio management and full cycle governance elements of the approach was developed working closely with NGT, and as a result they provide one of the richest examples of the implementation of these elements.

I am profoundly thankful to NGT and all of the Fujitsu Consulting clients who graciously agreed to share with you, our readers, how they used this new approach to improve the way they make and manage their business and IT investment decisions. We have learned a lot from them, and hope that we have captured some of those lessons.

I would be remiss if I did not also say a few words about those in our organization who carried the torch for this book, which was truly born out of passion and determination. Bringing together senior, experienced people in an organization, especially consultants, is no easy feat. Getting them to share their knowledge with the world deserves recognition.

This book represents a step forward in the process of continuously improving and developing the Benefits Realization Approach. We want to communicate our findings to a wider audience, testing them with new clients and exposing them to challenge in the broader market place of ideas. This is part of the necessary trial-and-error process of learning how to generate business results reliably from the growing array of IT applications in the business world.

We have indeed learned much in the four years since *The Information Paradox* was originally published. This edition includes a new Afterword in which we describe how we have applied what we have learned from working with clients across the world to evolve our thinking and practices. Building on the Benefits Realization Approach, we have developed a comprehensive approach to the broader subject of Enterprise Value Management, and particularly to the linkage between enterprise value and strategy. We also discuss how the lessons we have learned through implementing the Benefits Realization Approach to manage investments in IT-enabled change can, and indeed must, be applied to the broader realm of Enterprise Value Management.

The Information Paradox means that results cannot be taken for granted. The lack of measurable results from IT is a serious management issue and a potentially major barrier to our ability to succeed in the Knowledge Economy. We hope this book will help your organization navigate through the seas of technological change and become a successful Knowledge Economy enterprise.

May this book change, for the better, the way you look at information technology!

Michael Poehner
Chief Executive Officer
Fujitsu Consulting

ACKNOWLEDGEMENTS

This book is the product of a true team effort. The team putting this book together has been led by John Thorp, the head of Fujitsu Consulting's Center for Strategic Leadership. The Center's mission is to further the development of processes and techniques to apply information technology intelligently in a wide range of business operations. As business becomes more and more dependent on IT, and as technology is used to support more and more vital functions, the Center harnesses the expertise and intellectual resources of its management consultants worldwide and continuously leverages these into new applied knowledge.

The main collaborators of the team have been (in alphabetical order): Bronwyn Allen, who brought her unique skills at managing projects — and consultants — and acted as the safety net for the entire project and the lighthouse in tough times; David Bibby, who has shared his vast knowledge about how to apply this approach in implementing enterprise application packages. David also contributed to the research and development effort behind ResultStation™, our integrated set of methods and techniques for benefits realization; Lew Diggs, our editorial advisor who not only helped us structure our thinking for this book and helped the manuscript sing, but also guided us through key segments of the intellectual debate; David Forrest, who brought his practical sense about how to get started on this approach, provided important insights on the challenges of benefits management and lent his talented writing style as well as his skills in bringing the group down to earth; Vic

Kirby, who brought his creative ideas, critical analysis, pragmatism, fundamental focus on business value and an in-depth understanding of the necessary integration of business strategy, technology, organization, process and people. Vic was a major contributor to this book. He also brought us his experience on portfolio management, as well as helping organizations evolve successfully, through a value-based approach to investment in, and management of, information technology. The concept of Investment Value Management was Vic's brainchild, through his work at Nova Gas Transmission; Andrew Lamb — IT strategy and management consultant extraordinaire — who brought us his unique expertise in accountability and business process re-engineering, as well as lending his own special brand of British humor; Bruce Macrae, who brought to the table his experience in ongoing governance, operationalizing progressive resource commitment, how to develop effective benefits realization programs and a wealth of client experience; Julie Monette who stepped in to take over the management of the book project, and who made the new Afterword actually happen; Scott Swink who picked up the editorial advisor role for the new Afterword, to which he brought both insight and clarity; Jean Truax, one of the key builders of ResultStation™ and father of the Results Chain™, now lending his benefits realization skills directly with clients, who brought to the team his rigor, in-depth knowledge and experience of the process and techniques behind the approach and also provided important insights on the fundamentals and challenges of benefits management; and Tim Warner, who was responsible for the benefits realization practice within the Center, brought his knowledge of measurement, the art of executing benefits realization programs and a sharp perspective on business and IT executives' issues.

We also want to acknowledge other key consultants who contributed their time and thinking to further the Benefits Realization Approach and the content of this book, and the new Afterword (in alphabetical order): Daniel Beaulieu, Paul Blackburn, Jacques de Broux, Ricardo Buenaventura, Russ Caple, Mary-Rita Chapman, Ron Cox, Graham Cuckow, Benoit Dôme, Don Duval, David Eyre, Yvette van Delft-Denis, Srini Giridhar, Alan Hansell, Peter Harrison, Gary Hadford, Anne Hudson, Bob Hudson, Richard Hudson, Ken Joslyn, Luc Laroche, Bruce Linaker, Jim Love, Dave Mackenzie, Jeff McCracken-Hewson, James Morrison, Guy Piché, David Rosewall, Jim Sabuda, Alan Shefveland, Randy Smith, Attracta Uibhroin, and Wendy Turpin.

We owe special thanks to Jacques Pigeon and Jean-Marc Nantais — our marketing whizzes — who championed, launched and believed in this project from day one. Also to Ken Grant, Vice President for Strategic Consulting, who provided invaluable input to this book during the editing process.

It would all have been for naught without the extraordinary generosity of our clients in freely sharing their experiences, challenges and successes. In this respect, we must cite, in the United States: The Boeing Company, Bank of America, Oregon Department of Transportation; in Canada: Nova Gas Transmission, Ericsson, SaskTel, Alberta Pool, National Bank of Canada, Montreal Police Department (Service de police de la communauté urbaine de Montréal), Quebec Workers Compensation Board (Commission de la santé et de la sécurité du travail); in Europe: Royale Belge, Sollac, Barclays Bank; in Australia: SUNCORP-Metway, Qantas Airlines, Education Department of Western Australia.

Nova Gas Transmission (hereinafter referred to as NGT) deserves special mention. The organization adopted the Benefits Realization Approach, adapted it, improved on it and institutionalized it, under the name "Investment Value Management" (IVM). The views and logical thinking process of the people we worked with at NGT helped us shape our Benefits Realization Approach and further the concept of a Value Management Office. We are deeply indebted to NGT.

Finally, we wish to thank our publisher McGraw-Hill Ryerson for believing in this work and supporting its publication.

Books are not just built on ideas. We owe extreme gratitude to the spouses, partners and children of everybody who worked on this book for the days, nights and weekends we spent away from home while continuing with our day jobs.

This has truly been a group effort by individuals from many backgrounds and countries. In the end, we have learned much from each other and we hope this product — based on a rigorous research and development program begun in 1991 and years of field practice — reflects a successful melding of these different cultures and experiences.

This book is dedicated to the memory of Raoul Malouin,

a great mind, a true colleague and a valued friend.

The world is a lesser place without you.

Table of Contents

Introduction — Information Technology: Better Times and
  Worse Times. xvii

PART I — THE INFORMATION PARADOX AND
THE BENEFITS REALIZATION SOLUTION

Chapter 1 — The Information Paradox. 3
  The Impact of IT on the Economy: The Productivity Issue 4
    Measurement Error. 5
    Small Installed Base 5
    Poor Quality Software and Information Systems 5
    Learning Lags 6
  The Impact of IT on the Business: The Profitability Issue 7
  The Impact of IT on Knowledge Workers: The Individual
    Performance Issue 10
  Information Technology Projects: The Delivery Issue. 11
  A Balanced View 12
  Evolving Applications of Information Technology 13
    Automation of Work 15
    Information Management 16
    Business Transformation 18
  Management's Lagging Mind-set 20
    Silver Bullet Thinking. 21
  Management Blind Spots: Four Critical Dimensions of Complexity. 23
    Linkage. 23
    Reach 23
    People. 24
    Time 25
  The Management Challenge: The Evolving Complexity of IT
    Applications 25
  Business Transformation and the Knowledge Economy 28
    Selection and the Problem of Relative Value. 29
  Window on the Real World: Client Stories. 30
    A North American Utility. 31
    Alberta Pool 32
  Summary. 34

Chapter 2 — The Benefits Realization Approach 37
   Managing IT-enabled Technological Change: The Benefits
      Realization Process. 39
   Cornerstones of the Benefits Realization Approach 40
      Three Fundamentals. 42
      Three Necessary Conditions. 45
   Two Techniques to Support Benefits Realization. 46
      Modeling 48
      Value Assessment Technique 51
   Managers Must Have Patience: This is Not a Quick Fix. 54
   Window on the Real World: Client Stories 54
      Ericsson. 56
      Sollac 57
      A Regional Bank in Asia-Pacific 58
      National Bank of Canada. 59
      Quebec Workers Compensation Board 60
   Summary. 61

PART II — THREE FUNDAMENTALS

Chapter 3 — First Fundamental: Program Management. 65
   Project World: The Blinkered View 66
   Program Universe: The Big Picture 68
      Meshing Technological and Organizational Change 69
      Three Core Components of Program Management 70
   Defining Program Scope: The Blended Investment Perspective . 71
      IT as Part of the BTOPP Business System 72
      Programs that Produce Results. 74
   How to Assess Program Value: Multiple Dimensions 75
      Translating the Four "Ares" into Measurements 76
   Designing and Managing Programs: Getting from Here to There . 77
      Define Benefits and Articulate Linkages 78
      Define Program Scope 80
      Design Program: Map the Benefits Realization Process . . . 81
      Design Program: Select the Best Benefits Realization Path . 83
      Define Accountabilities 86
      Address the People Factor 87
      Recognize the Time Factor. 88
      Prepare for Risk and Uncertainty. 91

Window on the Real World: Client Stories 94

    Royale Belge 95

    SUNCORP-Metway 96

    Bank of America 98

    SaskTel 99

Summary 100

Chapter 4 — Second Fundamental: Portfolio Management 103

The Manager's Dilemma: Too Many Choices, Too Few Resources . 103

    Budget 104

    Delivery Capabilities of the IT Group 105

    Delivery Capabilities of the Business 105

    Capabilities of the Business To Absorb Change 105

Program Selection Challenge 105

Lagging Management Mind-set 106

    Three Selection Blind Spots 107

The Manager's New Weapon: Portfolio Power 108

Selecting and Managing Portfolios: Getting from Here to There . 109

    Categorize Programs 110

    Prepare Value Cases for Business Opportunity Programs . 112

    Manage Risk to Increase Value 117

    Manage and Leverage Program Interdependencies 119

    Adjust Portfolio Composition 121

Window on the Real World: Client Stories 123

    Transportation Development and Operations Branch,

       Oregon Department of Transportation (ODOT) 124

    Boeing Shared Services Group, Supplier Management &

       Procurement 127

Summary 129

Chapter 5 — Third Fundamental: Full Cycle Governance 131

A Major Change in Management Processes, Structures and

    Attitudes: Practical Steps 133

    Value Cases 135

    Stage Gates and Progressive Resource Commitment 136

    Program Decision Options and Portfolio Composition . . 145

    Organization Structure and Decision Making 148

Window on the Real World: Client Stories 151

    Nova Gas Transmission 151

Summary 153

PART III — THREE NECESSARY CONDITIONS

Chapter 6 — First Necessary Condition: Activist Accountability . . 157
Three Routes to Activist Accountability. 158
    Understand the Essence of Activist Accountability. 159
    Introduce Seven Plus One Key Conditions for Activist
        Accountability. 160
    Introduce the Accountabilities Required for Full Cycle Governance. 165
Succession Management. 173
Window on the Real World: Client Stories 175
    Nova Gas Transmission 175
Summary. 176

Chapter 7 — Second Necessary Condition: Relevant Measurement. . 179
The "New" Manager: Navigating in the Program Universe. . . . 180
    Four Measurement Blind Spots 181
Benefits Realization Approach to Measurement 182
Results Chain Models: A Unique Perspective. 183
    Managing the Four Dimensions of Complexity with Good
        Measurement Systems. 186
Designing a Measurement System 186
    Make Sure Measures Exist 187
    Measure the Right Things 188
    Measure Things the Right Way 190
    Managers Must Make Sure Measurement Systems Guide
        Decisions and Action 192
    Benefits Realization and Other Measurement Approaches . 194
Window on the Real World: Client Stories. 196
    Nova Gas Transmission 196
Summary. 198

**Chapter 8 — Third Necessary Condition: Proactive Management
  of Change. 201**
Making Results the Leverage Point of Change. 201
Business Sponsor Responsibility. 202
Only the Business Application of Technology Can Deliver Value . 203
Results-Focused Change Programs: Managing the Four
    Dimensions of Complexity 206
    First Dimension of Complexity: Linkage. 207
    Second Dimension of Complexity: Reach. 207

Third Dimension of Complexity: People 210

Fourth Dimension of Complexity: Time 213

Window on the Real World: Client Stories 214

Montreal Urban Community Police Service 215

Barclays Bank 217

The Boeing Company 218

Qantas Airways 220

Summary 222

PART IV — CONCLUSION

Chapter 9 — Getting Started 227

Define Your Challenge 227

Range of Solutions 228

Program Management 229

Portfolio Management and Full Cycle Governance 229

Support from the Top 230

Practical Steps: Getting from Here to There 231

Explore the Potential of Benefits Realization 232

Define Scope 236

Get Organized 237

Manage Change 240

Implement Full Cycle Governance (or Program Management) . 242

Surviving and Thriving in a Changing World 247

Afterword: Enterprise Value . . . The Next Step 249

Moving Beyond Benefits Realization to Enterprise

Value Management 251

Applying Lessons Learned to Enterprise Value Management . . 270

The Road Forward 278

Glossary 281

Bibliography 291

Index 297

INTRODUCTION —
Information Technology:
Better Times and
Worse Times

In the four years since *The Information Paradox* was first published, we have helped many organizations across the world better select and execute investments in IT-enabled change. The adoption of the Benefits Realization Approach, as described in this book, has enabled these organizations to make better decisions and to drive greater value from their investments. However, across the board, it is clear that investments in IT-enabled business change are still not being consistently translated into business value. If anything, the problem has gotten worse. Four years ago, Enterprise Resource Planning packages (ERPs) were the highly publicized failures. Since then, the dot.com bubble has burst, implementation of Supply Chain Management systems has slowed, and significant challenges have cropped up with Customer Relationship Management (CRM) Systems. Overall, the lemming-like rush to the e-business cliff of the dot.com era has slowed to a more rational crawl.

The transparency of the digital world makes failures increasingly visible. Household names such as FoxMeyer, Hershey, National Australia Bank, Nike and Whirlpool, and public sector organizations such as the

IRS, UK Passport Office, and NZ Police, to name but a few, have shown that the potential for costly and highly visible failure is high. Such failure can severely damage an organization's reputation, or even threaten its very survival.

While the link between large-scale IT-enabled investments in business change and business results continues to be unclear, our experience in working with many clients across the world implementing the Benefits Realization Approach has led us to understand that the issues with IT are merely a symptom of a larger problem. The reality is that the link between any investment in change and business results is unclear. The success rates of major changes including Business Process Re-engineering, and mergers and acquisitions are no better than those of IT investments.

This edition of *The Information Paradox* includes an Afterword that introduces a new approach called Enterprise Value Management. Enterprise Value Management goes beyond the challenge of realizing IT value — the Benefits Realization Approach — to address the essence of overall organizational governance. Enterprise Value Management builds on and extends benefits realization with a value-driven strategy process. It integrates Enterprise Architectures in structuring programs of change, and it identifies a dynamic, "sense and respond" Strategic Governance system to help organizations manage what is, in most cases, "an uncertain journey to an uncertain destination".

At the heart of the problem is the fundamental change in how organizations are using information technology and the information provided by that technology. The early applications of IT were primarily automation of routine work — an extension of industrial-age mechanization. They processed data, hence the term electronic data processing, but produced very little information, and what information they did produce was not widely used. As technology evolved and became more accessible, its application to managing information increased. Initial applications provided information to support existing work but subsequent applications provided information to fundamentally redesign how work was done or, to use the more popular term, to re-engineer work. Today, with the availability of ever-more sophisticated information handling systems, we have moved beyond the simple implementation of IT applications to an age of IT-enabled change — dramatic change in the very nature of businesses and indeed of entire industries.

The Information Paradox

The rapid pace and scope of IT-enabled change continues to create dilemmas for management. More and more information is being delivered by more and more technology, to the point where many people now feel that they are drowning in information — or being forced to work with the wrong types of information. An increasing amount of money is being spent on new technologies that will deliver even more information as time goes on. Yet, neither the information nor the technology dollars are being consistently translated into business value. This is the Information Paradox, a phenomenon that has been drawing attention since the late 1980s. It arises from the conflict between the widely held belief that information and investment in IT to provide that information is a "good thing," and the all too frequent reality that we cannot demonstrate a connection between money spent on IT and business results.

To understand the Information Paradox, we need to explore the relationship between information and information technology. A long-standing business mantra is that information is good. The belief arising from this is that if information is good, then more information must be better. There is a hidden assumption that information is cheap, even free, so the demand for information grows. On the supply side, new technologies are now able to produce and distribute vast quantities of information at apparently little cost. This in turn stimulates demand even further. More money is being spent on IT, and more and more information is being produced, but the link to business results is not clear. It is hard to demonstrate how a dollar spent on IT, or on producing another piece of information, translates into economic value.

The Information Paradox can be viewed through a number of lenses. One of these shows the information overload that is troubling front-line workers and managers. Although they may be drowning in information, they often do not have the specific information they believe that they need to do their work. While the frustration is evident, the costs of this information overload are hard to pin down and rarely measured in dollars. Looking at the Information Paradox through another lens reveals what we call the "IT value view." This has historically been the view seen by CEOs, CFOs and senior management. With the IT value lens, the costs are easier to pin down and measure. These costs are coming under increasing scrutiny and will continue to do so. In this book we have chosen to view the Information Paradox primarily through the IT value lens. We believe that while the application of IT will continue to evolve, and trends and fads will come and go, the question of value is an enduring one. An approach to answering it will be of long-term value to managers. More importantly, viewing the Information Paradox through the IT value lens, using the approach we present in this book, will be of practical importance to managers whose performance is still measured more on how they manage dollars than on how they manage information.

In order to better understand the question of value, let us take another look at the evolving application of information technology. In the early days, when the focus of automation was manual production operations, the problem of measuring value was less acute; the benefits were usually clear, predictable and measurable. The problem has become more serious with the growth of the capabilities of information technology: capabilities that are used to capture, create, manipulate and distribute increasing amounts of information. Networked computers and electronic commerce via the Internet are more exciting than an automated payroll processing system or a stamping unit in an auto parts plant, but they are also more risky IT applications, with broader business impacts. The benefits are potentially much richer, but at the same time, less clear and harder to predict. They require significant changes that go well beyond the implementation of technology and the availability of information. Similarly, transforming the infrastructure of a factory-to-store supply chain is far more ambitious and requires far more significant changes than automating a few operational islands, such as a manual assembly line at the factory or the bookkeeping at the store.

While the application of technology has evolved, and as its impacts have become far more dramatic, our management mind-sets have unfortunately failed to keep pace. They have remained rooted in the industrial-age mentality of work automation, with its clear and predictable benefits, requiring little more than the plugging in of the technology for results to be achieved. This is a far cry from the challenges presented today where benefits are neither clear nor easily predictable.

It is the heightened risk and lack of predictability surrounding business applications of information technology that is the key practical facet of the Information Paradox, with major implications for all business managers investing in technology. Seen from this standpoint, the paradox revolves around a basic statistical fact: to date the increasing amounts of money invested in IT do not appear to have produced corresponding increases in economic value. There are striking success stories, but there are also spectacular failures, and there is no consistent statistical relationship between IT spending and various measures of value over time.

In the case of the economy as a whole, professional economists remain divided about whether huge investments in information technology across virtually all sectors have actually increased economic productivity. This is a visible management issue since, in the 20 years preceding the burst of the dot.com bubble, IT expenditures have grown at rates of 20 to 30 percent annually and, despite the recent slowdown, still account for about 50 percent of annual business equipment expenditure in the United States. In the case of individual firms, a number of experts have noted the surprising lack of correlation between high spending on IT and various measures of business performance such as profit margins, return on assets and return on investment. Both top performers and poor ones spend a great deal on IT. Indeed, some highly profitable firms spend less on IT than their lower-ranked competitors.

Source: DILBERT reprinted by permission of United Feature Syndicate, Inc.

As you might expect, there is much learned debate about the precision of the numbers, exceptions to the averages and future trends. While there are many plausible explanations, the Information Paradox as an abstract statistical phenomenon does reflect some commonsense observations about the track record of IT.

The Best and the Worst of Information Technology

Taking a quick bird's-eye view of how information technology has been applied in the business world, what we see is both the "best of times" and the "worst of times." At the best of times, IT works productivity miracles and produces logistical breakthroughs. Examples include the automation of manual paper processing and manufacturing functions, the number crunching feats of supercomputers and the silent efficiency of the airline reservation and credit card systems. IT has transformed entire economic sectors, including telecommunications, air freight, banking, global payments processing and retail distribution. In these and other sectors, a variety of information technologies have proven their value many times over. Their main contribution has been to solve production problems, driving down costs and massively upgrading basic service standards. In a number of cases, including organizations such as Dell, FedEx, UPS, and Wal-Mart, the adoption of IT has fundamentally changed the business model.

At the worst of times, information technology falls down on the job, sometimes disastrously. Most visibly, and to many people's embarrassment, mission-critical systems fail and not only in Apollo 13 films. There have been brownouts of utilities and banking machine networks and trading halts on major stock exchanges. Less visible, but far more important in economic terms, are the many cases where perfectly good technology is poorly applied to business problems. For example, a Customer Relationship Management system is installed in a company without adjusting the ground-level work processes that service representatives follow every day to solve "live" customer complaints, and the required adjustments force an expensive redesign of the software interface. Or, in another case, a corporate Internet site features the latest in expensive graphics to attract shoppers' attention, but it is not integrated with plain-vanilla transaction processing systems, so the site generates no sales and no revenue. As well, top flight information systems are designed with the users' every need in mind, but they don't make it to market on time. They are delivered years late and over budget, lessening their economic value. The IT world has its share of "runaway" projects and white elephants.

Finally, there is the gray zone of information technology, a large basket of everyday problems that fall in between the best and the worst. A perfect example is the mundane but expensive problem of technology that is not used or is misused. People don't know and are not effectively taught how to use new software interfaces and information systems. Often, they do not understand what to do with the information that these provide. As a result, expensive new technology and intelligent software sits on their desktops, producing zero — or worse, negative — economic value, while they learn what to do with it. Time is lost and in business lost time means lost money.

The trend toward the increasing use of information technology across the economy is relentless. The demand to provide more information about more things in more ways to more people in more places, and to provide this information in real-time will continue. The technical potential to deliver this information, as measured by sheer memory, processing power and network capacity, continues to grow and become cheaper. Yet, the commonsense observation, confirmed by experts looking at the Information Paradox, is that buying expensive IT tools will not make you more productive unless you know how to apply them. In business, we are still learning how to apply IT and how to manage the information that IT provides. That is the central challenge.

The Odds of Success in Information Technology Investments

The biggest practical problem for managers confronted with the Information Paradox today is the dollars and cents issue of how to manage large information technology budgets and justify new IT spending. Based on our experience, we find that many executives today, despite the supposed inevitability of technological change, are increasingly hesitant to commit funds to large-scale IT investments. All too often, they feel like gamblers in a casino when making these investment decisions. They may not be winning, but they have seen others win, and may have occasionally won themselves. So, they keep playing the odds, albeit more cautiously in the current economic climate. Similarly, organizations may not be sure that they are winning in the casino, but they have seen, read or certainly been told by vendors about the stories of other organizations that have placed successful bets. Often they have at least one good win to show for it, especially if they automated a major manual process some years back. Or, they may conclude that their competitors are in the game, so they can't afford to disappear from the table. So, just like our gamblers, organizations keep playing the odds of the Information Paradox, which are 50-50 at best and more often in the 20 to 30 percent range. Gambling with these odds is an expensive proposition.

The challenge for organizations is to move from the gambler's world, where risk can be managed to some extent but luck remains the major factor, to a world where the dependence on luck is reduced to improve our odds to those more normally associated with business risk. In doing so, it is important to set realistic expectations. The risk associated with technological change cannot be eliminated, but it can most certainly be better managed. By this we mean it can be reduced systematically and brought into a stable relationship with expected rewards. A reasonable goal, we believe, is for business decision makers to learn how to bet more intelligently and with better knowledge of the odds. We must get rid of the old unquestioning faith in technological infallibility. Trusting to the gods will not improve the odds. Business managers must improve the management of risk associated with IT investments.

When it comes to managing risk, there are encouraging precedents in business going back hundreds of years and there are numerous examples of how businesses have been transformed through risk management. Actuarial science has made modern life insurance possible. The development of insurance syndicates made it feasible to insure shipping and many other types of commercial transactions. The modern banking system is able to finance and assume liability for international trade processes using risk management methods. And modern portfolio selection and management methods have, with the exception of the dot.com aberration, transformed stock and bond market investing, replacing seat-of-the-pants stock picking similar to a casino model, with more rational management of risk/reward relationships.

Managing the risks of investing in information technology is a business risk management challenge which can and must be met. It is similar to basic financial risk management in many ways. Consider these two points of comparison:

- Investment professionals can improve their earnings through better knowledge of individual firms, industries and stock market performance histories. Similarly, business decision makers can develop better knowledge of various technologies and how they actually produce business results. In both cases, investors better understand the odds of success through insights into key risk/reward relationships.

- In finance, risk is diversified through portfolio selection methods. Businesses can diversify IT-related risk by investing in a variety of technologies at the same time. In both cases, investors avoid "betting the company" on a single investment. They can maximize rewards at any chosen level of risk and choose to diversify away unwanted risk.

The Information Paradox introduced the idea that the methods used for monitoring and managing financial portfolios from day to day and adjusting portfolio composition as market conditions change can also be applied to IT and related business investments. With the current economic slowdown, and increasing focus on value or, more often, cost reduction, the portfolio management approach to IT investments has gained considerable momentum. Unfortunately, much of the writing and talking about portfolio management is missing the point. The primary focus still appears to be on the technology project, and the major activities are selection and tracking of these technology projects. In reality, value does not come from technology projects. Technology only provides a capability. Value is only realized when this capability is applied and managed as part of a program of business change, including changes to business strategy, business processes, how people work, organizational structure, and technology. If organizations are to seriously tackle the question of value with a portfolio management approach, they must focus on programs of business change, and apply all the fundamentals of the Benefits Realization Approach, as described in this book. The end result will be better risk/reward relationships and a much better overview of an organization's IT-business investment portfolio. We will be able to move from today's world of casino gambling, with its associated odds, to a new world of managed business investments.

How can organizations invest intelligently — like a financial portfolio manager — in information technology? They can start by providing consistent answers to several important questions:

- How can our organization's information technology investments produce measurable benefits?

- What are the processes that link "upstream" IT investments with "downstream" business results, such as productivity gains, increased revenues, market advantage, better job performance and improved product and service quality?

- How do we determine which IT-enabled business transformation projects are the most important for us?

- How do we ensure that our IT projects and other business initiatives support each other? How do we make sure our technology, people, processes and organization work smoothly together?

- How do we get more bang for our IT buck?

These questions used to be of interest primarily to a small group of IT specialists who spent a lot of time talking to each other about possible answers. Today, the Internet, and electronic commerce have become a part of the everyday vocabulary of business. In some way, almost all managers now have responsibility to manage IT, or at least to manage the intelligent use of the information that IT provides. So it should come as no surprise that more questions are being asked about IT by more people more often, and senior business executives are doing more of the asking. The pressure to find credible answers is intensifying as we move inexorably towards the Knowledge Economy.

Managers Confront the Knowledge Economy

Management's growing interest in technology is not just a matter of "management by magazine" or vendor-driven hype, although over the last decade hype has played far too large a role. Today, organizations can touch and feel the Knowledge Economy. They see technology more often, in such forms as a new intranet or desktop software. More managers are technologically literate, and the range of information technology choices and applications is getting broader.

Much more is being attempted with information technology. Much more is being asked of IT. Often, much more is promised as well. And, naturally, there is more complexity and more risk. This is especially true of the large-scale investment projects and major IT-enabled initiatives such as electronic commerce, Customer Relationship Management, and Supply Chain Management. To produce results, these initiatives require further supporting investments in long-term change initiatives such as Business Process Engineering (BPR), quality management, continuous learning and change management. We are learning fast that much more is involved in the Knowledge Economy than technology.

This is a scary picture but one that is also full of opportunity for organizations that learn how to apply information technology intelligently. This will require fundamental changes in our approach to investing in IT. Organizations must recognize that they are no longer making IT investments — they are investing in IT-enabled change in the overall business system. There will be many opportunities for such change. The challenge for organizations will be to:

- Pick the winning opportunities

- Understand all that must be done to realize the value from those opportunities

- Manage the opportunities through to the delivery of value.

To do so, they must recognize that while the availability of evolving new technologies fuels our apparently insatiable appetite for information, the information provided is only of value when it is used intelligently. Increasingly, beyond having the right information in the right place, this requires a clear understanding of what business outcomes an organization wants to achieve, what information supports the attainment of these outcomes and what changes are required in how an organization operates in order to achieve these outcomes. Only when these requirements are understood and managed will the true value of information and of information technology be realized.

In the Afterword, we explore how our thinking has evolved beyond the challenge of IT value to the essence of overall organizational governance. Our experience has led us to the realization that organizations must both recognize and deal with a number of critical issues if they are to realize value from their investments, both IT investments and any other type of investment. These issues include:

- Recognizing that the leadership challenge today is one of continually implementing change … major cultural change

- Defining and articulating clear and focused strategies to set the direction for change … with clear understanding of the value driven business outcomes that the strategies are striving to achieve

- Acknowledging, surfacing, and coming to grips with the complexity of strategy execution

- Implementing governance processes to effectively manage what is, in most cases, an uncertain journey to an uncertain destination.

The new approach, Enterprise Value Management, builds on and extends our original Benefits Realization Approach to include a value-driven strategy process, to integrate Enterprise Architecture in structuring programs of change, and to introduce a dynamic, "sense and respond" Strategic Governance system.

The Information Paradox is not a technology challenge, it is a business challenge. To deal with the Information Paradox, organizations must treat it as a full-bodied business management problem. This is not just a challenge for the CIO and the IT department, it is a challenge for all business managers, from the CEO down. Business managers must recognize that they all have a responsibility for successfully managing investments in IT-enabled change. It is only with this recognition that organizations will be able to successfully resolve the Information Paradox.

THE INFORMATION PARADOX AND THE BENEFITS REALIZATION SOLUTION

In Part I, we introduce our Benefits Realization Approach which has been developed in hundreds of consulting assignments with clients of the Fujitsu Consulting in response to their asking us: "Where are the business results? When will we reap the benefits from IT investments? And how?"

Chapter 1 describes the Information Paradox as seen through the IT value lens, focusing on the questions surrounding the business value being produced by the ever-increasing investments that organizations are making in information technology. We look at four viewpoints: the economy at large; industries and individual organizations; knowledge workers; and information technology projects. We discuss the evolution of the application of IT from automation of work through information management to business transformation. The Information Paradox is explained in terms of the management mind-set having lagged behind the evolution of the application of information technology. This lag has resulted in a failure to understand and manage critical dimensions of complexity and the increased risk associated with the application of IT to enable business transformation. The implications in terms of the emerging Knowledge Economy are explored, and the case for a new approach is made.

Chapter 2 introduces a new benefits realization mind-set and the cornerstones of our Benefits Realization Approach. These are the three fundamentals: program management; portfolio management; and full cycle governance, and the three necessary conditions: activist accountability; relevant measurement; and proactive management of change. Program management moves you beyond the project world into the broader universe of blended investment programs, ensuring that all actions required to deliver business results are identified and included. Portfolio management broadens your view further, moving from "free-for-all" competition for resources to selecting programs clearly aligned with your business goals and desired results and diversifying risk. Program and portfolio management represent significant shifts in the management mind-set. Full cycle governance operationalizes both program and portfolio management, continuously monitoring performance and adjusting portfolio composition through a staged process, premised on progressive commitment of resources. These three fundamentals can only be implemented by organizations that meet the three necessary conditions. Effective benefits realization requires activist accountability, supported by relevant measurement systems. Successful management of the entire benefits realization process requires, and must be introduced by, proactive management of change.

THE INFORMATION PARADOX

Managers at all levels in organizations confront the Information Paradox every day. It takes a variety of practical forms. Expensive new information systems are delivered, but they don't work properly; or people have not learned how to use them effectively; or, most often, the technology is working smoothly on the surface but, for some reason, it does not produce the expected business results. Sales are not increasing, customer complaints are up and the organization is still being managed pretty much the way it was before. All this, while increasing amounts of time and money are being spent on new technology.

There is a growing body of evidence that new and improved technology has not *consistently* produced business results over a period of several decades. The reality of Information Technology has not lived up to the promise at four levels:

1. Productivity performance of the economy at large

2. Business results of companies and other organizations

3. Workplace performance of individual knowledge workers and work groups

4. Reliability of IT project delivery.

3

The Impact of IT on the Economy: The Productivity Issue

What's in IT for the economy? In the words of Nobel prize-winning economist Robert Solow, "You can see computers everywhere but in the productivity statistics."

Over the last 20 years, information technology expenditures — including hardware, software, IT services and telecommunications networking costs — have grown strongly. In the United States, for example, prior to the burst of the dot.com bubble, annual corporate expenditure on IT rose by 20 to 30 percent in real terms *each year*. Despite the recent slowdown, in many cases, IT and telecommunications spending continues to rank as the single largest capital item and one of the largest operating expense items, after salaries and benefits.

A 1997 Compass report estimated that worldwide spending on IT averaged seven percent of total corporate costs and that about 60 percent of corporate operations depended to some extent on IT systems. A March 2002 Forrester Research report estimates United States spending on IT in 2000 at approximately $587 billion, and forecasts that it will continue to grow, albeit at a slower rate than in the past. The Aberdeen Group, as reported by Antone Gonsalves in *Internet Week*, estimates global IT spending in 2003 at $1.26 trillion. Despite this continuing strong growth in expenditures and in the use of IT, economists and other experts are at best divided as to its economic impact and have difficulty in correlating this ever-increasing investment in IT to growth in productivity.

A 1996 Gartner Group report by B. Stewart suggests that the net average return on investment from information technology from 1985 to 1995 was a mere one percent. In *The Corporation of the 1990s*, Michael Scott Morton notes that "no impact from information technology is yet visible in the macroeconomic data available. A very few individual firms are demonstrably better off, and there is a larger group of isolated examples of successful exploitation in particular individual functions or business units. However, on average, the expected benefits are not yet visible."

In his book *The Squandered Computer,* former CIO and consultant Paul A. Strassmann states: "It is safe to say that so far nobody has produced any evidence to support the popular myth that spending more on information technologies will boost economic performance. The presumption that more IT spending is better remains one of the most cherished beliefs of computerdom. It took experimental science to dispel

the dogmas of the ancients. It may take better research and better metrics before executives will come to recognize that IT is a subtle influence where an overdose of what works can also disable."

Experts have advanced a number of explanations for this phenomenon which are summarized by Pam Woodall in *The Economist,* "Survey of the World Economy: The Hitchhiker's Guide to Cybernomics," and a *Scientific American* article by Wayt Gibbs called, "Taking Computers to Task." The four most commonly mentioned explanations are:

1. Measurement Error
2. Small Installed Base
3. Poor Quality Software and Information Systems
4. Learning Lags.

Measurement Error

Some economists advance the argument that conventional productivity statistics fail to take into account many of the improvements in economic output brought about by IT such as faster service, more varied products and services and better access to business information. If this is true, productivity growth over the years may be underestimated by the figures. Moreover, productivity is notoriously hard to measure in the service sector where IT has been extensively applied. Historically, productivity measures across entire economies move at glacial rates. To make a very long story short, the jury of econometric experts is still out on the measurement issue.

Small Installed Base

Rapid growth in IT spending by business has created an optical illusion that IT is "everywhere" in today's organizations. In fact, it may not be. Economic measures indicate, for example, that computer hardware accounts for only two to five percent of U.S. firms' capital stock. That figure is disputed, since it does not include the costs of software, telecommunications and IT experts' salaries that are a big part of IT spending and could bring the amount to 12 percent. Here again, the jury of measurement experts is still hearing the evidence and deliberating. But nobody is seriously questioning the figures on growth in IT spending.

Poor Quality Software and Information Systems

A growing body of literature points to examples of new technologies and software interfaces which people find hard to use and hard to learn to apply at work. This obviously can delay, or even cancel, applications of IT to increase business productivity. Examples of such problems have become much more visible in today's organizations as IT has been applied across more and more functions and as new software has been introduced with increasing frequency. More IT applications produce more problems with IT, a trend to be expected. Measuring the extent of this family of problems and their long-term impact on economic productivity will be a primary focus of attention for many years.

Learning Lags

Many economists and IT practitioners agree that the newer generations of IT — including all those desktop PCs, workstations and Internet connections — will only produce business results when organizations restructure to take full advantage of them. True electronic commerce, for example, is not an add-on to conventional retail bank branches and storefronts. Restructuring organizations, even figuring out how to do so, takes time. This leads to what the economists call a learning lag. While this emerging IT phenomenon is hard to measure at the moment, there are instructive examples from economic history. Electric motors, first installed by Edison in 1881, took more than 40 years to boost U.S. productivity growth appreciably. In fact, only half of American plants were wired for power by 1919 and it was later still that most factories reorganized their production lines to exploit electric power fully. The first commercial computers were introduced about 40 years ago and the first personal computers appeared in the early 1980s, so a similar learning lag may be at work today.

****

As practicing consultants, we will not attempt to take a position in the measurement debate concerning the Information Paradox. Rather, we will try to use it to gain insight into the practical issues facing decision makers and managers. While all explanations of the productivity paradox have some truth, the one that we observe firsthand most often is the learning lag. People are still learning about information technology and what it can do. Across the economy, we are still low down on the learning curve about how to apply IT to create business solutions.

As Michael Scott Morton says: "One major explanation of this lack of impact lies in the enormous strength of historical precedence. The Western economies have had more than half a century of doing business in a certain way. These ways are very hard to discard, and it appears to be harder yet to learn new ones." Our experience confirms this observation. It can take many years, even decades, for business to learn how to fully exploit the potential of new technologies. It is not enough to acquire technology, you also have to learn to apply it intelligently. New ways of thinking, managing and working are required.

It is important to keep the productivity issue in perspective. The broad economic studies do not claim for a minute that all IT is unproductive. They do, however, indicate serious problems with it in a significant proportion of cases. These problems are significant enough to prevent the very real successes from showing when the averages are compiled.

The Impact of IT on the Business: The Profitability Issue

What's in IT for the company? Here the issue shifts from overall economic productivity to corporate profitability. The economic findings are confirmed when we talk to individual business executives. Chief executive officers (CEOs), chief financial officers (CFOs) and boards of directors all find it difficult to measure the impact of IT investments on business performance, return on investment (ROI) and productivity. Many senior executives have expressed their frustration that they can solve problems in other areas of their business but not with IT.

CFOs have notorious problems measuring returns from large-scale IT investments, whether in a data center or 500 new PCs that were purchased to boost desktop automation. It is hard to link a one-time cost decrease or revenue increase back to a specific IT investment. This problem is partly a matter of measurement methods, but it also reflects several other facts of IT life:

- IT investments blend with many other factors to produce business results, as Scott Morton points out, except in the most simple cases of automating manual functions.
- IT is also being applied to more varied business functions in more varied ways, so it is hard to use old rules of thumb from the mainframe/automation era of IT history.
- Finally, it is hard to allocate costs and revenues when the IT infrastructure supports an entire business, division or multinational corporation. Many user groups complain, for example, about usage fees that appear to make no sense.

Source: DILBERT reprinted by permission of United Feature Syndicate, Inc.

In a series of biennial surveys of CEOs, CFOs and other senior business executives conducted in the 1989-95 period, *Computerworld* asked to what extent they agreed with the following statement: "I do not feel my organization is getting the most for its information systems investment." The responses over time were consistent. Throughout the first half of the 1990s, about 50 percent — at times more — of the executives agreed, or strongly agreed, with the statement.

A 1997 A.T. Kearney study paints a more positive picture, but in so doing, further feeds the Information Paradox. The study found that 74 percent of senior executives are "very satisfied" or "fairly satisfied" with the return on IT investments, yet, at the same time, only 44 percent of companies say they have been successful in actually measuring IT's contribution to the bottom line.

The division of executive attitudes about the payoffs from IT investments reflects the ambiguity of actual business performance figures. There can be no doubt that some companies and public sector organizations have engineered major performance improvements with IT. Overall, however, the data indicate little or no correlation between levels of IT spending and various measures of business performance such as return on investment, return on assets and Economic Value Added (EVA®). IT consultant Paul Strassmann notes that spending levels on computers have no consistent relationship to whether results are inferior or superior. High-performing firms do not consistently allocate more money to information systems than low-performing firms, and this pattern holds across many sectors.

A series of statistical studies have begun to show a positive relationship between information technology spending — measured in a variety of ways — and business performance in specific sectors, such as banking and telecommunication where IT has transformed core operational processes such as payments processing and call switching. (Within the banking sector, however, the top performers are not invariably the heaviest technology spenders.) A positive relationship also appears in certain studies when specific categories of IT spending are correlated to specific operational performance measures such as firm-level output, labor productivity and production costs.

There are solid reasons why the relationship between IT spending and measures of economic value is hard to establish. IT changes how organizations handle information, and that information, in turn, is an input to many different business processes, some simple and many quite complex. It is not computers alone that make a difference but the people and work teams who know what do with them. As Strassmann points out: "Business productivity has its roots in well-organized, well-motivated and knowledgeable people who understand what to do with all the information that shows up on their computer screens. It would be too much to hope for such excellence to prevail in all businesses. If computer expenditures and corporate profits show no correlation, it is a reflection of the human condition that excellence is an uneven occurrence."

In view of the complexity of these issues, it is safe to say that the measurement debate on business performance like the one about general economic productivity will continue for a number of years. In the meantime, business managers will commit billions of dollars more to build, maintain and upgrade the IT infrastructures of their organizations. What do all the statistics around the Information Paradox mean to them in everyday practical terms? On the ground, it means that a handful of IT project teams and their sponsors are clearly picking winners, while a few less-fortunate teams are struggling to bring some losers under control. And the majority just aren't sure how things will turn out when they deliver the new technology or information system upgrade they are working on. Will users be happy? Will senior executive sponsors be satisfied? Will business results improve in some measurable way? Will the IT shop get credit or blame? In too many cases, it is just too hard to say.

More troubling than any short-term problem with a specific information technology is the long-term impact of all this uncertainty and questioning around the practical cases of the Information Paradox. The lack of convincing, positive and measurable returns from IT investments over long time periods erodes credibility. While most critics may focus on financial returns and the bottom line of major investment projects, the most damaging long-term impact is on the organization's collective ability to manage IT effectively. When it comes to positive results, as we have been told many times, "people just don't believe they will happen."

Top management is concerned because the amount of IT investments will continue to grow with the advent of the Knowledge Economy. The installed base of IT in most organizations is now large, meaning that basic software maintenance costs can amount to millions of dollars annually, before new investments are factored in. The stakes continue to grow as well. In short, IT will have a greater and greater impact on how we manage.

The Impact of IT on Knowledge Workers: The Individual Performance Issue

What's in IT for knowledge workers? Many individual IT users are not satisfied with their information technologies. They have trouble becoming proficient quickly and then, just when they thought they had mastered an important business application, a new version hits! Reliability, usability and friendliness of the IT working tools are the focus of regular complaints by knowledge workers, not to mention their kids at home and at school.

Beyond the level of individual complaints, software usability is becoming a key business and economic issue because of the growing evidence of its impact on workplace productivity. In a 1997 survey commissioned by SCO, a software company, Harris Research found that every employee who uses a personal computer can lose the equivalent of three weeks' working time every year as a result of problems with the technology. Two of the most commonly experienced reasons were network and software upgrade problems. According to T. Austin of the Gartner Group, the average employee wastes significant time "futzing" (futz factor) with computers, rather than working on them. SBT Accounting Systems in San Rafael, California, found in a survey of 6000 persons, that office workers average 5.1 hours futzing every week. In our experience, and based on the reaction of other individuals and groups, not only does this indeed appear to be the case, the numbers are likely understated.

Even such successful technologies as airline reservation systems are not immune from these problems. One of the contributors to this book recently had to make a change to an airline ticket. It was a relatively simple change but one that resulted in a different fare. In addition to the computer system, it took three agents and a reference manual, with much use of a pencil and notepad, over 45 minutes to complete this transaction. The frustration of the agents, not to mention our contributor, was evident — and certainly a lot more visible than the usability of the system.

One product of the Information Paradox, as experienced by knowledge workers and work groups, is the seemingly endless debate about "who is to blame" for software usability problems. Is it designers, the people using the system or just the inevitable software bugs? Such debates do not solve IT productivity problems and, in fact, often seem to perpetuate them.

Despite IT marketing hype, there is a significant community of dissatisfied users when new technologies are introduced. It is clear after several decades that technological change imposes significant new learning challenges on knowledge workers every day, in very practical ways. This comes on top of — and in addition to — any "technology problems" that may arise in implementing new information systems. This can prove to be a serious barrier to rapid adoption of new information systems and ways of working. While complaints are to be expected when any new technology is introduced in the workplace, the fact is that mundane user problems may help account for part, and, in certain cases, a big part of the Information Paradox.

Information Technology Projects: The Delivery Issue

As if all that weren't enough, there's also the track record of IT project delivery. New business applications do not just appear. They are purchased out of business units' budgets, developed and customized. The delivery process itself can be expensive and error prone. This problem is intimately linked to the business management and individual software usability problems discussed above.

For years, IT groups have been concerned about the reliability of processes for building information systems. Engineering standards have been slow to develop and even slower to be adopted. Project management performance has been abysmally inconsistent. Now, business managers are equally concerned, or if they are not, they certainly should be. All too often organizations have sunk millions of dollars into "runaway" projects that deliver less functionality than promised, significantly later and for considerably greater expenditure than planned. In the worst cases, some projects end up being cancelled.

A notable case in point is the cancellation of a five-year project to introduce electronic securities registration and transfer operations to the London Stock Exchange. This cancellation resulted in millions of pounds of losses and the resignation of the chairman. Other examples include long delays in the delivery of complex systems for air traffic control, tax collection and — one of the more publicized cases — the automated luggage handling system at the Denver International Airport. These delays resulted in significantly increased costs.

Unfortunately, these are by no means isolated cases. According to a survey by the Standish Group reported by Julia King in *Computerworld*, 73 percent of corporate America's IT projects in 1996 were "challenged" in that they were late, over budget or cancelled. Project failures cost an estimated $145 billion. The latest Standish Group survey, as reported by Scott Berinato in *CIO Magazine*, found almost no change with 72 percent of projects in 2000 being challenged. While the cost of these failures is significant, the more important impact is the lost opportunities and anticipated business benefits. Assuming that these projects were thought to be good investments at the time, this lost opportunity cost could likely amount to trillions of dollars.

Once again, apart from the dollars and cents, organizations need to be concerned about the impact of these project delivery problems on business managers' perceptions of IT and everyone's collective ability to get results from it.

A Balanced View

Up to this point, we have painted a somewhat bleak picture of the IT world. Clearly, this is not the complete picture. We have seen the proliferation of IT into every area of business over the last 30 years in part because it can deliver value. There are many IT success stories in the productivity and profitability statistics, and these are at least as impressive as the failures.

In many cases, including applications to automate high-volume, paper-intensive clerical operations like check or insurance claim processing, IT has produced productivity breakthroughs. Error rates have fallen, processing quality has improved, unit costs have dropped and the bottlenecks of manual production have been eliminated. In other cases, IT has produced logistical miracles, including customized software that automates complex systems for booking airline reservations, controlling in-flight guidance systems, routing truck and train traffic or creating industrial designs. Manual number crunching became history, accuracy and data processing speed increased by quantum leaps and time and distance became less of an obstacle.

The results create varied attitudes and opinions about IT. Both organizations and individual managers tend to divide into optimistic and pessimistic camps. Often, the optimistic camp is comprised of the vendors and IT professionals — the providers of the IT "solutions" — while the pessimistic camp is just about everyone else in business — the receivers of the IT "problems." Over time, the views of these camps have become so entrenched that in many organizations, they have resulted in the creation of IT and business ghettos. Business blames the IT shop and the vendors for all the problems with information technology, while IT experts complain that business managers do not devote enough attention to IT. In most cases, there is some truth to both of these views. The resulting conflict, however, often verging on open warfare, has not served organizations well in their search for effective business applications of IT that result in clear and demonstrable benefits to the business.

In our experience, the overall track record of IT investments supports neither the optimists nor the pessimists. When viewed in a balanced way, the history of IT shows extreme variability, creating both opportunity and risk. It indicates, moreover, that the risks are manageable. Most cases of the Information Paradox do not result from technology that is defective or broken. The new generations of IT are more powerful, reliable and capable of doing more things than before. It is not the technology itself that is the issue, but the business application of the technology to achieve clear business objectives. We are still learning how to get the most from IT by reorganizing, redesigning business processes and learning to work in new ways. We must work through the learning lag identified by Scott Morton, just like those factory engineers and assembly line workers had to learn to apply electric power for the first time in the early twentieth century.

To see where today's organizations stand in the learning process, let us consider the evolution of IT applications over the last 30 years.

Evolving Applications of Information Technology

As outlined by Scott Morton and other writers, such as Shoshana Zuboff, the application of IT has evolved and is continuing to evolve through three stages:

1. Automation of Work

2. Information Management

3. Business Transformation.

This evolution involves major leaps in the complexity of tasks that IT is being designed to perform. As we review this evolution, a consistent pattern of change emerges in the business application of IT. As we evolve from automation of work through information management to business transformation, the strategic importance of IT applications increases and that the amount of organizational change required to realize the benefits of an application is also greater. Specifically, an increasing number of changes are being made to elements of the business system beyond IT such as business processes, organizational structure and even business culture. At the same time, the number and complexity of applications (or potential applications) also increases. The three stages of evolution are summarized in Table 1-1.

TABLE 1-1
Three Stages of IT Evolution

Stage	Impact	Benefit	Examples
Automation of Work	• Getting work done • Doing the same things more efficiently	• Operational efficiency	• Payroll • Check processing • Basic order processing • Basic airline reservation systems
Information Management	• Restructuring work and work processes • Doing things differently	• Operational and tactical effectiveness	• Customer information systems • Airline yield management systems • Executive information systems
Business Transformation	• Defining the business • Doing different things • Changing the business/industry rules	• Strategic effectiveness and positioning	• JIT inventory systems • Electronic commerce • OLAP

Automation of Work

The first applications of IT in business involved the automation of work tasks such as census data calculations, check processing and payroll as well as basic order processing and reservation systems. An automation application, such as payroll, is not a strategic application (see Figure 1-1), and while it is certainly necessary, and failure to pay employees would have serious consequences, it is not an application that provides strategic advantage. The benefits were largely in the area of operational efficiency. A few new jobs were created to program, operate and support the technology itself and some manual jobs, such as pay calculation and check processing, were replaced. There was also limited change to people's jobs or to business processes, but the overall change to the nature of work was not significant. Learning requirements were relatively simple and narrow, focused on how to use the technology. Change was generally limited to one or a small number of functional areas. In the case of payroll, little if any change was experienced outside of the payroll department. The most important thing was that the payroll

FIGURE 1-1
Strategic Importance of IT for Automation of Work

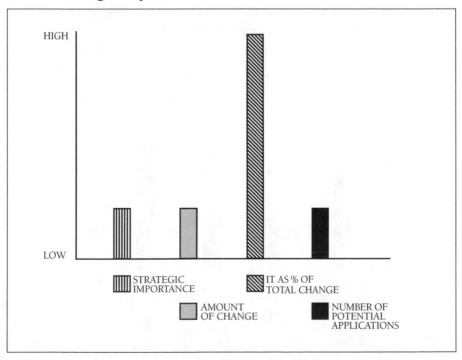

application ran correctly. If it did, you were most of the way to getting benefits.

The self-sufficiency of computerization was reflected by the physical reality of the mainframe, where computers were isolated behind data center walls — and operated invisibly by IT experts. Applications were often limited to those conceived by those same experts, with little understanding of technology by the broader business community, or how it could be applied.

Information Management

Automation applications created information as a by-product of automating work. In the early years of the automation stage, this information was not generally used, certainly not in any widespread formal way. As we moved into the information stage, the opportunities to use this information began to be recognized. With the wider distribution of desktop computer terminals, IT was increasingly applied to provide information to support improved decision making, to move it "closer

FIGURE 1-2
Strategic Importance of IT for Information Management

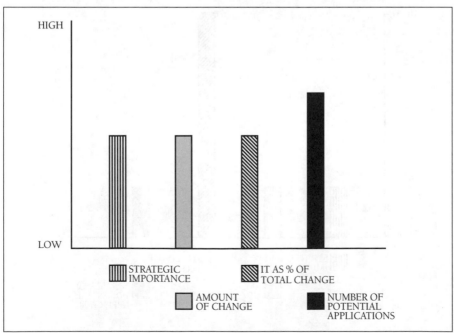

to the customer" and to support new service and product design. Here we saw the introduction of advanced order processing systems, airline yield management systems, customer information systems as well as the start of so-called executive information systems (EIS). Benefits moved beyond operational efficiency to operational and tactical effectiveness. Information could be used to make tactical, and in some cases, strategic decisions (see Figure 1-2). Initially, information was used to enable workers to do their jobs better. Their jobs changed somewhat, but primarily they were required, and had to be trained to take largely predetermined action based on the information provided.

As this information stage advanced, benefits were premised on workers improving how they analyzed and applied information to their work. In the case of order processing, seasonal variations in demand might be noticed, and adjustments made to order levels. In the case of customer information systems (or customer information files in financial institutions), information was used to increase the value of "customer moments" by cross-selling and target marketing of certain services. Airline systems moved beyond basic reservation systems to sophisticated yield management systems. In the later steps of the information stage, automated information bases provided opportunities to design new products, such as today's multitude of mutual funds and numerous volume-based discount plans for valued customers. It was no longer sufficient to simply provide the application and make sure that it worked as specified. For these benefits to be realized, the nature of people's work had to change. Business processes had to be restructured and better integrated. Reward systems had to change. Significant learning was required. The changes crossed functional boundaries, and in some cases, changed or eliminated them.

Physically, personal computers emerged from behind the walls of the central data center. PCs began to appear everywhere in organizations and to be operated by nonexperts. The number of potential applications of technology increased dramatically. Many of these were conceived outside of the IT world, by the broader community of business managers and front-line technology users.

Business Transformation

Information management applications enable organizations to rethink and redesign their business processes and how they carry out their business. As more and more computing power is distributed, and as advanced communications capabilities continue to erase the constraints of time and distance, the very nature of businesses, and even entire industries, is being redefined. Benefits have moved beyond operational and tactical effectiveness to strategic effectiveness and positioning (see Figure 1-3).

Business transformation applications, such as just-in-time (JIT) inventory systems and advanced electronic commerce, enable organizations to rethink not just how they do things, but also what they choose to do. For example, JIT ordering and inventory management systems are fundamentally changing the value/supply chain and shifting the balance of power among stakeholders. The emergence of Internet and virtual banking is redefining the financial industry by removing century-old barriers to entry and blurring financial product boundaries. Airlines are

FIGURE 1-3
Strategic Importance of IT for Business Transformation

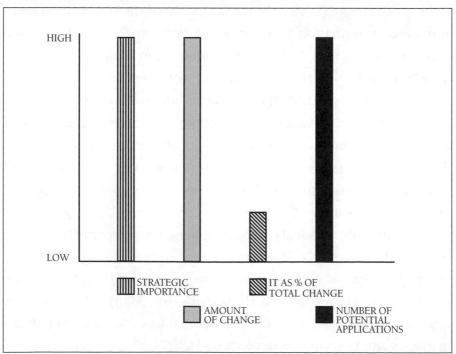

now offering passengers direct access to reservations systems and more, fighting for ownership of the client with travel agents, and thus redefining the travel agent business. Amazon.com is helping to redefine the book industry. It not only selling books electronically and offering a wider selection than is possible in physical bookstores, it is using the power of computers to repackage — and eventually transform — a range of services that were historically spread across multiple businesses, including the reference capabilities of libraries, the retail display and selection expertise of bookstores, the efficiency of volume discount distributors and the knowledge of professional book reviewers.

All these applications have significant strategic implications. While technology enables these benefits, most of the required change is beyond the realm of IT. Changes are required in the mission, the very raison d'être of organizations. The organizations carrying out these changes will, in many cases, be redrawing traditional industry boundaries or, at minimum, changing industry structures and rewriting industry ground rules. In doing so, they will harness IT with the aim of "competing for the future," in the sense proposed by Gary Hamel and C.K. Prahalad in their book of the same name.

The potential of transformational applications is tremendous, but to realize it will present organizations with new and significant challenges. Automating payroll processing was primarily an engineering question, whereas creating a virtual bank branch or bookstore is primarily a business one. These challenges will not be met as quickly as the hype would lead us to believe, but it will happen.

****

The evolution illustrated above has clear implications for the delivery methods embedded in IT projects. As you will recall, these methods are one key element of the Information Paradox. In the era of automation, stand-alone management of IT delivery projects was a necessary and largely sufficient condition for success. As we move beyond automation of work to information management and business transformation applications, sound management of IT projects remains necessary but is no longer by any means sufficient. In the case of financial customer information files, for example, employees have to learn new skills, assume new responsibilities and accept different reward systems. Cross-selling to banking customers means astutely interpreting customer profile information and cultivating personal relationships, rather than efficiently handling transactions and answering routine questions to shorten waiting time in a branch line-up. Such changes in management practice and workplace culture are just as important as new IT — though perhaps less visible — to any organization's ability to make a successful transition to the Knowledge Economy.

Organizations that have recognized this, and changed their management practices accordingly, have been relatively successful with their IT investments. In those organizations that have not — the majority, unfortunately — the failure to recognize these changes has caused management practices to lag behind the evolving nature of the application of IT.

Management's Lagging Mind-set

While the application of information technology has evolved significantly over the last three decades, our approach to managing it has not. When the primary application was automation, management thinking was still rooted in the industrial age. The mind-set meant that you went ahead and built the system, plugged it in and made sure it was running, like a new machine on a manufacturing assembly line or a new electrical appliance. Then, the benefits would flow automatically. Business cases, if required, were one-off affairs, which generally did not include the full costs of the investments, and paid cursory attention to benefits. The subsequent implementation focused almost totally on the IT project, with little consideration of other factors.

This approach was reasonably successful for managing implementation of self-contained automation applications, such as payroll, check processing or even basic airline reservation systems. Unfortunately, as the application of IT has moved beyond automation of work all the way to business transformation, our management approach has remained rooted in industrial-age thinking. Management thinking has failed to understand the implications of the evolving role of IT in business and how critical IT decisions will affect elements of the overall business system beyond technology. Many still think in terms of payroll processing systems that can begin depositing money in employee accounts on day one. In fact, we are delivering customer information systems that will only produce results gradually on day 50, day 100 or day 365, after people are trained and motivated to use the new application when serving customers.

Silver Bullet Thinking

The persistence of the industrial-age mind-set leads to what we call "silver bullet thinking" about the business capabilities of IT — and, more specifically, about the power of IT *alone* to deliver business results. Organizations rush to purchase IT "silver bullets" in the form of customized business solutions, enterprise application packages and other ready-to-wear IT solutions in the naive belief that they come neatly packaged and stamped "benefits inside." Again, the idea is that all you have to do is plug in the technology and, magically, the benefits will flow.

Silver bullet thinking has been found to be a contributing factor in the failure of many large scale business initiatives. In their 1997 *Sloan Management Review* article, M. Lynne Markus and Robert I. Benjamin use the term "magic bullet" to describe this thinking and in so doing, state: "The magic bullet theory hides one of the most important characteristics of information technology. IT is a package of ideas about how people should work differently." They go on to add that "the magic bullet theory does not tell us who should aim and fire the gun."

Twenty years ago, the "package of ideas" about how people should work differently was simple and simple to apply. The evolution of IT applications, and the shift from an industrial economy through an information economy to the emerging Knowledge Economy — characterized by IT-enabled business transformation — demands a new approach to the management of IT investments. In fact, the term "IT investments" is misleading. Given current trends, labeling investments as "technology," "BPR" (business process re-engineering) or "outsourcing" investments is misleading in the majority of cases. Any new approach must recognize that investing in IT is no longer primarily buying a piece of hardware or software, it is investing in the *process of change itself*, a process of change in the overall business system. This is a much more complex undertaking than the relatively simple delivery of an IT system.

Industrial-Age Business Cases   An industrial-age management practice that encourages silver bullet thinking is the use of one-off business cases to support IT investment decisions. Often, these are based on incomplete data and untested assumptions about the future business environment. The approach is to make a rough stab at forecasting future business trends, win project approval and then — frankly — to forget the forecast as quickly as possible. In the process of approving projects this way, managers embrace a "rite of passage" approach and move away from rational decision making.

This traditional one-off approach was never ideal, but it could be tolerated in the era of automation applications, implemented in relatively stable business environments where the executive peer group knew the business intimately. Today, it is often proving disastrous as organizations attempt to manage investments in major IT and business transformation initiatives, in unstable environments. The business cases for such initiatives need to be more comprehensive, flexible and durable. This will allow them to remain relevant even when there are:

- Moving IT targets that result from rapid technological change and the constant arrival of new generations of IT and new technical standards, which can affect an organization's entire technology infrastructure
- Moving business targets that reflect shifting markets, organization structures and business strategies
- Increased complexities that result from the wide range of choice in the technology marketplace, the variety of business functions supported by IT and the multiple linkages in large-scale business transformation initiatives.

Traditional one-off business cases simply sidestep the complexity. They radically oversimplify reality. For this reason, they do not help improve the odds of a successful investment in IT-enabled business transformation. In today's IT environment, they are more likely to produce those runaway projects and software interfaces that real people will not use. These, as we know, are the route to low-return IT investments.

Industrial-Age Project Management   Another facet of silver bullet thinking is that most, if not all, of the delivery and implementation focus is on the IT project, with blind faith that any other required changes will fall into place. Even large-scale, enterprise-wide projects may be managed on a stand-alone basis, with the primary focus being on delivery of a new technology as quickly as possible. When the new equipment is plugged in, the project team holds a victory bash and walks away. Users show up the next day. But the implementation party is really just starting. Not surprisingly, we encounter cases where advanced information systems were delivered on time and within budget, but the benefits still did not materialize as expected. Truly, as some of project teams have noted, the operation was successful but the patient died.

This way of viewing and thinking about IT leads to investment myopia, which is rooted in industrial-age project management practices and methods. While the engineering components of these methods are advanced in many ways, we believe they are too narrowly focused for today's world. Bringing major investment projects in as specified, on time and on budget remains essential. But it is only one necessary condition for success and not by any means a sufficient condition in itself.

Management Blind Spots: Four Critical Dimensions of Complexity

When we recognize that we are not just dealing with IT projects in isolation, but with the process of business transformation, we can then ask the following questions: What are the key things we overlook when we view the IT world using outdated mind-sets? Where do we focus our corrective efforts? In our experience, current management practice fails to adequately address the impact and resource implications of four critical dimensions of complexity. These blind spots in traditional management mind-sets are: linkage, reach, people and time.

Linkage

This refers to the linkage between the expected results of an IT investment and business strategy, and between the IT investment and investments required in other areas of the business in order to realize the benefit. Understanding and addressing linkage requires a clear appreciation of the ultimate benefits and of the full scope of the investment required to achieve the benefits.

Reach

Reach refers to the breadth of change required by an IT investment, meaning how much of the organization is impacted. It also refers to the depth of change — the degree of impact and of organizational change required to realize the benefit. Addressing reach requires understanding what areas of the organization, other organizations and stakeholders will be affected, what the impact will be and how it will be managed.

TABLE 1-2

Management Blind Spots

The Four Critical Dimensions of Complexity

Dimension	Key Elements	The Price of Forgetting
Linkage	• Alignment with business strategy • Contribution to benefits • Integration with other initiatives	• Lack of clear identification and understanding of desired benefits • Lack of clear and measurable contribution to benefits • Overlap/underlap between initiatives • The "project that grew to take over the world"
Reach	• Areas of organization/ supply chain impacted by change • Extent of impact	• Underestimating scope and depth of change • Failure to understand cross functional process implications • Inappropriate/ineffective accountabilities • Scapegoating • Lack of buy-in
People	• People affected by change • Current competencies • Attitudes, motivation, know-how • Readiness for change	• Thinking that "one size fits all" • "Done to" not "done with" • Steep IT and organizational learning curves • Significantly underestimated training effort • Late, inappropriate, ineffective change management • Resistance to change
Time	• Time it takes to manage all dimensions to realize benefit • Change in dimensions over time	• Unrealistic and unachievable expectations • Unexpected time lags between delivery of capability and realization of benefits • Not "staying the course" • Not knowing when to quit

People

A large number and diversity of people must be motivated and prepared to change. This critical factor in business transformation is often underestimated. We need to understand who these people are, where they are today, how they will have to change and what interventions will be required to effect the change. We need to ask how these interventions will be managed for people with different starting points, attitudes and motivations.

Time

In business transformation, time is always of the essence, but realistic time frames are notoriously hard to estimate. We need to ask — and ask again and again — what the realistic length of time is for all the necessary changes to occur and for the full benefits to be realized. We must base these estimates on understanding the previous three dimensions. There must also be a recognition that the dimensions of linkage, reach and people will change over time. This will further affect business transformation time frames. These dimensions are summarized in Table 1-2.

The Management Challenge:
The Evolving Complexity of IT Applications

These dimensions of change have become increasingly complex as the applications of IT have advanced through the stages of automation of work, information management and business transformation.

In the automation stage, the four dimensions were fairly straightforward and posed few problems. In the case of automated payroll systems, for example, there were few linkages, organizational reach was limited and few people were affected. Time was required to deliver the technology, but once it was installed the time to realize the benefits was short or, at least, the time frames were easily predictable in advance. Finally, benefits were easy to measure.

As we moved through the information stage, there were more linkages, not all of which were obvious, and those linkages became more complex. In the case of financial institutions' customer information files, for example, the availability of information did not produce benefits without additional investments in areas such as training, organizational structure and reward systems. These investments required change across more parts of the organization, not just in how work was done, but in what type of work was done and in business processes. More people had to change how they thought, managed and acted. These changes took time, and the precise amounts of time were not easy to predict in advance. As time went on, both the internal and external environment changed and the project delivery schedule had to be adjusted. Benefits did not automatically flow when information applications were delivered, and they were more difficult to measure. Many organizations still wrestle with these issues today as they develop and implement advanced information management applications.

In the transformation stage, there are multiple complex linkages, many not at all obvious. The reach of change affects all areas of organizations, and reaches beyond organizations to customers, suppliers and other business partners. New businesses are defined and, as pointed out above, industry ground rules can be completely rewritten. People from the line worker to the customer have to change how they think and act. All levels of management up to the CEO have to change how they think, manage and act. Learning is continuous. Time to reach the ultimate benefits is unclear. Business transformation is an ongoing process. The growth of complexity across the four dimensions of change is summarized in Table 1-3.

Any new approach to managing investment in IT-enabled change must address these four dimensions of complexity. In doing so, the approach must further recognize that the linkage, reach and people dimensions themselves will change over time. The business environment will change, both externally and internally. Technology itself will certainly change. And, last but not least, the players — and, with new players, the agendas — will change. Addressing them once and then forgetting them, as in the case of traditional one-off business cases, will not cut it.

Just consider a few of the challenges involved in managing IT-enabled business transformation in the banking industry. The automated banking machine networks of the 1980s were fairly simple cases of automating core banking deposit, withdrawal and funds transfer operations. At first, those networks were literally add-ons installed in the outer walls of bank branches, hardly affecting the line-ups and branch tellers' jobs next door. Even today's simple Web sites are relatively self-contained. Customers use these virtual channels or not, while the rest of the organization continues with business as usual in the physical world.

What happens, however, as customers catch on and want more and more services to be delivered electronically? Consumer loans, bill payments, discount brokerage and the negotiation of mortgages are increasingly handled via ATM, telephone banking services, PCs and Internet sites. One day soon, critical mass will be reached and significant

TABLE 1-3
The Three Stages of IT Evolution and the
Four Critical Dimensions of Complexity

Application	Linkage	Reach	People	Time
Automation	• few • simple • obvious • easily measurable results	• few units within organization • minimal change in work activities	• few occupational categories • limited worker job loss • simple and narrow learning for other employees • limited management process impact	• immediate results • clear time frame
Information	• larger number • more complex • less obvious • less easily measurable results	• large number of units, mainly within organization • changed work processes	• crosses occupational categories • worker job change • mid-management job loss • major impact on managment processes • broad learning	• longer term results • less clear time frame
Trans-formation	• many • very complex, multiple • hidden, hard to pinpoint • many measures of value • multiple and variable paths to results	• all organization and extended enterprise • change major business processes • change nature of business /industry • create new businesses	• crosses organizational & occupational boundaries • job change, loss and creation at all levels • significant management process change • complex and continuous learning • executive challenge	• long-term results • open-ended time frame

customer segments will end up conducting the majority of their trans-actions via PCs, telephones and electronic kiosks. At this point, they will no longer have a traditional banking relationship with a home branch but rather a remote banking relationship with the virtual bank. In consequence, electronic banking technology will no longer stand alone. The virtual customer-bank relationship will drive not only IT investment but the re-engineering of customer service processes, the reorganization of sales and service groups and changes to many bankers' jobs. Some of the best sales people will be in call centers and sitting in front of PCs. Clearly, electronic banking on this scale raises significant new issues of linkage, reach, people and time.

Business Transformation and the Knowledge Economy

The potential risks and rewards associated with such cases of business transformation show what is involved in engineering our transition to a Knowledge Economy. The opportunities include expanding geographic scope, expanding electronic commerce and creating virtual companies. We are moving toward an economy that is on-line, interactive, instan-taneous, inter-networked and knowledge based. It is an economy that will require new organizational forms and which will dramatically change the nature of organizations and work.

The emergence of this new economy involves business trans-formation — fundamental changes in value chain management and the application of new technologies to support "networked" organiza-tions that share knowledge, insight and experience effectively. Some experts predict that chief executives will become knowledge capitalists who manage the knowledge assets of their organizations. Knowledge will not just be limited to your organization; it will come from outside it, as well. In addition to managing investments in IT-enabled change in your own business system, you will have to manage change in an extended business system which includes customers, suppliers, financial institutions, regulators and many other intermediaries, all of whom will themselves be in a state of change.

While the opportunities created by business transformation are awesome, the risks can be daunting to investment decision makers. Today's large-scale IT projects and organizational change programs will be viewed as relatively simple initiatives compared to the sophisticated business transformation ones that will be required in the Knowledge

Economy. These will raise significant new issues of linkage, reach, people and time. To manage these dimensions of complexity successfully, business transformation initiatives can no longer be viewed as traditional projects. They will need to be treated almost like mid-size businesses within the business, as programs that are managed continuously and proactively over long periods of time.

Selection and the Problem of Relative Value

Another central facet of the Knowledge Economy, which is already in evidence, is the multiplication of ways to apply IT to enable business transformation initiatives. These opportunities, the fruit of technological progress, will far exceed the capabilities of organizations' resources. This challenge is reviewed in depth in Chapter 4.

Any new management approach must deal with the challenge of determining the relative value of all the opportunities for harnessing IT. In contrast to the mainframe automation era, almost any business initiative proposed today involves IT in some way. This places a great demand on IT resources, and since they are not all created equal, this tends to place an excessive demand on a few key resources — be they gurus with expert knowledge, veteran project managers or project teams used to working together. Even if IT resources can be made available, IT is becoming a smaller part of major business initiatives because much of the required change is in other elements of the business system. Organizations have a finite capacity for absorbing the change required by these initiatives, especially considering that they have a business to run every day while all this is going on.

While, as discussed in Chapter 4, all potential initiatives promise some benefit for organizations, there is a limit to the amount of good organizations can deliver and absorb at any one time. If 20 are proposed, and realistically you can do only five, which five should you do? Which will deliver the greatest value to the organization? This is a potential "bet your business" decision. When Jeff Bezos, the founder of Amazon.com, was setting up his business, he considered both CDs and books. He chose books because there were thousands of publishers and a wide-open market for new services, whereas the music business was dominated by just a few labels that might not support a new on-line venture. Choosing the right business, in this case, was the primary "relative value" decision to be taken.

Again, our industrial-age management approach fails us here. Decisions are generally made in the environment of a competitive free-for-all among stand-alone IT projects, each championed by an executive sponsor interested in pushing his or her pet project. Too often, lobbying, horse trading and selling skills win the day. While it would be naive to believe that these skills do not have their place, the result is that too many IT decisions are made with no greater chance of success than the average gambler in a casino. Yet, these decisions could determine the success or even the survival of organizations in the Knowledge Economy.

Of course, you can carry on managing in this traditional way, leaving realization of the benefits to chance. It happens all the time. When it does, however, chance does its work, resulting in the 20 to 30 percent success rates characteristic of the Information Paradox. We believe that success rates of 80 to 90 percent, exceptional by today's standards, can nevertheless be achieved but only through consistent, proactive management. Again, a new management approach is required that significantly improves the odds of success in IT investment.

Window on the Real World: Client Stories

A striking example of the impacts of silver bullet thinking is the problems some organizations have encountered in implementing enterprise application packages. These packages, supplied by such companies as Baan, Oracle, PeopleSoft and SAP, are intended to replace automation era legacy systems with new integrated systems designed to provide broad information-sharing capabilities. Such capabilities are widely viewed as establishing the foundation for business transformation and the move into the Knowledge Economy.

Enterprise packages, however, can cost many tens of millions of dollars to purchase and implement effectively. They also require organizations to make fundamental changes to the way they do business. If treated as silver bullets, these packages can actually become silver cruise missiles — packing a lot of power that can become dangerous if their business guidance systems are not properly adjusted. Enterprise package implementations are not industrial-era automation projects. Leading with the IT solution, even if it is the most visible element, can be a costly mistake.

The technology is sound. The primary problem is how it is being applied in a business setting. Integrating data across many applications and business units is more than a technical problem. There are business, organizational and process challenges. It takes people time to understand how to apply these new packages to improve business performance. The active involvement and support of many business units and other stakeholders is essential.

To illustrate this point, consider two recent cases where IT managers implementing enterprise packages understood the issues and applied the Benefits Realization Approach, explained in Chapter 2, to manage implementation successfully. After extensive discussion and planning, traditional stand-alone IT projects were replaced with investment programs which ensured that all the complex linkages between the components of the software package, the supporting IT infrastructure and the other elements of the business system were defined and understood. In both cases, traditional business cases were judged incomplete and were supplemented with comprehensive benefits plans. These are examples of managing IT projects as part of broader information management and business transformation initiatives.

A North American Utility

As the scope of the undertaking became clear, the head of information services saw that his group would have to prepare more than the traditional one-off business case.

A large power utility located in North America had a policy of buying off-the-shelf software rather than building it from scratch. In fact, its IT group had to demonstrate why they should *not* buy a software package that appeared to meet the company's needs rather than custom developing one in-house. It was no surprise, then, that the utility contemplated implementing an enterprise application package. Selection and implementation became much more than a technical challenge, however, when the IT group realized that the total cost of the project would exceed that of many of their investments in power lines. It was a striking example of information infrastructure becoming as important as industrial-age infrastructure in the capital-intensive energy generation and transmission sector.

The utility was moving rapidly into the new, deregulated energy distribution marketplace. To prepare for regulatory change and new competitive markets, separate accounting systems would have to be implemented for transmission, distribution and generation. At the same time, business units wanted IT integration to help improve customer service. As the scope of the undertaking became clear, the vice president of information services saw that his group would have to prepare more than a conventional one-off business case for the project. Applying insights gained from bene-fits realization, he decided that only a comprehensive business benefits plan would satisfy the many stakeholders in the company and secure their commitment.

The benefits plan would clarify linkages between projects and benefits, rigorously test assumptions, assess risk and define accountabilities for realizing benefits. The plan would be used throughout the life of the project. "The problem is that benefits are usually estimated at one point in time — or worse — assumed," the vice president of information services commented. "Organizations forget to follow up and address 'how' to realize them. In this case, we couldn't afford to assume that benefits would be a one-time event."

The planning exercise pointed to the need for a full-fledged business program with software implementation as just one com-ponent. The IT project was linked to a series of business initiatives to redesign business processes and introduce new ways of doing work. Defining these projects and building them into the benefits plan had the effect of stimulating business groups to jump on the bandwagon.

A number of scenarios were developed for implementing the package where the main variable was the commitment obtained from business groups to change the way they worked. The utility estimated that by taking a completely passive approach to package implementation, it would realize several million dollars in cost sav-ings. By being more active and doing the supporting business projects, it would realize more than twice that amount in addi-tional benefits.

The benefits plan gave the CEO a clear understanding of probable long-term returns on the company's investment. It pro-vided a valuable decision-making tool, focusing the company's attention on activities that would deliver the greatest benefits. Just as important, it provided a tool for active benefits harvesting over time, and a new model for business-oriented management of major technological change. The IT group used the plan to quickly retire aging systems, reducing operating costs and scoring quick hits. And because most of the expected benefits were contingent on business initiatives, the plan provided a clear road map for business teams involved in the change to commit and coordinate their effort.

Alberta Pool

A standard business case was prepared to support the purchase of an enterprise software package. The key issues troubling the chief infor-mation officer were simple: Will we actually get these benefits? What are the risks?

Wholesale grain handling is a fast-changing global business where advanced IT plays a role at virtually every stage of a complex supply chain that runs from receiving and storing to handling, blending and worldwide shipping.

Alberta Pool, a highly successful Canadian grain co-op located in Calgary, Alberta, offers fully integrated grain handling, marketing and agricultural business services to farmers through a network of grain elevators and agro-centers. The Pool was looking to upgrade its operational and logistics capabilities in order to compete in a global market characterized by price wars. In 1995, it committed over $100 million to revitalize its business processes and technology base and increase efficiencies in an industry where JIT procurement of grain products will become an operational reality. A significant portion of the budget was earmarked for IT upgrades. The aim was to use new technologies to improve customer service and to better integrate operations — tightening links, for example, between grain procurement and marketing operations. A standard business case was prepared to support the purchase of an enterprise application package. Reducing the cost of information technology, addressing the Year 2000 conversion problem and standardizing information systems in such areas as sales, accounting, finance, human resources and materials management were fundamental strategic goals.

The key issues troubling CIO Rand Ayres were simple: Will we actually get these benefits? What are the risks? Ayres knew from previous experience that business processes and people would be affected by the new software. As he says:

> Most organizations have seen cases where a large project is proposed, a business case is put together, approval is obtained from senior management and a plan is assembled for implementing the system over, perhaps, several years. But along the way something seems to happen. People get under pressure to meet installation dates, achieve budgetary targets — to basically get the thing done. The only problem is, they forget to manage the benefits over time and keep an eye on all the things that cause the benefits to happen. We felt we had to do better. In addition, we knew that the parts of these projects relating solely to IT are relatively simple to manage when you compare them to the human issues surrounding re-engineered processes.

The answer was to design an investment program, using the Benefits Realization Approach, that linked software package implementation to business process, cultural and human/organizational changes. The organization learned that implementation of an enterprise application package can sometimes trigger very sensitive discussions. Benefits realization made it possible to deal objectively with risks and benefits. When planning was raised to the senior management level, the IT project could be coordinated with other activities in the organization.

"This [Benefits Realization] Approach," Ayres says, "brings you face to face with a lot of things you have to do to get value." Building a Results Chain produced a comprehensive road map of all the initiatives that would be required to lever the IT investment and harvest benefits over time. It also brought the business organization to the table with the IT group, so that everyone agreed up front on what needed to be done.

Summary

The Information Paradox is evident in economic productivity, in business profitability, in knowledge worker performance and in project delivery performance. The lack of convincing, positive and measurable returns from IT investments over long time periods is raising many questions. As we enter the Knowledge Economy, managers increasingly ask: Where are the business results? When will we reap the benefits from these investments? And how?

This is understandable. The overall track record of IT investments over 30 years shows extreme variability. As a result, many executives making IT investment decisions today feel like gamblers in a casino. In our experience, the primary reason for this variability is that information technology is not being applied properly to achieve clear business objectives. This huge variability of business results is not a technology problem — it is a business management problem. The immediate challenge for business is to reduce the variability and, in so doing, to improve the odds of getting business results from IT investments. Organizations need to move from today's world of casino gambling, with its associated odds, to the world of managed business investments.

The answer to the Information Paradox lies in changing our management mind-sets. While the application of IT has moved beyond automation of work all the way to business transformation, our management thinking has failed to understand the implications of this evolving role of IT in business and how critical IT decisions will affect all elements of the overall business system beyond technology.

This lagging mind-set leads to silver bullet thinking about the "magical" business capabilities of IT and, more specifically, about the power of IT alone to deliver business results. In doing so, it overlooks four critical dimensions of complexity — linkage, reach, people and time. Consequently, it fails to provide a context for evaluating choices between a growing number of potential ways to apply IT. To date, silver bullet thinking and its associated behavior has been a frustration and an embarrassment. It has had an impact on organizations' bottom lines but has not generally posed a threat to their survival. It has cost some CIOs their jobs. The result has been the Information Paradox and high failure rates of IT initiatives.

As we enter the uncharted waters of the Knowledge Economy, these problems will become more acute and will threaten the very survival of organizations. The need for a new approach to the management of IT investments becomes critical. As Peter Senge said in *The Fifth Discipline,* "Learning disabilities are tragic in children, but they are fatal in organizations. Because of them, few corporations live even half as long as a person — most die before the age of 40." Today, the need for organizations to learn how to better manage their investments in IT-enabled change has never been greater. The life expectancy of those organizations that do not learn will be greatly reduced.

Solving the Information Paradox should be a business imperative for executives and for all business managers today. It is part of the continuing challenge of reinventing organizations to compete for future leadership of their industries. Those organizations that solve the Information Paradox, including those few that have already solved it, will be the winners in the emerging Knowledge Economy. Those that do not will be history.

****

In Chapter 2, we introduce Fujitsu Consulting's approach to solving the Information Paradox, our Benefits Realization Approach. We introduce the cornerstones of the approach, three fundamentals: program management, portfolio management and full cycle governance, and three necessary conditions: activist accountability, relevant measurement and proactive management of change. We present two supporting techniques: a modeling technique, the Results Chain™, and a value assessment technique, the four "ares."

THE BENEFITS **2** REALIZATION
APPROACH

As we enter the Knowledge Economy, the challenge of effectively managing technological change in organizations and indeed across entire industries is becoming acute. This is not primarily a technology issue, nor an issue of interest only to IT managers, it is an issue for all business managers. The traditional industrial-age approach to managing automation-focused projects has become a relic, leading to silver bullet thinking about the new generations of IT and how they can be applied to support advanced information management and enable business transformation. The end result is unacceptably high failure rates in applying new technologies. We need a new approach.

The Benefits Realization Approach provides a new basis for using information technology to deliver business results more consistently and predictably. It proposes two interrelated shifts: in mind-sets about IT and in management methods. Silver bullet thinking is replaced with a new benefits mind-set that focuses on integrating technology into the business system. Its central tenet is that IT alone, no matter how technically powerful, cannot deliver business results.

Before we describe the approach, it is useful to note that while the focus of this book is on investments in IT-enabled change, the Benefits Realization Approach that we describe in this chapter, and all through the book, is applicable to any major investment in organizational change. Our examples throughout the book have a strong IT component, but the astute reader will observe, as many of our clients have done, that the approach and its underlying fundamentals have much more general applicability. And it is important to note that initiatives which at first appear to be dominated by technology, on analysis, prove to be exactly the opposite. The client story of Ericsson is a case in point. There, 80 percent of the work proved not to be IT related.

The benefits mind-set underlying the Benefits Realization Approach is based on the following premises:

- *Benefits do not just happen.* They don't just automatically appear when a new technology is delivered. A benefits stream flows and evolves over time as people learn to use it.

- *Benefits rarely happen according to plan.* A forecast of benefits to support the business case for an investment is just an early estimate. It is unlikely to turn out as expected, much like corporate earnings forecasts. You have to keep checking, just as you would with a financial investment that fluctuates in value on the securities market.

- *Benefits realization is a continuous process* of envisioning results, implementing, checking intermediate results and dynamically adjusting the path leading from investments to business results. Benefits realization is a process that can and must be managed, just like any other business process.

The benefits mind-set forms the basis for a major shift in management methods and practices that is the main focus of this chapter. The industrial-age approach to project management described in Chapter 1 focuses almost exclusively on the delivery of technology, on time and on budget. In contrast, the Benefits Realization Approach focuses on all the projects and initiatives required to produce business results, whether they involve training or technology, change management or software engineering. It focuses on managing the continuous benefits realization process.

Managing IT-Enabled Technological Change: The Benefits Realization Process

The benefits realization process includes traditional project management processes, which are well understood and documented, but it reaches well beyond the "design-develop-test-deliver" cycle of conventional project management. Upstream from traditional project design, the benefits realization process reaches to the initial hatching of project concepts. At the other end of the cycle, it includes the ultimate harvesting of end results, which occurs far downstream from traditional project completion landmarks such as the delivery of new software, networks and information systems. Viewed this way, the process includes all phases of investment decision making, project management, delivery, implementation, monitoring and continuous adjustment. In contrast to traditional project management cycles, it reaches from "concept to cash" rather than from "design to delivery."

All organizations today have a benefits realization process whether they know it or not. It is probably not a formal process and therefore is neither known nor understood. It almost certainly does not work very well. It is a passive process, not a managed one. We have found that, like manufacturing or product development processes, the benefits realization process can be designed and engineered systematically to improve business performance.

The Benefits Realization Approach is designed to provide proactive management of the benefits realization process. By continuously improving the benefits realization processes of many organizations, we can envision the day when the success rates of investments in IT-enabled change will rise to 80 — then 90 percent and beyond – considerably higher than the casino odds prevailing today. Information technology will be recognized as delivering demonstrable business value consistently and predictably.

The Benefits Realization Approach is designed to help people build a shared vision of the benefits realization process. It gives senior management a clear understanding of what business results are to be achieved through a major investment and of IT's contribution to those results. It gives middle management a clear understanding of the resources required to get these results and of their role in achieving this goal. All employees and work groups develop an understanding of how they will contribute to results and how they will use new technologies to do their work in new ways. With the Benefits Realization Approach, organizations will only embark on IT-enabled change with both a clear road map depicting the paths that lead to beneficial results and the capabilities required to realize those benefits.

The Benefits Realization Approach is not just another academic theory. It is a practical approach, much of which was developed, tested in the field and successfully used in the U.S., Canada, Europe, Australia and New Zealand in organizations that include telecommunications companies, energy utilities, banks, insurance companies and manufacturers. It has been used to meet a variety of business transformation challenges, such as:

■ Ensuring that benefits are understood and realized from large, complex and expensive software investments, including enterprise application packages such as SAP, Internet related applications and Knowledge Management initiatives

■ Understanding, managing and realizing benefits from major business process re-engineering programs

■ Managing complex portfolios of investment programs and projects

■ Providing a focus on results to guide major organizational change programs.

Cornerstones of the Benefits Realization Approach

There are three fundamentals that define the core of the Benefits Realization Approach. To implement it successfully, organizations must also meet three necessary conditions. These are outlined below.

Three Fundamentals

1. Shift from stand-alone IT project management to business *program management.*
2. Shift from free-for-all competition among projects to disciplined *portfolio management.*
3. Shift from traditional project management cycles to *full cycle governance.*

Three Necessary Conditions

1. *Activist accountability* in order to identify business sponsors with active, continuous ownership of investment programs.

2. *Relevant measurement* systems to measure the things that count in the benefits realization process.

3. *Proactive management of change* to give people ownership stakes in programs.

 The fundamentals and necessary conditions are illustrated in Figure 2-1.

FIGURE 2-1
Cornerstones of Benefits Realization Approach

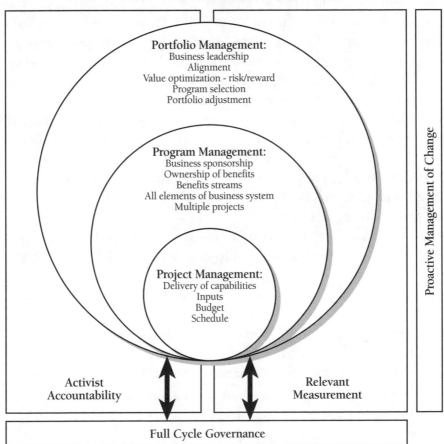

Portfolio Management:
Business leadership
Alignment
Value optimization - risk/reward
Program selection
Portfolio adjustment

Program Management:
Business sponsorship
Ownership of benefits
Benefits streams
All elements of business system
Multiple projects

Project Management:
Delivery of capabilities
Inputs
Budget
Schedule

Proactive Management of Change

Activist
Accountability

Relevant
Measurement

Full Cycle Governance

Three Fundamentals

The three fundamentals underpinning the Benefits Realization Approach, aimed at changing the way people think and manage, are: program management, portfolio management and full cycle governance.

First Fundamental: Program Management. Organizations need to make the shift from stand-alone project management to managing blended business investment programs, including all elements of the business system. To understand the magnitude of this change, it is important to make the distinction between projects and programs.

Projects are a structured set of activities concerned with delivering a defined capability to the organization based on an agreed schedule and budget. Major projects common in the IT world include construction of an Internet Web site, installation of a new software package and design of a customer information system and automated response system for a call center. In terms of the benefits realization process, the focus of projects is on the inputs, costs and time required to produce intermediate outcomes. The typical project management cycle ends with delivery of the technology. The capability does not translate into benefit for the organization until it is combined with others delivered by other related projects. Some of these may be IT projects while yet others are business projects which will deliver capabilities in the other elements of the overall business system.

Programs are structured groupings of projects designed to produce clearly identified business results or other end benefits. The projects cited above would form important parts of blended investment programs. Here's what three of them could look like:

1. The program around the interactive Web site would include all projects required to generate a minimum number of hits and achieve a predetermined sales revenue target within 12 months of the launch.

2. The program around the new software package would include related initiatives to help business units achieve well-defined process improvement objectives in manufacturing, finance and sales within 24 months.

3. The call center program would include staffing, training, marketing and launch projects designed to achieve clear operational, sales and profitability goals over the first 24 months of operation.

In terms of the benefits realization process, the focus is on all the steps required to deliver business results. To reinforce this view, the term "blended investment program" (explained fully in Chapter 3), is used. These programs include many types of projects: IT delivery, training, marketing, organizational change and business process redesign. All these projects are managed and monitored from concept to cash. Consequently, well-designed programs extend, in time, well beyond the delivery of technology to the desktop or data center. Benefits are realized because the process is continually managed from end to end. Program management will be explored fully in Chapter 3.

Second Fundamental: Portfolio Management Organizations need to make the shift from free-for-all competition for resources among stand-alone projects to disciplined portfolio management. This involves managing all blended investment programs as part of a portfolio with clear performance objectives.

Portfolios are structured groupings of investment programs selected by management to achieve defined business results, while meeting clear risk/reward standards. The classic example in business is a financial portfolio which groups stocks, bonds and any other financial assets together into a blended investment, offering a single rate of return. Ideally, the portfolio can be selected to maximize the expected return for any level of risk that the investor is prepared to accept. Investment risk is reduced through diversification. The investor gets a whole new menu of investment choices, rather than being limited to buy/sell decisions on a single stock or category of securities.

The idea is to manage an organization's blended investment programs as part of a portfolio that produces a stream of benefits, similar to investment returns. Using this approach, the organization seeks to build the best portfolio mix of programs. This is happening to a limited degree today. Some companies, for example, manage portfolios of IT applications through the coordination of technology acquisition, development, maintenance and retirement processes. Major information systems may pass through defined life cycles as part of this process. The Benefits Realization Approach goes farther and suggests that the portfolio should include investments that touch all elements of the business system, not just IT. More specifically, and as indicated above, the portfolio will be composed of investment programs that blend IT investments with related business initiatives.

In terms of the benefits realization process, the portfolio focus is on the alignment of high-level outcomes of the major investment programs with business objectives, the costs incurred and the risk exposure associated with those outcomes. The portfolio focus is strategic. In a period of rapid technological and economic change, the portfolio represents the future of the business.

Moving beyond stand-alone projects to blended business investment programs allows organizations to define the full scope of such programs. Few organizations, however, have the luxury of working on only one program at a time or of "freezing" the internal and external environment during the life of the program. In reality, there are many potential programs, some of which will be underway at any given time. As programs are better understood, and as there are changes to the internal and external environment, the anticipated benefits from a program — and, as a result, its relative value — will change.

Organizations need to take the same approach as investors on the stock market. They need to select and manage a portfolio of business assets. This involves determining the desired mix of investments, and monitoring the investments based on changing returns and "market" conditions. Current investments may be increased, decreased or withdrawn, and new investments may be added. The composition of the portfolio will change over time. Portfolio management will be explored fully in Chapter 4.

Third Fundamental: Full Cycle Governance. Organizations need to move beyond myopic project management cycles to full cycle governance, an integrated management system that operationalizes the concepts of program and portfolio management.

Full cycle governance is the actual management process that goes beyond traditional project management in order to implement the Benefits Realization Approach. Like program management, it is distinguished by its long time frame that supports management of the benefits realization process from the conception of projects to the harvesting of benefits — from concept to cash. It is also distinguished by a process of progressive resource commitment in which resources are committed to programs in small increments.

To manage progressive resource commitment, full cycle governance employs a set of defined "stage gates," decision points at which clear decisions are made to continue, modify or cancel programs. Stage gates are designed to encourage the search for new benefits opportunities as the business environment around a program changes. It also allows for the incremental management of risk, since programs applying new technologies only bet the company one step at a time. Full cycle governance will be explored fully in Chapter 5.

Three Necessary Conditions

There are three conditions necessary for effective implementation of the Benefits Realization Approach, both of individual investment programs and of entire investment portfolios. These conditions require organizations to manage and act differently. The three necessary conditions are: activist accountability, relevant measurement and proactive management of change.

First Necessary Condition: Activist Accountability. Accountability must be assigned in a more active mode to clearly identify business sponsors of the investment programs that produce benefits, as well as the people responsible for specific projects and tasks. Full cycle governance makes business managers clearly accountable for delivering business benefits and IT managers accountable for delivering the right tools and technological capabilities. There must be a strong focus on destroying old ghetto walls between business and IT. We must move to activist accountability that includes the concept of ownership. By ownership, we mean active, continuous involvement in managing a program and, most importantly, clear ownership of each measurable outcome and the associated benefits. Accountability must be appropriately positioned in the organization, with business accountability for blended investment programs and their target benefits. Accountability will be explored fully in Chapter 6.

Second Necessary Condition: Relevant Measurement. Measurement systems must be adjusted to measure the things that count in the benefits realization process and to give the people who are accountable the information they need to make decisions and act upon them. Full cycle governance requires measurement of new domains of organizational performance, moving beyond the traditional measurement of inputs to measuring outcomes, with a primary focus on key business outcomes. Measurements must clearly link the contribution of investments to outcomes, and themselves be linked to clear lines of accountability. Measurement will be explored fully in Chapter 7.

Third Necessary Condition: Proactive Management of Change. The third necessary condition applies generally to the success of any attempt to implement the Benefits Realization Approach. It is a condition that is designed specifically to ensure that people think, manage and act differently, and therefore to help them make the transition.

This condition is the proactive management of change. Change management methods must be applied effectively both to introduce the new benefits mind-set and to support all phases of full cycle governance. As with accountability, a far more activist approach to managing change is required for organizations to take charge of the benefits realization process. The major change processes of benefits realization must be actively structured and visibly led by senior management. Their leadership role must be shared with program and project managers. The concept of ownership in major investment programs, introduced to sharpen the focus on accountability, includes the idea of ownership in key change initiatives. It conveys the sense that people can proactively direct the course of change. Managing change will be explored fully in Chapter 8.

Two Techniques to Support Benefits Realization

Organizations face two practical challenges when implementing the Benefits Realization Approach. These are designing programs and assessing the relative value of programs. There are two techniques to meet these challenges: modeling and value assessment.

Modeling:

- Supports program design through improved understanding of the linkages between investments and benefits in the benefits realization process, as well as many organizational reach issues, and
- Supports dynamic management of the benefits realization process over time.

Value assessment:

- Supports valuation and selection of programs, and
- Supports ongoing management of the portfolio, including dynamic adjustment to the programs composing it.

FIGURE 2-2 ODOT Results Chain

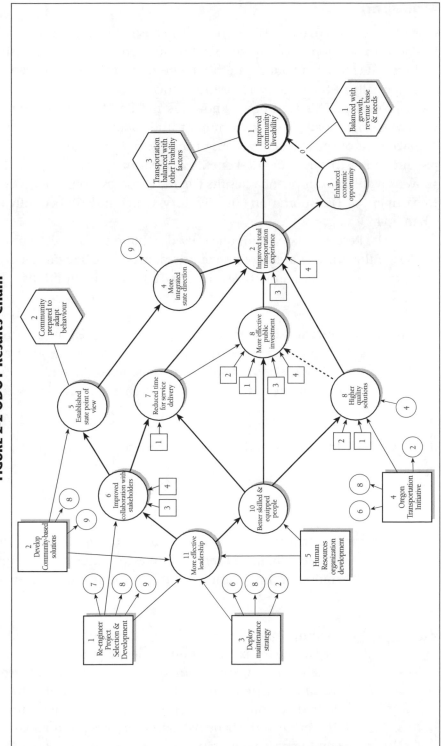

Modeling

One of our distinctive contributions to the cause of benefits realization has been to develop a technique to help you prepare a comprehensive and accurate model of your organization's benefits realization process — and especially of the benefits realization process specific to large investment programs. This technique, known as the Results Chain, enables you to prepare "road maps" that support understanding and proactive management of the four dimensions of complexity (linkage, reach, people and time) throughout the benefits realization process. Figure 2-2 shows a real life example of a Results Chain. It comes from the Oregon Department of Transportation (ODOT) story, which is described fully in Chapter 4.

The Results Chain technique is used to build simple yet rigorous models of the linkages among four core elements of the benefits realization process: outcomes, initiatives, contributions and assumptions.

 Outcomes: the results sought, including either intermediate outcomes in the chain, those outcomes that are necessary but not sufficient to achieve the end benefit, or ultimate outcomes, the end benefits to be harvested.

 Initiatives: actions that contribute to one or more outcomes.

Contributions: the roles played by elements of the Results Chain, either initiatives or intermediate outcomes, in contributing to other initiatives or outcomes.

 Assumptions: hypotheses regarding conditions necessary to the realization of outcomes or intiatives but over which the organization has little or no control. Assumptions represent risks that you may not achieve desired outcomes. Any change to an assumption during the course of the benefits realization process should force you to revise your map.

The Results Chain for a program isn't just another externally created piece of documentation. It is developed through a process of extensive interviews and workshops with business stakeholders. The process of developing a Results Chain promotes discussion, consensus and commitment. It develops a shared understanding of the linkages between IT initiatives and initiatives related to other elements of the business system. Understanding of linkages exposes reach and people impacts, which then allows the time dimension to be realistically assessed. Its power is in making implicit thinking explicit, and bringing hidden assumptions to the surface, thus facilitating communication and enabling better decision making.

To illustrate these points, let us review just one small fragment of a program model built using the Results Chain. It comes from the plan of a printing firm that was experiencing a drop in sales. They were also receiving complaints from some customers about the length of time required to fill orders. The company felt that this problem was contributing to their decline in sales and that they needed to reduce their order processing cycle time. To accomplish this, they decided to develop and implement a new order entry system. The initial, simple Results Chain for this case is illustrated in Figure 2-3.

FIGURE 2-3
Illustration of a Simple Results Chain

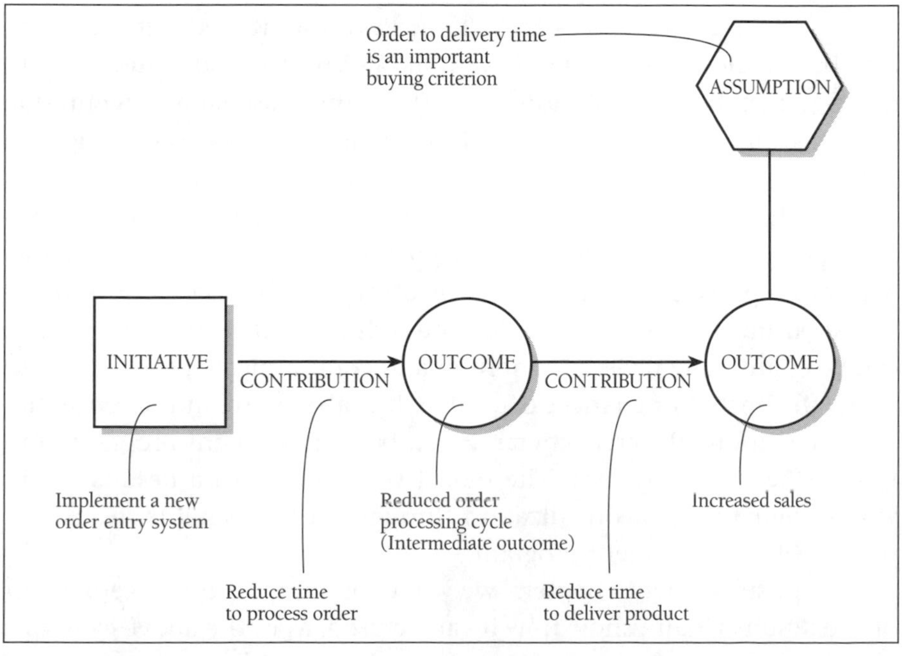

In Results Chain terminology, the company undertook an *initiative* to develop and implement a new order entry system. The objective of the new order entry system was to reduce the time it took to process an order. This reduction was expected to *contribute* to reducing the order processing cycle, an *intermediate outcome*. The reduced order processing cycle was in turn expected to contribute to increased sales, the final *outcome*. This expected contribution was also premised on the *assumption* that, based on customer complaints, order to delivery time was an important buying criterion.

In reality, the true Results Chain behind such a case would be much more complex. As currently modelled, this is a clear case of silver bullet thinking about how quickly the new order processing system can increase sales because it is unlikely that it alone will reduce the order processing cycle.

In the Benefits Realization Approach, this model would become the starting point for fleshing out other initiatives. It is likely that some re-engineering of the order entry process itself would be required. The assumption around the impact of delivery time on sales would need to be tested. Other initiatives that might be included are training, changing physical layouts, defining new roles and responsibilities and designing a new reward system. Along the way, further intermediate outcomes and assumptions would surface. These are all required for this to become a true blended investment program.

Different ways or "paths" to achieve the desired outcome may also be revealed. The Results Chain allows you to model and identify these paths. In combination with the value assessment technique described in the next section, a Results Chain lets you select the best path and to switch paths in response to changing conditions.

The Results Chain model is more than an abstract map of business reality. When completed, it becomes a living model of the benefits realization process. It is not just a one-off model that is used, like traditional business cases, and then forgotten. It is living in the sense that it can be continually revised to monitor and communicate progress and to assess the impact of changes over time. It is also living in the sense that it can be modified to reflect changes in both investment programs and the business environment. The model you build with a Results Chain will accompany your organization throughout the benefits realization process of an investment program.

In subsequent chapters, we will expand upon the development of the Results Chain, show how it can be used, as in the above example, to define programs and demonstrate how it can further be used to support program management, including accountability, measurement and ongoing communication.

In the past, in the era of relatively simple automation applications of technology, such a model may not have been required. Today it is essential. It will become even more so in the Knowledge Economy when organizations are managing the complex web of initiatives involved in business transformation (including such endeavors as the implementation of large enterprise application packages, major IT-enabled re-engineering efforts, implementation of the virtual value chain through advanced electronic commerce applications and the creation of entirely new knowledge-based businesses).

Value Assessment Technique

The Results Chain provides the model for benefits realization. It shows the desired outcomes and the possible paths that can be taken to reach those outcomes. It does not, in and of itself, help you decide the relative value, including the opportunities and risks, of the various paths within a program, or of the potential programs within a portfolio. As such, it does not help you select programs. For that, the value assessment technique will assist you in gauging the odds of success for a specific investment program.

The Four "Ares". There are many questions that need to be asked as you develop the Results Chain and try to assess the relative value of paths and of programs. What you need are a structured framework to organize the questions and instruments to provide more objectivity to the answers, permitting comparable measurement of the answers.

The structured framework is in the form of four basic questions — the four "ares":

Are 1: Are we doing the right things? This question addresses the definition (or redefinition) of business, of business direction and the alignment of programs and the overall business investment portfolio with that direction.

Are 2: Are we doing them the right way? This question addresses organizational structure and process, and the integration of programs within that structure and process.

Are 3: Are we getting them done well? This question addresses organizational capability, the resources available and supporting infrastructure required to get work done efficiently.

Are 4: Are we getting the benefits? This question addresses the proactive management of the benefits realization process as a whole.

The four "ares" are summarized in the Figure 2-4.

FIGURE 2-4
The Four "Ares"

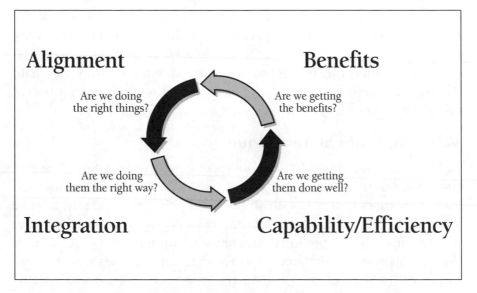

The four "ares" provide a rich framework for assessing value. To be truly useful in the benefits realization process, we have to drive these questions down to a greater level of detail and incorporate them into measurement instruments that are practical, easy to apply and that allow some degree of consistent — and therefore comparable — measurement.

From practical experience, a good approximation of the four "ares" can be developed with more detailed questions and measurements along three dimensions: alignment, financial worth and risk. For example, in the case of Nova Gas Transmission, one of North America's largest natural gas pipeline companies, the four "ares" have been used to determine how well programs contribute to current business objectives, to achieving the future strategic vision of the company and to supporting the goals of the parent organization. Financial worth is calculated using traditional accounting methods, and program risk is again measured with respect to the four "ares." In Chapters 3 and 4, we will expand further on these dimensions and their supporting instruments.

The most important thing that organizations must do if they are to master the benefits realization process is to ask the right questions and to ask them over and over again. All too frequently, organizations rush forward blindly, basing their decisions on superficial answers to the wrong questions and never revisit the questions except to lay blame. Taking the time to formulate and ask the right questions and continuing to ask them is critical to an effective benefits realization process.

Tough questioning is also critical to get rid of silver bullet thinking and lose the industrial-age mind-set that is proving extremely costly to organizations. Asking the four "ares," in particular, helps to define the business and technical issues clearly, and thus to better define the distinctive but interrelated roles of business executives and IT experts in the investment decision process. Are 1, Are we doing the right things? and Are 4, Are we getting the benefits? raise key business issues relating to both strategic direction and the organization's ability to produce the targeted business benefits. Are 2, Are we doing them the right way? raises a mix of business and technology integration issues that must be answered to design successful blended investment programs. Are 3, Are we getting them done well? directs attention to the ability of business groups to deliver change projects as well as to traditional IT project delivery issues.

In the days of automation of work, attention focused mainly on "getting it done" (Are 3), with the IT group deciding whether proposed projects were executable and supported by accurate technical resource estimates. There might also have been discussion of "doing it the right way" (Are 2), ensuring compliance with the technology architecture and standards. To develop information management applications, the questions of integration (Are 2) and benefits (Are 4) became more important. To design business transformation programs, all four "ares" must be asked often. For benefits realization to be effective, business managers — including senior business executives — are needed to ensure that strategic alignment and benefits questions (Ares 1 and 4) are asked and answered. They also need to deal with the business aspects of integration and delivery (Ares 2 and 3). The IT group must continue to take the lead in answering the delivery question (Are 3), as related to IT projects, while participating more actively in discussion of all the four "ares."

The Results Chain and value assessment techniques are innovative creations. However, it is important to recognize that they are only tools that are used to support the much bigger job of proactively managing the benefits realization process. This approach requires the use of a much more diversified tool kit and, most importantly, the commitment of all levels of management to understand and shape the way that benefits are realized over a period of many years.

Managers Must Have Patience: This is Not a Quick Fix

In today's increasingly complex world, very few things worth doing are easy. This is no exception. The Benefits Realization Approach is not a quick fix and certainly not a silver bullet. It involves a long-term, sustained change effort for organizations and managers in how they think and look at the world, how they organize and manage and how they act and execute. This approach is not a cookbook. It must be adapted to each organization, indeed to each of its major IT-enabled change programs. To succeed, however, all organizations must apply the three fundamentals and observe the three necessary conditions.

One final word of caution. The Benefits Realization Approach should not be considered as a purely mechanistic process. It is an approach to *support* business judgment, not to replace it. The future changes every day. It is the continuous nature of the approach that ensures that organizations can detect and react to change as it occurs.

Window on the Real World: Client Stories

The Benefits Realization Approach has been applied to meet a variety of business transformation challenges. Those described in the client stories that follow include: the redesign of core business processes; major IT conversion projects; and the management of IT investments with long-term business impacts that were hard to forecast and control.

Whatever the starting point, however, the path to success was not clear and there were pressing concerns about the risks of failure. The common core of issues included the following:

- *Project scope* was broad and unclear, since it included both technological change and business process redesign
- *Contribution of IT* was unclear in some areas and not universally understood in the organization
- *Traditional business cases,* cost/benefit analysis and project management methods appeared inadequate to deal with these issues.

In all cases, key decision makers and project managers recognized that new game plans, road maps and models were needed.

Benefits Realization Process

Although the exact approach differed from case to case, all the clients whose stories appear here built a Results Chain model of the initial project and possible related projects. The process of building the model included the following steps:

- Reviews of written strategies, business plans and budgets and the status of projects

- Interviews with key executives and managers involved in setting objectives and designing programs to determine high-level *objectives* and *outcomes*

- Interviews with a cross section of senior and middle managers to flesh out the *initiatives, contributions, assumptions* and *intermediate outcomes.*

The Results Chain models were built through an iterative process of discussion, preparing rough drafts, validation and the progressive detailing of programs and projects. There was a substantial element of consensus building around the model that emerged.

Results

As was the case with the initial problem, the specific results varied. But again there was a common pattern revolving around the recognition that the vast majority of project work in all these business transformation programs was not IT related. This discovery by project teams led to several positive results:

- Tighter meshing of Business Process Re-engineering (BPR) and IT projects in blended business investment programs

- Better transition plans built into programs

- Broader value cases and cost/benefit perspectives.

In addition to these technical results, these organizations developed a new mind-set about technological change and BPR. Closer cooperation between business managers and IT flowed from the validation and consensus building process required to build the Results Chain model. At the end of the day, there was universal recognition that the shared vision of change was more important than the paper model.

Ericsson

The projects appeared to be dominated by technology, but benefits analysis pointed to the opposite conclusion: almost 80 percent of the work was *not* IT related.

The telecommunications industry is faced with constant competitive pressures, sophisticated and demanding clients and smaller and smaller windows of opportunity to introduce new products. More than ever, time to market is a critical success factor for players in telecommunications.

Ericsson, headquartered in Sweden with operations in over 100 countries throughout the world, is a global provider of advanced telecommunications technology and the leading supplier of digital cellular systems. The challenge facing Ericsson was dramatic. The high-tech engineering teams at its Montreal development center for advanced cellular system equipment needed to achieve two goals: reduce the time to market for new products by 50 percent, and collapse the cycle time for fixing product bugs reported by clients by 95 percent. These goals were ambitious, to be sure, but they reflected clear messages coming from the sophisticated telecom carriers purchasing Ericsson cellular systems. Time was of the essence in a wide-open market where they had to get new cell phones and services in consumers' hands quickly, or lose out to their competitors.

Ericsson concluded that a major re-engineering of core development and quality control processes was required to protect its global market position. Testing for software bugs and correcting them appeared to be the major time-consuming activities. The re-engineering planners zeroed in on two key areas for improvement: the product testing process at the back end of the manufacturing process for cellular switching equipment, and the process for diagnosing, solving and deploying software solutions for product bugs reported by clients, a prime customer service indicator.

The question asked by Ericsson managers was how to best design these two business process re-engineering (BPR) projects — known as advanced verification environment (AVE) and modification handling (MH). "These were not clear-cut BPR projects," recalls director Luc Mayrand "The road to success was not clearly mapped in advance. We were concerned about risks of cost overruns, delays and failure to achieve targeted benefits."

The Benefits Realization Approach was used to gain a better understanding of the risks and success factors. The investigation produced some surprises. At first glance, both the AVE and MH projects appeared to be dominated by IT and changes to advanced technology production environments. In fact, analysis pointed to the opposite conclusion: almost 80 percent of the required initiatives were non-IT related.

As the perspective changed for the project teams, and a benefits mind-set began to shape senior management perceptions, the original BPR projects were expanded into complete blended investment programs. "We focused on business processes, organizational change, technology and people aspects. Scope and timing were key issues," recalls program manager Patrick Forslund.

The approach allowed them to achieve commitment and consensus, share a common understanding of the changes to be put in place and select the highest value initiatives. But above all, it allowed them to determine the entire sequence in which all projects had to be realized over three years in order to maximize value and speed the realization of the benefits.

The exercise brought to the surface critical new projects that would be required to reduce the targeted cycle times and helped the company plan for an orderly transition to the new environment. Benefits realization showed the most effective grouping of initiatives into action programs and clearly mapped the linkages between key projects. Using this information, the programs were designed to avoid conflicts and delays.

The results were impressive — and measurable. With the two programs six months away from completion, time to market for new products was already down 50 percent, and the time required to deploy modifications to clients was reduced by 70 percent.

Sollac

The Benefits Realization Approach made IT visible to senior management and made it clear that "there's no such thing as an IT project anymore."

In the new economy, traditional heavy manufacturing industries are under just as much pressure to redesign their core business processes as are advanced technology firms. Benefits realization can be used to help structure blended investment programs that get results from these complex and critical initiatives.

Sollac, located in Paris, France, is the flat-products branch of Groupe Usinor Sacilor, Europe's largest steel producer, and the world's third largest. Sollac provides steel products to various industries. Sollac decided to adopt the Benefits Realization Approach when it began to reorganize its business around the automobile industry — its largest client segment. This was a major business transformation initiative with impacts on all major processes, from product design to billing. That meant a major effort by the IT group, as 11 of the company's 12 information systems needed to be changed. Traditionally, Sollac had used the same systems and applications for all of its clients. Now, within a few years, it would have to tailor systems from one end of the supply chain to the other — including order processing, manufacturing, inventory management and billing — to meet the needs of an automobile industry that was undergoing rapid change.

"This was a large program for us," says Jean-Pierre Corniou, Sollac's director of systems and information technology. "We knew there would be risk and a sizable impact on both our systems and the way the organization works. A program like this touches the 'heart' of the organization. There is always a risk of rejection, just like when a surgeon transplants an organ into a patient. We had to minimize the risk of rejection of our IT systems. We needed a safety net."

The Benefits Realization Approach gave the business units and the IT group an integrated, big picture view of how all of the change programs would interact over time. It helped with project sequencing and prioritizing and facilitated communication with all of the stakeholders.

Corniou observes that while historically IT has been a side-line player in many organizations, the big picture view discloses a different reality: "This [Benefits Realization] Approach makes IT visible to senior management, especially as there's no such thing as an IT project any more. IT is all interrelated now with work processes, the culture, the people, other technologies in the organization etc. IT projects are blended investments, and they need to be viewed and treated as such."

A Regional Bank in Asia-Pacific

Benefits Realization linked the introduction of new technology with business process redesign, cultural change, bonuses based on results and the transformation of the teller's role into that of financial advisor.

Regional banks must compete in a world of global and national giants that have all the advantages of financial and technological scale. To build a competitive position in the Asia-Pacific market and measurably increase shareholder value, a regional bank launched an ambitious redesign of several dozen business processes, combined with an IT conversion program aimed at improving both customer service and cost performance.

Like most banking institutions, this regional bank was critically dependent on information technology to effectively serve its business and retail clients. Not surprisingly, it identified its information systems as the most promising area for improvement: the area most likely to have an impact on the bank's overall efficiency, revenues and profitability. When the systems were targeted for replacement as part of the whole strategy, management recognized that every part of the bank would be affected, and that the systems conversion could not be managed like a typical IT project.

Benefits realization was used to link the introduction of new technology with a wide range of other change initiatives, including business process redesign, cultural change, bonuses based on results and the transformation of the teller's role into that of a financial advisor. What emerged, of course, were several blended investment programs.

The new approach transformed the bank's decision-making and management process by:

- Articulating high-level outcomes with senior executives
- Developing a common language and perspective that could be shared by banking and IT executives
- Defining less tangible, but strategically important outcomes, such as increased cross-selling of bank services
- Getting the executives involved to commit to delivering the expected benefits.

Benefits realization was integrated into the regional bank's project initiation and management methods. It has been used to assess all new project proposals, define programs, assign account-abilities, measure outcomes and track the delivery of benefits using a benefits register.

National Bank of Canada

The Results Chain model became a powerful communication and selling tool.

One of the classic causes of silver bullet thinking is that many investments in information technology are simply invisible to the business side of the organization, as are the immediate impacts on end users and customers. This is only to be expected, given that in most cases, there is a long and complex chain of linkages leading from the IT investment, through other elements of the business to end results.

The challenge is twofold. First, these linkages must be speci-fied and articulated so managers know how and when they will get the benefits. Second, linkages to supporting business initiatives must be clarified, communicated and sold. Results Chain modeling helps IT groups to meet these challenges. The models are particularly valuable when large investments must be made in so-called enabling IT infrastructure, which are platforms that only technology experts see and touch and that are generally invisible to the rest of the organization.

The National Bank of Canada is the sixth largest chartered bank in Canada, with 637 branches and offices and assets in excess of $66 billion. National Bank of Canada's decision to invest in a multiyear migration toward a PC-based, client-server development platform in one of its departments was a perfect case in point. The new platform would be far upstream in the production supply chain. Its new hardware and software tools would be used by IT professionals to create the business applications that bankers would use. While invisible, it promised to produce benefits for years, many of them hard to forecast with 100 percent accuracy.

To build understanding and stakeholder support, the IT group decided to amplify the standard cost/benefit analysis used to justify the investment. "Even if the budget is secured," says André Piette, senior project director of payment systems, "you still need a thorough picture of all the things that need to get done to make a success of such a large investment. What about training? What are we going to do with all the applications built with the old platform? What change programs need to be put in place? How do we get commitment from all stakeholders?"

National Bank developed a Results Chain model that provided an accurate picture of the linkages leading to many potential benefits, and identified new paths for maximizing returns on the investment. The model became a powerful communication and selling tool, demonstrating the value of the investment all the way downstream in various units of the bank. Once the program was under way, the bank was able to use the model to make dynamic adjustments to key program parameters, based on changes in the business and IT environments.

Piette says that using the Benefits Realization Approach allowed the bank to clearly map the proposed program, identifying benefits sought, business changes required to reap the benefits, ways of achieving them and obstacles to implementation. The result is the ability to more objectively evaluate and prioritize initiatives.

Quebec Workers Compensation Board

The method solidly supports the concept of "thought before action."

The Quebec Workers Compensation Board enforces the laws governing the protection, compensation and rehabilitation of workers in Quebec, Canada. The Quebec workplace health and safety plan is a social contract between over two million employees and their employers. When the Quebec Workers Compensation Board began to look at replacing legacy financial systems, it found itself embarking upon a sensitive blended investment program. The two key systems used for budgeting by the accounting and finance departments needed to be updated. The IS directorate wanted to resolve the situation quickly to keep users satisfied and systems performing smoothly. But it needed a reliable game plan and found its standard cost/benefit, PERT and critical path methods to be too static. A more comprehensive method was needed to clearly define the expected results and provide a logical framework that could be used to monitor development and implementation.

The directorate — a recent winner of an award for excellence in public administration — used benefits realization to develop a transition plan that took into account:

- The consequences of removing the existing systems

- Scheduling and prioritization issues

- Interdependencies between the various pieces of the puzzle

- The need to bring the IT group and users closer together by creating a common vision and identifying the anchor points of the program

- The need to manage process and people factors as well as computing issues.

The new systems are now in place after a smooth transition. Jean Houde, IS department director, says that one of the key benefits of the Results Chain was that it provided a tool for communicating with users — an effective way of showing what had to be done, and of monitoring progress over time. "Based on our experience," he says, "this method works well in an environment in which people have to anticipate problems and plan multidimensional implementations — beyond simple computing issues. Indeed, this method solidly supports the concept of *thought before action.*"

Summary

A strong focus on results is the starting point of the Benefits Realization Approach. This results focus is the energy source that drives everything else. Benefits Realization does not eliminate risk. In business terms, however, it ensures better risk/reward relationships and an intelligent overview of your business investment portfolio, which includes a mix of IT and business projects. It does this by drawing on the financial risk management methods mentioned in the Introduction. Consider these points of comparison:

- *Program management* gives investment decision makers better knowledge of how different technologies produce business results as part of the overall business system, similar to financial investors' search for good information on individual firms, industries and stock market performance histories. The end result of program management is a better appreciation of risk/reward relationships.

- *Portfolio management* gives organizations methods of diversifying risk by selecting a variety of technologies and investment programs. They can also tailor their portfolio to suit their own risk tolerance, just as financial investors do when selecting a portfolio. The end result of portfolio management is that decision makers don't need to "bet the store" on a single stock, industry or IT-enabled change investment.

- *Full cycle governance* provides better methods of managing projects, programs and portfolios from day to day. It is an operational system of continuously monitoring performance and adjusting portfolio composition, similar in concept to the systems used by financial investment managers to manage mutual funds. The end result is better month-to-month performance as the future unfolds.

In commonsense terms, the approach to benefits realization helps you understand more clearly the benefits that you are trying to achieve. It gives you a better understanding of what you have to do to achieve the benefits. It provides a disciplined process to help you manage your way along the path to achieving the benefits.

> *Does it position you better to get results? It certainly* does.
> *Does it guarantee that you will get results? No. That is* your *job.*

****

It may be hard at first for you to learn the benefits mind-set, but it will certainly be easier to learn than to adopt. Program and portfolio management represent a significant change in management thinking. New processes and organizational structures will be needed to operationalize the new mind-set through full cycle governance. Major changes will be required in the areas of accountability, measurement and the process of change itself. In Part II, we discuss these changes in greater detail.

THREE FUNDAMENTALS

Part I, we introduced the Information Paradox, the problems associated with it and the lagging management mind-set that contributes to it. We made the case for a new mind-set, and a new approach to managing information technology investments and introduced our Benefits Realization Approach, with its cornerstones, the three fundamentals: program management; portfolio management; and full cycle governance; and the three necessary conditions: activist accountability; relevant measurement; and proactive management of change. Part II discusses each of the three fundamentals of the approach in depth.

Chapter 3 describes program management, showing you how the program view gives you the big picture, as we move beyond the project world to the program universe. It enables you to define the scope of programs and design them to address the increasing complexity introduced as IT applications evolve beyond automation of work to information management and business transformation. The program view helps you manage these variables, to more accurately assess program value and improve your chances of success while reducing risk.

Chapter 4 demonstrates how portfolio management can be used to deal with the problem of too many potential programs chasing too few resources. It builds on program management, using the value assessment technique to select the right set of programs. It helps your organization assign the best players to each program and ensure they play as a team in establishing their budgets and setting their strategies. It gives you an overview of the action and the ongoing ability to make adjustments as circumstances change.

Chapter 5 moves on to full cycle governance which operational-izes program and portfolio management into a true flexible system that makes programs and portfolios work on the ground. It gives you the framework to make disciplined decisions about benefits and risk. We introduce the stage gate approval process, which enables you to pro-gressively commit resources to programs, and to make changes in portfolio composition. We discuss the organization structures that are required to support full cycle governance.

FIRST FUNDAMENTAL: PROGRAM MANAGEMENT

In the film *Field of Dreams,* an inspired visionary builds a baseball diamond in the middle of a cornfield. While the power of his imagination is impressive, there are a few realities to face. There is no team. No coach. No marketing program. No brewery or other sponsor who provides financial support. The motto of this visionary is: "Build it, and they will come."

Both the baseball visionary and most managers are caught in the project world. They take a blinkered view of the work and focus only on constructing the artifact, whether it's a baseball diamond or a computer system. The difference is that in the dream world, people did indeed come. They came because, in fiction, we can create happy endings without allowing reality to intrude. In the real world, we do not have that luxury.

Unfortunately, too often we act as if we do. Most information systems are built on a similar principle: "Build it, and the benefits will come." It is assumed that the desired business outcome will happen automatically, through faith. With industrial-age projects — for example, installing new production capacity to address market growth — the faith is often rewarded. With IT projects, it's much more of a gamble, and as the opening chapter indicated, the odds are getting worse as we move toward more sophisticated IT applications through the evolution from automation of work through information management to business transformation.

Viewing IT projects today as magical silver bullets that alone will deliver required business outcomes is a root cause of the Information Paradox.

Source: DILBERT reprinted by permission of United Feature Syndicate, Inc.

Project World: The Blinkered View

Improving the odds of delivering business benefits requires more than just better project management. We have to take off the blinkers and look at the full program of activities involved in changing the business system, and then manage the investment program as a whole, with full knowledge of the linkage, reach, people and time issues involved.

The IT field of dreams is strewn with projects that did not reward the faith of their promoters. The narrow project focus leads to investment myopia. The following are fictional examples, with features adapted from real cases, of what happens when linkage, reach, people and time issues are not understood or managed.

- *Example 1:*

  A large bank called off a major electronic commerce initiative in midstream, with money down the drain, because upscale customers did not want to bank by phone or PC. They were a critical target market for the service and the project couldn't proceed in its current form without them. The turn of events was viewed as a "surprise delay" after several components of the system had already been built. In fact, the original business case assumed favorable customer attitudes toward new technologies, but it laid out no ways to explore this assumption, which is not surprising when you consider that it was prepared by the systems group, with few bankers buying in. This is an example of what can happen when you ignore the linkage, reach and people elements of even a modest business transformation.

- *Example 2:*

  A medium-size pharmaceutical company installed a new customer information system (CIS) at a cost of $5 million to improve sales force productivity and create a central database to improve targeting of prime accounts. Unfortunately, it would take this staff nine months to learn how to use the new system comfortably and, in the meantime, sales targets had to be met. Many sales people claimed they had no choice but to ignore the new system for the time being and continued storing valuable data on stand-alone personal laptops they bought for themselves. No one knew when or how that data would be transferred to the new system since salespeople often worked six and a half days a week. Months before, a few salespeople tested the CIS prototypes, but they happened to be PC wizards who were called in regularly for help with PC upgrades. This is an example of the impacts of misreading a typical people element of change: the ability to cope with new technology.

- *Example 3:*

  A complex software package was delivered for $30 million to a large retail chain. Thirty departments, warehouses and key stores had received extensive technology training courses given by experts from the package supplier. Unfortunately, some training sessions backfired. People walked out with the impression — right or wrong — that the new system was unreliable and could lead to unexpected inventory shortages while it was being "run in." The result was that the staff at about 20 front-line operating units refused to use the new applications right away and insisted on continuing to work with the legacy system for the time being. "We're hitting a sales peak this month and Christmas is just a few months off. Just leave the old terminals plugged in for now," they said. Meanwhile, a senior warehouse manager noticed that three key ordering processes might need to be redesigned from A to Z to make them compatible with the new package — a linkage that was missed. Realistically, in these conditions, it could take two years — rather than two months — to get everyone on board. This is an example of the importance of gauging and proactively managing the linkage, reach, people and time elements of major IT-driven programs.

In each of these three examples, the business investment was designed as a project. As we indicated in Chapter 2, projects are a structured set of activities concerned with delivering a defined capability to the organization based on an agreed schedule and budget. The focus of projects is on the inputs, costs and time required to produce the intermediate outcomes depicted on a Results Chain model, not on translating those outcomes into benefits for the organization. What was required in these examples — and in the Benefits Realization Approach — is a program view.

Program Universe: The Big Picture

Programs are structured groupings of projects designed to produce clearly identified business results or other end benefits. The projects in the above examples could have formed important and necessary parts of broader investment programs but were not sufficient themselves to realize benefits for the organization. The program focus is on all the steps required to deliver business results. It is the effectively managed, blended business investment program that delivers the benefits to the organization.

A good example of a program, in this sense, is the space program. While hardware may have dominated the budgets, the mission objective was human: to put people into space to get a job done and bring them back home again. Myopia was not an option. Consequently, it was easy to make a distinction along these lines:

Projects: Hundreds of individual projects delivered the thousands of pieces that were assembled into key deliverables: the space capsule, the missile, the computers and ground tracking stations. Projects also delivered trained people, public funding and so on.

Program: A single program was required that put all the pieces of technology together and placed them in the hands of a highly organized and skilled team of astronauts, with support from expert ground units. It ensured they all followed a shared game plan for landing on the moon, repairing a space station or other project and then coming back home.

Each space mission was managed like a program, reaching far beyond the individual projects and their technical deliverables. Project managers could afford to be myopic and obsessed with detail. Program managers had to keep their eyes on the big picture, as politicians and the astronauts' families would remind them from time to time.

Building business information systems is not as daunting as a space launch, but it has become complex enough to merit a program approach. For the comfortable project world, there are established ways of thinking and practices to guide the way. In the new, larger program universe, we need to think differently and use new tools. That is what investment programs deliver, and add, to the project world.

Meshing Technological and Organizational Change

The program view is more powerful than many managers expect when they first see it. It has proven its worth to clients who have used it, for example, to mesh organizational change with the introduction of new technologies.

Consider the example of the Education Department of Western Australia, which wanted to use new software to help in its effort to decentralize some of its human resource (HR) activities. The department wanted to reduce a long chain of handoffs for many HR operations, typically beginning with a teacher, moving to the school registrar and the central human resources group and then back to the school and the teacher. It believed a new HR software package would provide a solution. At first, it looked like a vision of technology-driven change.

The new system would drive a radical decentralization of responsibility to schools from the central HR group of several hundred civil servants, handling everything from the broad outlines of educational policy to the nitty-gritty details of compensation packages, processing leave and payroll changes, appointing relief teachers and handling the backlog of overpayments due to late processing of forms. This would be in line with pressure to streamline the department and reduce HR operating costs, all while improving the level of HR service to employees. Changes would be required at the individual, school and organization level.

It did not take long for department officials to realize instinctively what the Benefits Realization Approach makes explicit. As Adrian Stoffles, project manager notes, "the benefits being targeted were not inside the new package. And there was a big difference between a new technology that drives organizational change and one that enables change — along with many other elements of the business system. There were questions, in particular, about people and organizational issues. Would people feel threatened by the software project? Would teachers perceive the decentralization as extra work for them? What about computer literacy? How much resistance to change would there be?"

Department leaders diagnosed the problem early. They realized this was a business transformation initiative with broad scope and impact. The Benefits Realization Approach was used to expand a potential silver bullet project into a well-rounded change program. Says Bevan Doyle, project director, "we included not only steps to introduce the new software smoothly, with appropriate coaching, but also these key projects: preparing a detailed communications plan for all stakeholder groups; holding department vision workshops; developing a transition plan with well-defined accountabilities; and organizing discussion and feedback sessions."

Today, the pilot software is in 210 schools, and key HR tasks are being handled faster, with fewer errors and improved service. Typically 14 000 forms a month — which used to be sent to central office — are now being processed on-line at the school level. Achieving these early benefits has significantly advanced the change aspects of the program and the attitude toward the initiative from both a school and central office perspective. Some schools which at first resisted, later applied to serve as "lighthouses" in the program. More and more, the department's investments in organizational and technological change are complementing and leveraging off each other, demonstrating the power of the program view.

Three Core Components of Program Management

There are three core components to successful navigation in the program universe: defining program scope; assessing program value; and designing and managing programs.

Defining Program Scope

- Understanding the concept that blended investment programs replace the narrow project perspective
- Identifying all the elements of change that are needed to deliver benefits.

Assessing Program Value

- Moving to multidimensional measures of value (based on the four "ares" framework introduced in Chapter 2) in place of unidimensional financial measures, such as ROI
- Adopting evergreen value cases to replace one-off business cases.

Designing and Managing Programs

- Using the Results Chain technique to design the best program to achieve the objectives
- Establishing and managing mechanisms to track program performance and make corrections to deliver the best value from the program, even in light of changing circumstances.

We will address each of these components in this chapter. Before we delve into the new constructs of the program universe, though, a gentle reminder: Programs do not replace projects. In fact, good programs are built on a foundation of well-designed projects, executed with advanced project management disciplines. Bringing projects in as specified, on time and on budget, remains essential. In the more complex world of the Knowledge Economy, however, solid project management is a necessary condition — but not a sufficient one — for business success. The unique contribution of programs is to guide projects along the path to business results.

Defining Program Scope:
The Blended Investment Perspective

The first practical step is to define program scope. To do this, managers need to take a large mental leap. They need to embrace the new benefits mind-set that sees investments in IT as part of blended business investment programs rather than stand-alone IT projects. This is not a minor point, and it is not just playing with words. This is truly a change of mind-set based on a new understanding of how IT contributes as part of the overall business system to deliver results.

The traditional approach to managing IT treats it, in engineering terms, as a piece of equipment that is delivered and plugged in. But to create value, IT must not just be plugged into the wall socket. It must be plugged, in a much broader sense, into the overall business system. It is only when we see IT in the context of the overall business system that we will be able to deal with the often-overlooked, but essential, dimensions of linkage, reach, people and time.

IT as Part of the BTOPP Business System

What do we mean by the BTOPP business system? It is: business, technology, organization, process and people. We have found the following framework (see Figure 3-1), derived from Michael Scott Morton's *The Corporation of the 1990s,* to be helpful in understanding the business system and therefore creating sound programs that truly deliver the business benefits.

FIGURE 3-1
The BTOPP System

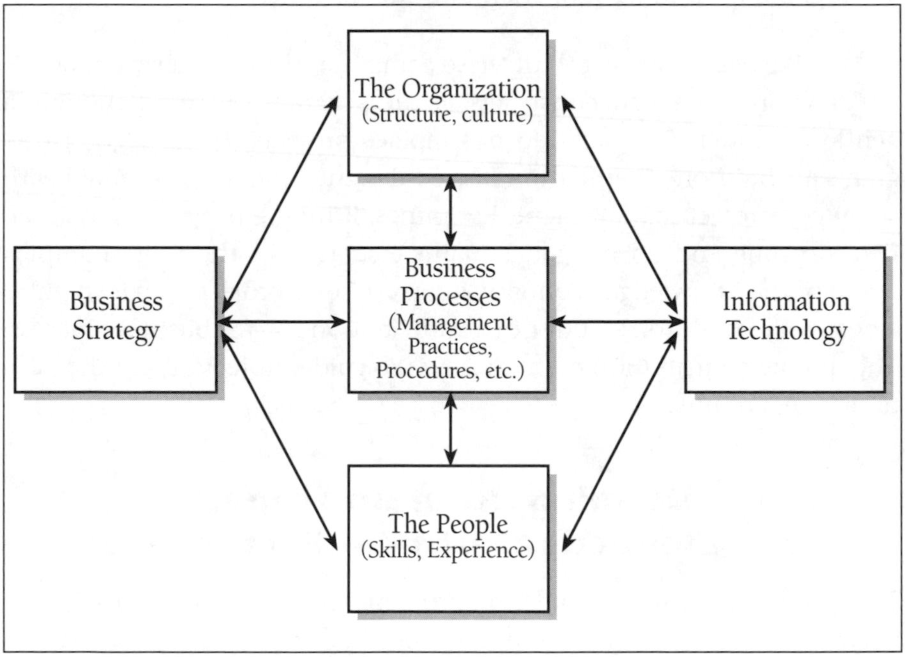

Source: Adapted from Michael Scott Morton, 1988

Let us review the elements of BTOPP in more detail from the perspective of an organization wanting to introduce new information technologies and ways of working them into its business system.

B — Business. Like all technologies, new information technologies need to align with a market need or opportunity. At a minimum, they should meet an internal need for information and thus strengthen the value chain that leads ultimately to the customer. Any planned application of IT must be tightly linked to — business strategy. Two simple questions are: Where is the market for the product, service or information produced by this technology? How realistic is your first answer?

T — Technology. Once the hardware is physically installed, the software must be working. The system must be configured and networked with other business systems to ensure that the right information can get to the right people at the right time.

O — Organization. Organizations must be structured and restructured to get the most from their IT bases. This means much more than downsizing. The location of work teams, offices and customer service facilities are all affected. The adjustment to new technologies can take months, even years.

P — Process. Business processes must be engineered to focus on end-to-end service delivery, recognizing and integrating the new capabilities of IT. After the first time, these processes must continue to be re-engineered often to reflect changing conditions. A wide variety of management practices and work procedures must be adjusted and changed to mesh with the major engineered business processes, such as product design and order processing.

P — People. Employees, customers and business partners must learn how to the use the information system. They must not only be comfortable with the software, they must also have the know-how, motivation and authority to use the capability, such as information they receive to get their jobs done. And that means not only getting their jobs done, but more importantly, improving how they do their jobs. They must know what their jobs are and how technology has changed them.

In the remainder of this book, we refer to the elements described above as belonging to the BTOPP model of the business system.

Organizations caught in traditional thinking focus their attention almost exclusively on the technology element of the business system. Even in the relatively new world of electronic commerce, a Gartner Group Research Note by T. Berg describing 55 electronic commerce case studies found that in only 35 percent of the cases were results measured in business terms (e.g., "reduced inventory costs" or "increased profitability"). The other 65 percent were measured in stand-alone IT project terms, addressing the questions: Did the technology work? Was it delivered on time? Was it delivered on budget? In most cases, the business element is dealt with by reference to a one-off, financially oriented business case that does not adequately value the business strategy link. The stand-alone focus on technology during the project gives little attention to the organizational, process and people issues that are so important to successful implementation.

The new blended investment mind-set requires learning and — possibly most important — unlearning. The clincher for most managers is the BTOPP view. When this view is seen, it becomes very apparent that 80 to 95 percent of most activities in "so-called" IT projects are not IT-related at all. They fall into the OPP categories.

Programs that Produce Results

The blended investment perspective has made a concrete difference to organizations trying to implement software packages, design BPR projects and meet other business transformation challenges. Projects no longer stand alone, as they did in cases of silver bullet thinking.

Consider the story of Ericsson, told in the "Window on the Real World: Client Stories" section of Chapter 2. This global manufacturer of telecommunications equipment was designing two BPR projects in a high-tech development setting. "These were not clear-cut BPR projects. The road to success was not clearly mapped in advance. We were concerned about risks of cost overruns, delays and failure to achieve targeted benefits," recalls director Luc Mayrand.

The Benefits Realization Approach, supported by Results Chain modeling, was used to gain a better understanding of the risks and success factors. The investigation produced some surprises. At first glance, both projects appeared to be dominated by IT and changes to the advanced technology production environments. In fact, the Results Chain models pointed to the opposite conclusion: almost 80 percent of the initiatives turned out not to be IT-related.

In another case, SUNCORP-Metway, an Australian financial group, wanted to introduce an advanced knowledge-based system offered by a third-party vendor that would enable the company's claims agents to quickly capture and reuse information on claims settlements. "Aside from system implementation, two key issues that arose were how to ensure ROI was properly measured and how knowledge workers were persuaded to buy into the new technology," recalls

Neil Singleton, general manager, Compulsory Third Party, SUNCORP-Metway. "About a third of the agents were comfortable with the technology. Another third needed some training. Another third were uncertain, with some expressing the opinion that 'a machine can't do the job as well as I can.' "

In the end, the solution took the form of a blended investment program of IT, communications, coaching and change management initiatives. "Most of the actual initiatives fell outside the IT area," Singleton says. "It was pretty much all around change management for people on the front line who would be interfacing with the new technology."

The full story appears in the "Window on the Real World: Client Stories" section near the end of this chapter.

How to Assess Program Value: Multiple Dimensions

The new BTOPP picture of programs can help managers develop a broader view of program value. This is becoming a business imperative as we move beyond automation applications to information and transformation applications — applications on which we are increasingly betting our businesses. Return on investment simply doesn't cut it as the only measure of value. As described in Chapter 2, a blended investment program can contribute many more benefits than pure financial returns — for example, the opportunity to bring about a new strategic capability.

An effective way of understanding value is to treat the prospective value of a program as being reflected in responses to the four "ares" questions introduced in Chapter 2:

1. *Are we doing the right things?* Are we clear what benefits we are seeking? Are the end benefits in line with our organization's goals and priorities? Will they remain so over the life of the program?

2. *Are we doing them the right way?* Will the program comply with all necessary technical and quality standards? Will it reinforce the general direction of other work in the area? Do all elements of the investment (business, technology, organization, process and people) blend well together?

3. *Are we getting them done well?* Have we identified all the work and have all players accepted the responsibility for their part in this work? Are there sound delivery plans and well-designed projects in

the program? Is the project work achievable with the planned resources? Will there be adequate quality assurance? Can all the "soft" organization, people and process initiatives be completed in time to take full advantage of technological changes?

4. *Are we getting the benefits?* Do the prospective benefits justify the costs? How certain are we about the estimates of benefits? Is there broad acceptance for the program? Is there a solid business sponsor, ready, willing and able to deliver the benefits? How much could the estimates be affected by factors outside the organization's control?

The four "ares" provides a rich framework for looking at value. To be useful in program management, however, we have to translate the concepts into terms that are practical, easy to apply and allow some degree of consistency in measurement.

Translating the Four "Ares" into Measurements

From practical experience, once the four "ares" are answered at a high level, you will need to normalize the answers so that they can be compared across programs. We have found three measurement dimensions useful in achieving this normalization. They are: alignment, financial worth and risk.

Alignment. Alignment is a measure of the degree to which the program supports the business goals and strategic intents of the organization. Alignment looks to measurements beyond financial worth. It aims to capture these other contributors to your organization's success, such as those suggested by Kaplan and Norton's *Balanced Scorecard.*

Financial Worth. Financial worth is a measure of the worth of the program in purely financial terms. This could well include newer financial measures such as economic value added (EVA®).

Risk. Risk is measured in terms of the fact that the program may not ultimately deliver all of the potential value, taking into account all of the contributing elements involved in the program's Results Chain.

We will return to the specifics of measuring value dimensions in the next chapter when dealing with the issue of how programs are selected and built into investment portfolios.

Designing and Managing Programs: Getting from Here to There

Understanding the concept of a program — how it is different from traditional projects and what it brings to them — is the first major step to embarking on the route to effective, proactive benefits management. The next step is to embrace a new view of value. Then comes the hardest part: bringing about change in long-standing management practices. As always, the biggest challenge — or at least the most time-consuming one — is getting from here to there.

The Results Chain technique plays a crucial role in the change process. It helps to design and continuously manage programs. It assists in identifying all that has to be done to deliver benefits, articulating the linkages between elements of the required program, and exploring the different program options available, both initially and as the work progresses.

What follows is a series of eight practical steps organizations can take to design and deliver a major blended investment program. This is not intended as a magic formula but a model that you can adapt and customize to suit your needs. You may choose to skip some steps or follow them in a different order. Indeed, some steps, if not all, are most efficiently done in parallel. Each step will be discussed in greater detail later in this chapter.

1. *Define Benefits and Articulate Linkages.* To increase your chances of achieving benefits, the first step is to clearly define what you are after, in meaningful, measurable terms. This is often overlooked in traditional projects which have many potential benefits. Once you have defined them, you then need to articulate the key linkages — the paths leading from the program investments to the end results. A clear view of benefits and linkages forms the broad outline of the big picture.

2. *Define Program Scope.* You fill in the big picture by defining the scope of work to include all projects (and any other activities) that will generate the desired benefits. By including projects from all areas of the BTOPP business system, you will naturally define a full-bodied program not just a traditional project.

3. *Design Program: Map the Benefits Realization Process.* Using the insights and information assembled in Steps 1 and 2, you map a

number of potential benefits paths specific to the program in question, using the Results Chain technique. Linkages, reach, people and time issues are tackled head-on as each path is mapped. The end product is a practical working model of the benefits realization process for a specific program.

4. *Design Program: Select the Best Benefits Realization Path.* You assess which benefits path you prefer to follow. You will need to make clear choices and may face tough strategic trade-offs.

5. *Define Accountabilities.* A core issue that must be settled is activist accountability for business results — a new concept for many organizations. This means that senior business sponsors must take ownership of the program and accept clear accountability for delivering benefits. Accountabilities become a management tool for successful benefits delivery, not a way to point the finger for failures.

6. *Address the People Factor.* Most benefits come from change. Change involves people and calls for their active commitment. But many prefer to avoid it. You won't get the benefits you are seeking unless focused change management is a part of your action plan.

7. *Recognize the Time Factor.* The simplistic assumption of immediate benefits delivery inherent in one-off business cases hides the need to look at a time-based profile of benefit streams. The benefits realization maps and paths will help people understand that profile and build it into the program.

8. *Prepare for Risk and Uncertainty.* There are factors under your control and others that are not. You need to recognize and monitor the factors you do not (or only partially) control. Benefits management can actually capitalize on the risk and change which occur in a dynamic business environment.

The relationship of each of these steps to the linkage, reach, people and time dimensions is shown in Table 3-1.

These steps are central to designing and delivering a major blended investment program. Let us now review each of these steps in more detail.

1. Define Benefits and Articulate Linkages

"It's easy to define the benefits we seek from this project. We are results-driven around here." We hear this statement often when discussing the benefits realization process with managers. Now, ask yourself

TABLE 3-1

Relationship Between Steps Toward Blended Investment Programs and the Dimensions of Linkage, Reach, People and Time

	Linkage	Reach	People	Time
1. Define Benefits and Articulate Linkages	X			
2. Define Program Scope	X	X		
3. Design Program: Map the Benefits Realization Process	X	X	X	X
4. Design Program: Select the Best Benefits Realization Path	X	X	X	X
5. Define Accountabilities		X	X	
6. Address the People Factor			X	
7. Recognize the Time Factor				X
8. Prepare for Risk and Uncertainty	X	X	X	X

whether it is really true when it comes to your IT investments. In other words, is your organization an exception? Do you truly articulate the benefits you are after and how what you are doing, or planning to do, will contribute to them?

Let's reconsider the example of enterprise application packages. They are often purchased based on one-off business cases that focus on such features as "integrated information" or "increased flexibility." But are these features true business benefits? The answer is no. Integrated information is, at best, a vague description of a new organizational capability delivered by the software package. As in the earlier case of a customer information file, it will be of no value unless other actions are taken to address problems or opportunities. Similarly, increased flexibility is an intermediate outcome with potential for transformation into a benefit. It is not the benefit itself.

When it comes to defining the benefits flowing from new capabilities and outcomes, there are a wide range of steps that can be taken to produce results with the new data-sharing capabilities. One possibility is to reduce head office staffing levels. Another is to reduce inventory levels as information on them is integrated across several locations. These are only two examples. There are many choices but not all are compatible.

Faced with the challenge of defining benefits, the first step is easy. Just ask (and keep asking): "So What?" This often forces the discussion to focus on the real business reason for the program. Relating back to the Results Chain model, it moves the discussion past intermediate outcomes toward end benefits, meaning the positive change in the key performance indicators associated with the organization. Benefits are therefore often more than just dollars and indeed will relate to other directional goals of an organization, as represented by such frameworks as Kaplan and Norton's *Balanced Scorecard.*

2. Define Program Scope

"We have been pouring money down a high-tech drain!" Many business executives have said this under their breath for years. Now, we are admitting that few IT projects deliver benefits, but before you jump to conclusions, let's expand the statement and the thought. Few IT projects deliver benefits in isolation, but they can do so as part of a blended investment program. In this regard, there are different types of projects with varying degrees of linkage to other elements of the BTOPP business system. In other words, some IT investments blend with the business more than others. Here is the progression:

- *Self-contained technical projects* can reduce the costs of IT performance. Installing a cheaper technology that runs exactly the same software as before, or getting a better lease arrangement on some hardware, are examples. In these few instances, benefits are virtually automatic, with few, if any, impacts on OPP elements of the business system. These projects are similar to old stand-alone automation projects.

- *IT management projects* such as outsourcing and the adoption of new technical/engineering standards may produce short-term benefits. Over time, they will produce new technical capabilities which can be used to benefit the business side with new applications and information. Realization of these benefits will have direct or indirect impacts on OPP elements and require linkages to be understood and managed.

- Most *information system projects* are ordered by business units to change organizational capabilities by transforming the way that a particular function can be done or by adding new capabilities. These capabilities, however, are only of *potential value*. They can be used, abused or simply left to rot. They will likely have an impact on many OPP elements. There will be complex linkages to be understood. The potential value of these projects will only be realized when they, and their complex linkages to other technology and OPP projects, are managed as part of blended business investment programs.

In a true blended investment program, the capabilities have to be exercised in a particular way, aligned with an overall business strategy. In almost all cases, this will involve making some business changes in the way people work, in business processes, in the organization and in the reward scheme. All of this has to happen before benefits flow.

We use the BTOPP model to paint the big picture of major changes that may be necessary. As we identify the change initiatives, the linkage and reach issues will be fleshed out. This step helps to root out the potentially wide range of changes that need to happen to realize benefits, and which must be managed within the program. Once we have defined the scope, we are in a position to model and design the program and its initiatives.

When it comes to improving the chances of success, it is far more effective to design the OPP projects into the investment program up front than bolting them on after the project is complete but not delivering benefits. How many IT projects end up looking very little like the original because of all the post-delivery "extras"?

3. Design Program: Map Benefits Realization Process

The benefits are now defined, the strategy and benefits linkages are articulated and the program outline is in hand. The next step is to flesh out and anchor the potential program with a model of the benefits realization process, prepared with the Results Chain technique and with a benefits management strategy. The model provides a map to help you see where you are going.

Let's take the case of an insurance company that wants to put in a customer information system. Its target benefits are cutting the workload generated by customer queries, and reducing the costs of this function by reducing staff. The system provides the capability of quickly accessing all relevant customer data when answering a call, but this alone is not enough to deliver the savings.

Certain other initiatives must be taken to use the capability to increase the number of customers processed per hour. For example, staff would need to be trained to use the system to access information quickly. The reward mechanisms would have to be modified to encourage shorter "customer moments." If the higher throughput causes problems in downstream processes, these will require streamlining. Using the Results Chain notation, the contributions can be represented as in Figure 3-2.

FIGURE 3-2
Delivering the Capability

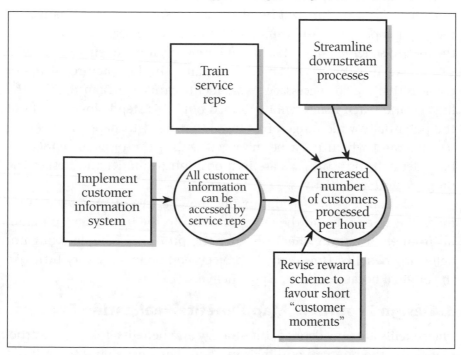

Just increasing the throughput rate may decrease unit costs, but it does not decrease staff costs. To achieve this benefit, initiatives must be taken to produce another outcome: staff reductions. To do this, in turn, the workload has to be reassigned (perhaps the rules for customer assignment might need to change). There might also be union negotiations and severance packages to consider. In short, more OPP projects need to be designed into the program (see Figure 3-3).

What we end up with is a Results Chain running from the original initiatives, through one or more intermediate outcomes (e.g., the increased customer processing rate), to the benefit realized by the final outcome (in this case, decreased operating costs). Some of the other initiatives may be IT projects (such as the streamlining of downstream customer processing systems), but most of them are business initiatives, such as revising the reward scheme and negotiating severance agreements.

FIGURE 3-3
Leveraging the Capability into Benefits

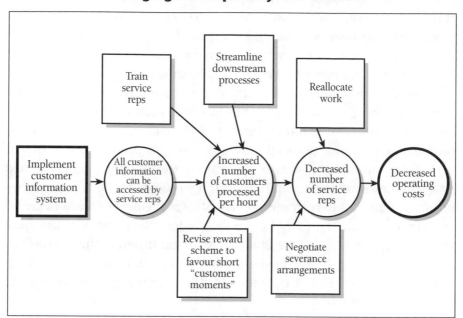

Indeed, in the case of enterprise application packages, our experience suggests that of the work involved in delivering benefits, 80 to 95 percent lies in the areas of organization, processes and people — on the business side. Like an iceberg, the real work lies out of sight, with only the IT group's work visible. No wonder we have had difficulty in delivering benefits. We have been trying to pilot a ship to its destination by locking ourselves in the engine room and just making sure the turbines are working well.

Once we have developed the Results Chain model, we come face to face with the issues of the reach dimension in designing the program. What areas will be impacted by the program? Where do we need buy-in? Are these people within the orbit of control of the person accountable for delivering benefits? Reach and people afford an organizational perspective, while linkage provides a conceptual view of the benefits realization process.

4. Design Program: Select the Best Benefits Realization Path

A primary contribution of the Results Chain model is to define your business options more clearly. With a high-level map of the benefits realization process, you can articulate choices — usually many more than you thought possible. The benefits paths appearing on the map are not "hardwired." They can be adjusted in response to changing conditions, and you can also choose to switch paths altogether. Understanding your options, and being able to revise or switch options dynamically, is one step towards improving your chances of success.

In the old project world, it was assumed that the benefits were fixed when you committed money to the project. In the program universe, we can see at least two quite distinct routes for exploiting the new informational capabilities offered by the customer information system example. One, as originally intended, is to cut the costs of processing customer queries by increasing throughput per service rep and reducing staff levels. Another option would be to use the capability of increased access to customer information at the time of a call to create customer intimacy, and use it to increase sales. Using the extra information, service reps would be able to understand better the customer's needs, establish credibility in the customers' eyes and suggest new products to meet their needs. Under the old scenario these possibilities would have never been raised.

It's the same project. The informational capabilities are the same, but the organizational, process redesign and people (OPP) projects are quite different. So are the linkage, reach, people and time issues, and, not surprisingly, the benefits are too. This is because the two blended investment programs are quite different even though the IT element is the same in both cases. The former, reducing customer moments to brief time windows, is mapped in the Results Chain shown in Figure 3-3. The latter (see Figure 3-4) involves giving the service reps some sales training and teaching them to lengthen customer moments to probe for sales leads. Training needs to focus not only on techniques of getting the information fast but rather on methods of using the CIS to pull it together and build a profile of the customer's needs. The reward scheme would have to award pay on the basis of yield per call rather than volume of calls handled.

Even though the CIS technology is virtually identical, we see two distinct sets of business results, each with its own distinct benefits path. The two programs are mutually exclusive alternatives, or at least could not be implemented together with the same group of service staff in the same period of time. To begin with, you couldn't have an effective reward scheme that promoted both speed and increased yield per call at the same time. Similarly, the initiative to reduce staffing levels runs counter to the desire to turn the service function into an important revenue generator.

FIGURE 3-4
Selecting the Best Path to Benefits Realization

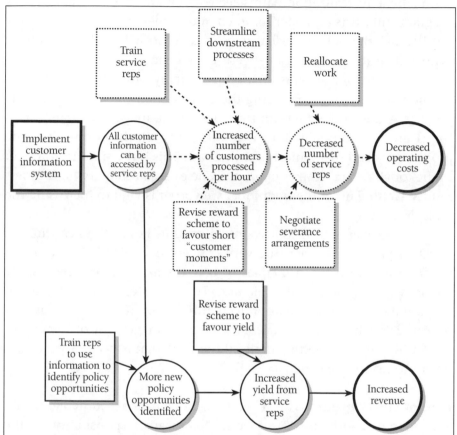

The job of the managers, who are accountable for delivering the benefits, is to identify the different benefits paths and to make the difficult choice of picking the best one for the organization. They can also make dynamic changes to the benefits paths as project work proceeds, learning occurs and conditions in the market place change. In the case of the insurance company, the initial aim of the CIS project was to reduce costs and service staff headcounts. However, some inventive service people showed them that the new technology actually generated a higher potential return when it was applied to increase yield via better telephone service and cross-selling. As a result, managers changed the scope and nature of the blended investment program.

How do you choose the best paths? By focusing on relative value assessment as described earlier. We will return to the issue of selection based on relative value in Chapter 4, when dealing with methods of selecting the optimal portfolio of investment programs.

5. Define Accountabilities

With a benefits realization path selected, you are a step ahead, but the program still exists on paper (or in computer memories) only. You now need to ask the organizational questions. Who will make it happen? Who will be accountable for delivering the benefits?

Technology appears at the tip of many program icebergs. The business initiatives — including the organization, process and people projects — are hidden beneath the waves. So it appears natural to hold the IT group accountable for the results. After all, they do most of the project work and spend most of the dollars. This is the simplistic answer to the tough and critically important issue of accountability for business results. Getting rid of the traditional viewpoint is vital to increasing the odds of success.

A new approach to accountability thus lies at the heart of any effective program. In fact, the very concept of a blended investment program based on the principles of benefits management necessarily changes the accountability picture. The key step is to distinguish accountability for individual projects from accountability for business results. The latter implies general business management ownership of the entire process of getting done all the work that is necessary and sufficient to realize the benefits.

Role of the IT group. The IT group must be held accountable, clearly and unambiguously, for IT projects. This means responsibility for the delivery of technologies as specified, on time and on budget. It also means delivery of the agreed informational and organizational capabilities flowing directly from completion of the technology project. Beyond this core responsibility, IT experts often provide leadership along with others in the organization in helping people understand desired business outcomes, and what it will take to achieve them. This should not imply, however, that they are accountable for delivery of targeted benefits and end results. In the new program universe, CIOs will have to leave behind some familiar roles—like chief magician of information technology, and honorable head scapegoat!

Role of the Business Sponsor. For each program, a business sponsor is needed who must be unambiguously accountable for targeted benefits, and thus for the overall program. Remember the space program: only the director of NASA could be held responsible for a successful space mission. Individual project managers could have meaningful accountability for their particular pieces, never for the whole.

This means that business sponsors must join CIOs in leaving behind some outdated roles. One is that of executive patron, the person who gets the money and waves the project through the tollbooth. Another is that of senior cheerleader, who waves magic pompons internally as the IT team performs more miracles. At the other extreme, business sponsors cannot become ardent buyers and proponents of a specific technology solution, such as enterprise application packages, client-server environments or intranets. Real accountability for results has been far from the minds of executives playing these traditional sponsorship roles, roles more closely associated with stand-alone projects.

The role of a true business sponsor is to lead proactive benefits management initiatives. He or she signs a contract with the organization along these lines: "If you grant me the resources to make this investment, I will deliver the proposed benefits, at minimum, and any more that I can find on the way." The business sponsor is truly the owner of the program — of the end benefits, of all the activities necessary to realize the benefits, as modeled by the Results Chain, and of the associated costs. As owner, the sponsor needs to ensure delivery of all the project deliverables and intermediate outcomes, including new organizational capabilities, within predefined times and budgets. The accountability for each of the intermediate outcomes needs to be assigned to clearly identified outcome owners. For their part, project leaders are responsible for delivering their pieces reliably.

Accountability for results is the hard core of program management. It is such an important issue in making benefits realization work that we devote a whole chapter to the topic later in the book (Chapter 6). For now, we will leave you with the thought that the business sponsor is the owner of a small professional-style business that will only turn a profit if it delivers on the benefits contract it signed with the organization.

6. Address the People Factor

People are everywhere in the new program universe you are entering. Few benefits arise automatically from IT investments — they come from making changes to the business. The only way these changes will come to pass, and produce the effects that you are seeking, is if the people involved adopt these changes and, in many cases, actively make them happen. The challenge is changing the way they think, manage and act.

Without an effective transition, all the good plans and benefits management activities in the world will not result in sustained benefits.

Getting people to make transitions is not easy. It takes time and effort, and the effects of that effort can get diffused through lack of focus. Yet, this is so critical to benefits delivery that we devote a whole chapter later in the book to the proactive management of change (Chapter 8).

7. Recognize the Time Factor

The traditional one-off business cases include forecasts of end benefits only for the sake of justifying project work. They also assume — in a drastic oversimplification of reality — that benefits can be switched on (like a tap or pipeline) once the project has been completed. Since benefits are assumed to be "automatic", there is little need to track them. They are either there or not there when the technology is plugged in.

Of course, we know that the new technologies of today cannot just be plugged in and left to run by themselves. Nor are they commissioned on a certain launch date like data centers, dams, aircraft carriers and new factories. Work units begin to use their technologies and get better as time goes on. Naturally, the benefits also flow in over time. It is what we refer to as a benefits stream. That stream does not always flow at a constant rate and, consequently, it needs to be measured and tracked systematically, just like a seasonal river flow.

Under the old, naive assumptions, benefits are deemed to start immediately after implementation and to flow at a constant rate. But this ignores the reality of "plugging IT into the business system." This means changing the way business is conducted. Adapting to a new work environment and tool kit takes time. Training takes time. And the effects of a new rewards system take time to percolate into an established, consistent pattern of performance.

Some people learn more slowly than others which leads to the learning lags mentioned in Chapter 1. As individuals and work groups learn new ways of doing things, and more importantly, unlearn old ways of doing things, their performance often dips. Looking at any one outcome in a Results Chain (for example, the increase in customer moments per person hour in the case of the insurance company's CIS), one might see a benefits profile somewhat like that illustrated in Figure 3-5.

It may be easy to predict when a certain organizational capability, such as easier access to customer data will be delivered, but it is much harder to forecast when it will combine with others — and the related intermediate outcomes — to produce the end results shown on a Results Chain. Information systems are delivered in one go, with immediate impacts and intermediate outcomes. Benefits can often take months or years to fully materialize, as in, for example, an enterprise-wide implementation of a major package solution.

FIGURE 3-5
The Learning Lag

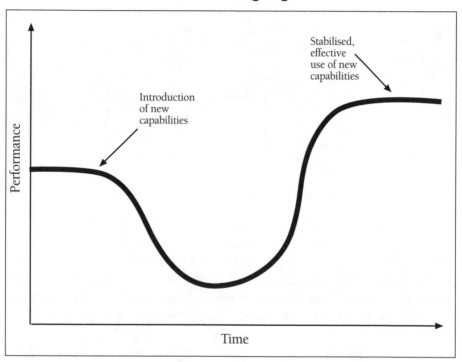

Clearly, benefits do not "switch on" at a point in time. We must incorporate a time-based profile of benefits into our benefits realization model (map) and use that profile to design the appropriate performance measures. All essential outcomes and contributions need to be tracked in order to manage benefits delivery.

Effective benefits realization requires forecasting and delivering the flow of benefits associated with the delivery of key organizational capabilities and the associated intermediate outcomes over time. The end-results forecast is used to judge how good a program proposal is while it is being designed. However, the real tools for continuing benefits management are the time-based profiles of expected intermediate outcomes. These intermediate levels are sometimes referred to as benefit plateaus, as illustrated in Figure 3-6.

FIGURE 3-6
Benefits Plateaus

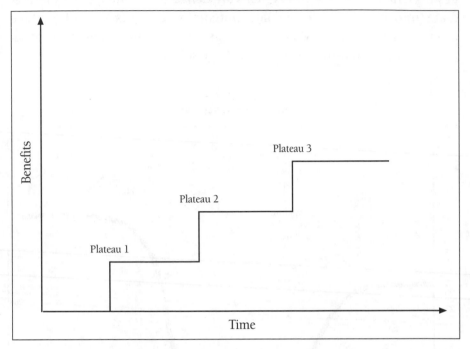

The plateaus will likely correlate to intermediate outcomes. They may also be a combination of a number of intermediate outcomes and partial realization of the final outcome. Plateaus move us away from the all-or-nothing thinking about benefits, and enable us to show how benefits will be realized over time — incrementally, in a measurable way.

Benefits Attribution. Lag time is one reason why we don't want to focus solely on the end benefit as the item that we measure to manage benefits realization. Another significant reason is the problem of benefits attribution. Consider the classic road death syndrome. Suppose we make some changes to driver education in a particular geographic area, with the desired end benefit of fewer traffic fatalities. If the fatality count goes down, was the program a success?

Answering that question can be as challenging as any in cost accounting or operations management. High-level benefits — such as the number of road deaths, revenue growth, market share — are influenced by a plethora of factors. The program in question is only one. We can't always measure the contribution of each factor directly. But we can use the Results Chain map as a working model for identifying the contributions of key initiatives, organizational capabilities and intermediate outcomes. We can measure the achievement of these outcomes and use the model to identify the contributions they make to end results. This perennial measurement challenge is covered in much greater detail in Chapter 7.

8. Prepare for Risk and Uncertainty

If only we could predict the future, we could better define benefits, articulate key linkages, design blended investment programs, assign accountabilities and just get on with the job of project delivery. We automatically would do a good-to-excellent job of benefits realization.

Unfortunately, life isn't that simple. As we said in Chapter 1, the future changes every day. The Knowledge Economy and the stormy IT environment of today resemble the stock and bond markets. The unexpected often happens. What's the impact of the unexpected on the bigger picture of benefits realization?

In traditional stand-alone project management, there is a touching faith that benefits will appear, as just reward for a job done well done in project delivery. Will you get benefits this way in the uncertain world that we face? The answer is maybe or maybe not. A few immediate benefits will come from delivery of a new technology or organizational capability, but these are minor compared to the kinds of benefits a complete program can deliver over time. The real prizes lie in the benefits that become possible from a more active Benefits Realization Approach, including adaptations to changes in the environment as the work proceeds.

Traditional approaches go for the low return of easy prizes and trust to the gods for the rest. They give you the same chances of winning, of realizing benefits, as a gambler in a casino with no knowledge of the odds. In today's world, where the bets are getting much bigger and the stakes much higher, this is not good enough. The time has come to take a more active approach.

Understanding What You Can and Can't Control. It is possible to manage risk and uncertainty and, in fact, to find opportunities in a volatile environment. This starts with a clear understanding of what you can and can't control. There are three main categories: delivery of capabilities, outcomes and assumptions.

Delivery of capabilities is the easy part. Delivery of capabilities is entirely under your control. The good news is that there is a well-established body of knowledge for managing projects to deliver capabilities. The bad news is that this body of knowledge is not universally applied.

Outcomes are more difficult. You can't control them directly. For example, you can't guarantee that your people will deal with customers faster. You can, however, influence the outcome through initiatives. Active benefits management thus involves picking the right initiatives, tracking the outcomes against forecasts and taking corrective action if the influence doesn't deliver as planned.

We make *assumptions* about environmental conditions (regulation, market trends, economy) and internal organizational conditions (culture, motivation level) necessary for realization of benefits. We do not control, or only partially control, these conditions. For example, we can do nothing about the general rate of inflation or the relative value that customers place on different characteristics of our products. Yet, they can have a huge impact on the success of our initiatives and programs, and on decisions about when and whether to undertake work. As we move down benefits paths, we need to track changing conditions closely and assess the impact of any changes on our assumptions. Based on this assessment, we can continue on our present path, alter the path or — in the worst case — cancel a program rather than throwing good money after bad.

Assumptions must also be incorporated into the Results Chain model to provide a complete picture of the benefits paths, and their exposure to risk. For example, in the case of the insurance company's CIS, we could add an assumption on the increased yield path around the potential for sales of new products to existing customers over the phone. We can't "make it so," but we can test the assumption and look at the impact of the assumption proving false on the Results Chain model for the predicted benefits (see Figure 3-7).

Managing Risk to Increase Value. With a clearer view of what we can and can't control, we can better gauge and manage the impacts of future variability on benefits realization plans.

In the midst of the CIS training program, for example, the regulatory environment could change. Large banks might be allowed into the insurance market with their relatively low-cost, large-scale distribution systems. In response, the company might switch from a low-cost to an upscale, niche strategy. The training program might be switched to a service/sales orientation in midstream. In short, another benefits realization path might be chosen. This is just one example of how the relative attractiveness of different paths may change over time as circumstances change. What seemed sensible at the outset may prove to deliver little, and what appeared unlikely initially may prove to be quite realizable. It is important to assess the value of different paths dynamically and make changes in real time.

FIGURE 3-7
Assessing the Impact of an Assumption

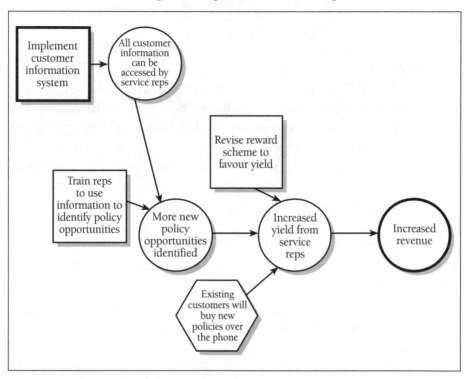

So far we've only addressed changes in the paths that had already been identified. These days systems are getting so complex, and so intertwined with the way business is conducted, that you can't be expected to think of all possibilities at the outset. It is quite common for additional benefits, that you had never anticipated, to emerge. The goal here is to identify these benefits, which perhaps are uncovered by a pioneering soul trying something different and tripping over a vein of benefits gold.

As the new capabilities are institutionalized by the organization, and as you acquire a higher level of understanding of the potential of a holistic business system, new emergent benefits may become possibilities, although they were never targeted initially. Again, to maximize the return on the investment, you must recognize and manage the delivery of these extra benefits across the organization.

Window on the Real World: Client Stories

Blended investment programs have been designed with Results Chain models to meet a variety of business transformation and information management challenges. In the client stories that follow, the challenges included: selection of the right technologies to support business process redesign; convincing professional knowledge workers to accept and use new desktop technologies; stopping "scope creep" that threatened to bog down an Intranet project; and improving the responsiveness of a large IT group to business needs.

While the starting points varied, there was concern in all these organizations about the issue of the *linkage* between the introduction of new technologies in the workplace, the redesign of business processes and improvements in business performance. There was a feeling that large IT projects were too complex to stand alone and that they would have to be embedded in some type of broader change program. The common core of issues also included:

- High stakes projects focused attention on the risk of failure.
- Many work units were involved but did not understand clearly where they fit in.
- Traditional business cases, cost/benefit analysis and project management methods did not appear adequate to deal with these issues.

As in the client stories told in Chapter 2, the path to success was not clear, creating demand for new game plans, road maps and models.

Benefits Realization Process

While the exact approach differed from case to case, all the clients whose stories appear here built a Results Chain model of the initial project and possible related projects. The modeling process focused on:

- The *linkage* of multiple *initiatives* with each other and *ultimate outcomes*
- The *scope* of IT projects and related Organization, Process and People initiatives.

As in all Results Chain modeling initiatives, the extensive discussion and validation of the model were as important as the model itself.

Results

While the specific results varied, there was a clear pattern of benefits that emerged in all cases as decision-making processes moved from being project driven to being benefits driven.

■ Blended business investment programs were designed to include all BTOPP projects and initiatives.

■ Programs could be managed to ensure better definition, sequencing, prioritization and timing of individual projects.

■ People were brought on board with complex change and process programs, significantly reducing the risks of derailed projects.

■ Project management and decision-making processes were improved.

In the process, the Results Chain model became a visible and ongoing communications tool, with one organization using a colored chain to show all units where they fit in a multiyear BPR program. A solid consensus was built among many stakeholders around the program.

Royale Belge

Royale Belge applied the Results Chain to capture all ideas in the cross-functional work group and link technology, BPR and other change projects in a unified re-engineering program.

Royale Belge of Brussels, Belgium, is the second largest insurance company in that country and offers all lines of insurance. Royale Belge wanted to reinforce its leading position in the insurance industry by reinventing standard industry practices and customer service standards. In a bold move, a group of change champions targeted a process lying at the core of the insurance business: claims processing. Their goal was to reduce the time it takes to process insurance claims from weeks to days (or less) while improving responsiveness to customers. They did not view these two objectives as contradictory as they believed that improvements in the quality of service would lead to a reduction in operating costs. In the end, they wanted Royale Belge to engineer a radical break with the past of the insurance industry.

A strategic decision was made to give soft benefits priority over costs in this BPR program, says Eric Huet, director of organizational development and a prominent change agent. "We felt those kinds of benefits were more important to our customers. In this industry, customer loyalty is a major influencer in getting new business. Price comes in only second."

From the outset, Royale Belge had searched both for new technologies and new process designs that could transform claims processing. It was a blended investment program in the making. The issues were to clarify objectives in precise operational terms and to design the program properly. Limiting the risk of failure or delay was a priority given the resources the company was prepared to commit. The Results Chain technique proved to be invaluable in addressing these concerns.

After surveying new technologies, digital imaging and work-flow were identified as the tools that would allow customer service staff to scan, store and retrieve images much faster from client files. When converted from hard copy to digital form, such items as photos of car accidents and home damages could be viewed instantly on workstation screens. Previous claims and forms would become instantly accessible, eliminating time-consuming searches. Speed would increase — the soft benefit originally sought. In addition, paper-driven costs such as shipping, handling and staff time would decrease, creating a measurable bottom-line benefit.

Royale Belge applied the Results Chain to capture all ideas in the cross-functional work group and link technology, BPR and other change projects in a unified re-engineering program. It also helped to sequence project implementation, create scenarios mapping alternate paths to achieve targeted benefits, and build consensus and commitment from all stakeholders as the program advanced.

The Benefits Realization Approach gave management at Royale Belge a new way of thinking and a new method for designing blended investment programs. It provided a clear big picture of the redesigned claims management process, aligned with the company's long-term vision of industry segment leadership. By reinventing the way it processes claims, the company has created a stream of benefits that it will continue to harvest over time.

SUNCORP-Metway

The Benefits Realization Approach was used to help diagnose the problem and propose a remedy which took the form of a blended investment program of IT, communications, coaching and change management initiatives. "Most of the initiatives fell outside the IT area. It was pretty much all around change management for people on the front line."

In the property and casualty insurance business, the process of settling claims lies at the heart of customer service, cost management, credibility and a reputation for fair business practices. The larger the company, the bigger the challenge of ensuring consistency and equity in the settlements awarded to clients. SUNCORP-Metway, an

Australian financial group with more than $8 billion in assets, faced just this challenge in handling claims arising from car accidents. The company's Compulsory Third Party division wanted to reduce opportunities for disparities to arise in settlement amounts for similar accidents, injuries and damages.

According to Neil Singleton, general manager of Compulsory Third Party at SUNCORP-Metway, the plan was to implement an advanced knowledge-based system, offered by a third-party vendor, that would allow company claims agents to quickly gather and reuse information on claim settlements. The system would walk the agents through standard questions about medical history, medical diagnosis, the accident and other issues. It would then use a repository of data on past settlements in hundreds of similar cases to recommend a "settlement range." The system was also designed to detect exaggerated and fraudulent claims.

"Aside from system implementation, two key issues that arose were how to ensure ROI was properly measured and how knowledge workers were persuaded to buy into the new technology," Singleton says. "About a third of the agents were comfortable with the technology. Another third needed some training. Another third were uncertain, with some expressing the opinion that 'a machine can't do the job as well as I can.'"

The Benefits Realization Approach was used to help diagnose the problem and propose a remedy which took the form of a blended investment program of IT, communications, coaching and change management initiatives. "Most of the actual initiatives fell outside the IT area," Singleton says. "It was pretty much all around change management for people on the front line who would be interfacing with the new technology."

The Benefits Realization Approach and the Results Chain technique helped SUNCORP-Metway gain a clearer understanding of the risks and develop risk mitigation strategies, highlight all the initiatives needed to achieve the benefits, indicate whether the organization's current thinking was appropriate and on track and develop a positive cross-functional group dynamic which allowed everybody to see where they fit in the overall process and why they were being asked to do what they had to do.

"Organizations often believe that business benefits will materialize automatically when they buy knowledge-based systems," Singleton says. "They forget all of the things that need to be put in place to realize these benefits. Even if our financial calculations indicated a good one year ROI, we needed a road map identifying the risk areas and assigning ownership of the things that had to be done. Our clients can win or lose large sums of money based on insurance settlements. We had to do this right the first time."

The Benefits Realization Approach has had the desired results. There is greater consistency in settlements, and the company has successfully implemented a measurement system that will track settlement performance over time.

Bank of America

The Results Chain provided a powerful vehicle for communicating the new vision of the IT unit's processes to all group employees.

The service levels delivered by IT groups to business users are a perennial issue. This is especially true in a large financial institution like Bank of America, the third largest bank in the United States and fifteenth in the world. The bank has one of the most extensive installed IT bases in the world and more applications than you can click a mouse at. Bank of America's Systems Engineering (BASE) services group had a critical but largely invisible role in a complex supply chain leading from behind-the-scenes technical work on software and information systems all the way to front-line action at ATMs and branch computer terminals. BASE was dedicated to clearly defining its role and working to continuously improve its performance, both technically and in terms of the value it delivered to the business.

After participating in a technical benchmarking study that revealed it to be a leader, BASE decided to radically re-engineer the three core processes that impacted service quality standards: responding to end-user requests for changes to current information systems, solving problems that disrupt service and managing overall systems engineering service levels. BASE realized that, while these three processes had historically been managed separately, they were highly interconnected. There would be significant gains in efficiency, productivity and user satisfaction if they could be successfully integrated.

For BASE, this amounted to a major process redesign program. But the re-engineering team recognized that it was much more than a technology problem. There were many stakeholders — other IT units and banking groups — that were impacted by these core service levels and that would have to contribute actively to process redesign initiatives. "We knew change would involve redesigning business processes, IT environments and organizational forms in many areas. We saw major risks such as resistance to change, cost overruns, delays and failure to achieve targeted benefits. We needed a road map," recalls Edward Hawthorne, senior vice president and BASE's general manager.

The group used the Benefits Realization Approach and the Results Chain technique to prepare a map to help managers visualize how the three processes could be integrated in a single work flow and to define the benefits of this change in terms of cost savings, productivity and user satisfaction. Quick hits were identified that were aligned with BASE's fundamental objectives. The map also helped to determine how other departments fit into the integration program, how initiatives would be sequenced and how progress would be measured.

The Results Chain also provided a powerful vehicle for communicating the new vision of BASE processes to all group employees. "We developed a colored Results Chain where everyone could see where they fit and how they contributed to the overall game plan. We updated the Chain every quarter to let people know how they were progressing," said Kathy Stout, system director. "Every manager in this program has a framed Results Chain in his or her office, which allows us to maintain strong commitment over several years."

Benefits realization has become an integral part of program management practice, giving managers the tools to manage a new dimension — benefits — in addition to the traditional tasking and scheduling of project management. This has influenced numerous decisions, and has helped to set expectations, leading BASE to extend the time frame for implementation of its program from two to three years to a more realistic three to five years.

SaskTel

The review prompted the intranet team to transform the project into a longer term program to change the channels for business information sharing.

A perfect example of the "field of dreams" mind-set is the recent wave of Internet cyber-construction, particularly of Web sites and intranet facilities. Many of these electronic publishing plants were built quickly, before it was clear what information would be published and the audiences who would use it.

SaskTel, a government-owned telecommunications carrier in the Canadian province of Saskatchewan, with 4000 employees and assets valued at more than $1.3 billion, took steps to bring its intranet program under business control early in the game. The initiative first saw the light of day as a typical IT project. A simple decision was made to build the facility, based on the understanding that people wanted to get rid of paper memos, policy manuals and binders and that the payback would take just a few months.

It did not take long for scope creep to set in. One reason was the volume and variety of information that could be published electronically in an organization that delivered more than 200 products every day and introduced new products on a regular basis. Front-line people needed quick access to everything from product information to competitive information, policies, procedures, news releases, organizational changes and job postings. Another cause was the variety of stakeholders in a workforce dispersed in more than 60 locations. It was also clear that the new technology would bring new ways of working and dealing with information. Roles, responsibilities and information ownership would have to be redefined along with the technology infrastructure.

While the business impacts were significant, attention had been focused largely on the IT project. SaskTel saw the potential problems early in the process and decided to rethink its approach using a Results Chain model for guidance. The review prompted the intranet team to transform the project into a longer-term program to change the channels for business information sharing. SaskTel's manager of corporate affairs, Dave Traynor, says the model provided an overview of the entire process of creating information and delivering it to employees. "It is not because you put information on a server that you will get results. You need a wider view, a comprehensive road map, to get these results. And there is a lot happening aside from technology that needs to be considered."

Kelly McCurry, director of SaskTel corporate affairs, says that the modeling exercise helped the company rethink how front-line employees are evaluated. Instead of assessing customer service representatives on the number of calls they take per minute, SaskTel is thinking about implementing an evaluation system based on the number of problems solved per client.

The intranet team ended up with clearer goals, well-defined information owners, broader stakeholder support, better prioritization of multiple projects and a realistic critical path. As a result, the intranet is up and running, paper flows have been reduced and information is being delivered more quickly. At the end of the day, there are far fewer binders kicking around.

Summary

The traditional project focus takes too narrow a view of the world. To get a handle on benefits realization for even just one initiative, managers need to open up their field of vision to encompass the program universe. It is an emerging macrocosm that captures the realities of applying IT for purposes of advanced information management and business transformation. Table 3-2 highlights the paradigm shift required to move from the project world to the program universe.

TABLE 3-2
Paradigm Shift

From Project World	To Program Universe
IT **Project** focus	Business-outcome **Program** focus
Projects deliver "automatic" benefits	Projects deliver capabilities, programs deliver benefits
IT is accountable for benefits	Benefits are a business responsibility
ROI is king	Broader view on what constitutes a benefit
Project business case	Program value case
Passive benefits realization	Active benefits realization
"Trusting the gods" to deliver benefits	Managing risk to deliver benefits Recognizing that there are choices in benefit paths and that even though the future is uncertain, investment returns can be maximized well beyond the completion of any IT project

There are three key components for successful navigation in the program universe: definition of program scope, assessment of program value and managing the full program life cycle.

The first is the broad definition of program scope that places technology in the context of the other four elements of the BTOPP business system: business strategy, organization, processes and people. Getting the right program scope is essential to the integration of IT and those critical OPP projects required to deliver benefits.

The second component is a well-rounded assessment of program value, based on answers to the four "ares" and measures of alignment, financial worth and risk. Getting the right assessment is essential to understanding all the benefits that blended investments can deliver over time, not just a one-time jump in ROI.

The third component is to follow the proper steps for designing and managing programs through the full program life cycle reaching from concept to cash. This cycle ends when the business sponsor of the program — whose central role has been highlighted in this chapter — turns the job of continuing responsibility for benefits realization over to an operating line manager.

In the old, predictable project world, it was easy for managers to know when the job was over. In the program universe, the rules have changed. A blended investment program is not over when its key projects are completed. The same goes for the job of business sponsors. Their benefits realization work reaches far beyond project delivery. It continues through the monitoring of outcome delivery and assumption testing and into the reconfiguration of benefits paths over time.

Does the job ever end? The point for the hand off of benefits realization from the business sponsor to operational managers is when the conditions needed for all selected benefits paths are met. From this point, benefits will still flow, but the responsibility for optimizing return is that of the operating manager. The sponsor has delivered.

****

In the real world, few managers have the luxury of dealing with only one program at a time. There are many programs underway at any given time and many potential programs vying for consideration. There are far more choices than there are resources available. Evaluating these current and potential programs presents a significant management challenge. We need to move beyond treating selection as a one-time event, making selections in isolation, and taking a narrow view of value we need to move to a portfolio approach. In Chapter 4, we discuss how the Benefits Realization Approach incorporates portfolio management to address this challenge.

SECOND FUNDAMENTAL: PORTFOLIO MANAGEMENT

The Manager's Dilemma:
Too Many Choices, Too Few Resources

When Nova Gas Transmission (NGT), one of North America's largest natural gas pipeline companies, sat down in the fall of 1995 to review the budget for the next year, they faced a daunting challenge. There were requests for 168 capital projects, representing more than double the amount of work that NGT had historically ever been able to complete in a year. The grab bag of projects covered a wide range of possibilities. There were requests to upgrade or replace PCs to cope with the next generation of office software. Some money was needed to expand information technology capacity to support growth in the business and changing regulatory requirements. There were also demands to expand network infrastructure to accommodate the introduction of an enterprise application package (SAP) and other organization-wide initiatives.

The technology base had to evolve, as well, to position NGT for a future vision of its operation. On top of all this, there were many proposals for new systems, addressing different needs such as electronic commerce, better maintenance of the company's pipelines and improved efficiencies in engineering work. The question was: "Which projects should we decide to do, and which to defer or drop?" The material available to justify the projects ranged in quality and depth, but there were very few that could be dismissed as not worth doing.

NGT struggled with the selection process, with many impassioned and prolonged arguments around the relative merits of projects. It wasn't that this problem was brand new. Deciding which work to do had never been easy. Over the years, though, NGT had found that the demands had grown larger, along with the stakes, in terms of business impact. NGT's experience is most definitely not unique. The evolution of the application of information technology has driven an increase in the number and complexity of potential applications. In addition to new applications, there is also a large installed base of legacy applications of technology that must be maintained and upgraded. The overload of choices competing for resources is growing. There will be more projects in the queue, an increasing amount of potentially beneficial work to do, and the business impact of much of it — the linkage, reach, people and time issues — is going to become greater. The problem of selecting the right work to do will become more difficult. For decision makers, it is a formidable challenge.

- More choice
- More complexity
- Greater business impacts
- More visibility
- Much more management and executive attention.

The selection challenge of NGT and many other organizations is driven not only by too many choices, but by the scarcity of key resources relative to all that demand. In the world of advanced information management and business transformation initiatives, there are a number of constraints that limit the amount of good that can be done, and these constraints will not go away.

Budget

This is the simplest and easiest constraint to understand. While some organizations have deep pockets, they are not bottomless. Budgets are limited relative to the many program proposals in the queue and the many potential applications of IT.

Delivery Capabilities of the IT Group

The IT group can have bottlenecks. There may also be a scarcity of certain critical human resources, notably IT experts with knowledge of the business and gurus with mastery of leading-edge technologies. Even if outside resources are employed, management may not be able to handle all the challenges involved in delivery of multiple IT projects.

Delivery Capabilities of the Business

In executing programs, 80 to 95 percent of the actual work falls in the lap of the business. Even if the IT group can deliver new technologies and organizational capabilities, are there enough business resources to do all the other organizational, process redesign and people projects (BTOPP) required to realize the benefits? And can they do all this and keep the business running?

Capabilities of the Business To Absorb Change

Even if your people can do the OPP project work, can they handle the changes that program introduction will bring? Can they keep the business running while managing change? This is the area where many organizations hit the wall. They've been through downsizing, re-engineering, empowerment, and they can't take much more. The best ideas in the world are of no use if the workforce can't handle any more change.

Hardware may be cheap, software may be perceived to be easy to install, but scarce financial and human resources are required to fit that technology into the business system, and to ensure that it produces value. As a result of these problems, project selection in some organizations has turned into a free-for-all. Here again, we need a new approach.

The first step is to systematically group projects into blended investment programs using the process described in Chapter 3. This will ensure, at least, that all those projects appear in logical families, grouped according to the business results which they are aimed at achieving. Even after this is done, however, all the evidence cited above indicates that there will be more investment programs in the pipeline than available resources can handle. The resource constraints will continue to be severe in the areas of delivery capabilities and the capability to absorb change.

Program Selection Challenge

The reality is that today most organizations have a backlog of projects and potential programs that exceeds their capacity to get the work done.

So, let's just increase the budget, you may say, or, let's just contract it all out. But this solution — standing alone — will prove short-lived. Spending more dollars on technology with an industrial-age mind-set will simply create more cases of the Information Paradox. We need to spend with an eye to the challenges of IT-enabled business transformation. Increased IT spending in the absence of new ways of managing will rarely improve business performance. The core problem here is that the projects already in the pipeline require changes to the business system that far exceed the organization's ability to absorb.

Returning to the imagery of space programs, there is no point for an IT group to launch a lot of new projects when the entire organization is not able to successfully land those projects. When investing for results, the core goal is not launching, but landing. That's the difference between just building a space capsule and completing the whole mission. This means that you have to make choices, and that problem is both real and ongoing. The trouble is that these choices are rarely obvious, much less so than even a decade ago. The options are not always easy. This all adds up to a major value assessment challenge for business.

If we accept, then, that program selection is an issue that won't go away, and indeed will become more acute, can't we just apply our existing selection methods to programs now, rather than projects? The answer lies in the lagging management mind-set described in Chapter 1.

Lagging Management Mind-set

Traditional selection tools were one-off business cases, designed to support, or in many cases justify, simple go/no go decisions about major projects. These tools are being overwhelmed by the challenge of too many choices chasing too few resources. In particular, they were never designed to optimize an organization's mix of investment programs. As discussed in Chapter 2, measures of value such as ROI are simply too limited to permit consistent comparison of a large number of blended investment programs.

The net result is inconsistency — an uneven playing field. There is no context in which to make informed business decisions. In the case of Nova Gas Transmission before they adopted the Benefits Realization Approach, Tom Whitehead, manager of planning and practices, says that the selection process was like an annual sweepstakes. "Everybody would send their best man in with gloves on once a year to win some money. It would be a euphemism to say that it was somewhat heated.

Not only was negotiation intense during the process, some decisions were being made based on issues such as equity and fairness, instead of the real issue: business objectives."

Three Selection Blind Spots

In our experience, the old tools and processes have three blind spots. They are: treating selection as a one-time event; making selections in isolation; and not looking at all aspects of value.

Treating Selection as a One-Time Event. Traditional approaches are typified by selection being part of an annual budget event. The world in which organizations operate, however, doesn't stand still. We have already seen how a changing environment creates the need to adjust benefits paths within investment programs. In addition, new ideas can arise at any time, often compelled by industry and technological changes. What is a right decision at one point may not be appropriate later. Reality says we need flexibility and the capability to respond to change.

Making Selections in Isolation. When we focus on the IT projects rather than the blended investment programs of which they are a part, we are looking in the wrong place to make business decisions. Lacking the wider program view described in Chapter 3, we have no context for understanding the business implications of investment decisions. Moving into the program universe is a necessary prerequisite for effective IT investment decisions.

Even when selecting investment programs (rather than projects), the old ways of thinking lead us to look at each opportunity in isolation. Just picking good programs individually doesn't mean that the overall viability or net effect of all those selected is optimal. We are not after optimization in each local business unit or work group, we want the best results for the organization as a whole, given the finite resource pool.

Not Looking at all Aspects of Value. In Chapter 3, we discussed the need for, and outlined an approach to, assessing value that goes beyond the usual simple financial measures (or gut feeling!) to encompass all aspects of prospective value of a program. In the absence of holistic measures of value, decisions are swayed by simplistic analysis, oratory or horse-trading.

The Manager's New Weapon: Portfolio Power

Investment decision makers are trying to handle the project overload using the traditional tools of single project selection like the one-off business cases mentioned in Chapter 1. These tools were originally designed to support simple go/no go decisions, and no longer reflect business reality.

We need a tool that reflects reality. It is the portfolio view. A portfolio, as defined in Chapter 2, is a structured grouping of investment programs selected by management to achieve defined business results, while meeting clear risk/reward standards. Portfolio management has been applied to financial investments for decades, helping decision makers choose among increasingly numerous and complex options in a volatile environment. The analogy with the financial markets is powerful. The IT and business environments are now fluctuating, much like the stock and bond markets and the current value of individual IT investments can change with those fluctuations. There are problems forecasting future values and benefits streams. The portfolio concept allows investors to select among complex options and adjust investment selections over time to meet defined risk/reward criteria. The time has come to apply this concept systematically to manage blended (BTOPP) investment programs. This means looking at the investments you make in IT-enabled change as a whole, and picking and managing an optimum set of programs — the portfolio — to fit within your means to meet the organization's diverse and potentially conflicting demands. It also means taking a panoramic view of needs and opportunities and not looking at each program in isolation.

A high-performance portfolio must be built on the foundation of solid programs that produce reliable benefits streams over time. As each program incorporates a big picture of benefits realization, so must the portfolio be anchored in an even bigger picture. The portfolio's composition reflects a balanced set of high-value opportunities that, together, promise the best overall return, in dollars and other benefits.

Portfolios are not static; their composition needs to be adjusted to take into account changes in the environment and better knowledge of investment opportunities. Portfolio management means active involvement, not just picking the expected winners and then going to sleep. The term "portfolio" indicates the need to have a balance of opportunities to deliver the most value over time, and allowing for the vagaries of the future. With a stock and bond portfolio, financial planners look for a balance of investments to thrive in most environments. And they never stop monitoring the performance of that portfolio. The same active involvement is required for a portfolio of blended business investment programs.

Organizations as diverse as Boeing, Oregon Department of Transportation (ODOT) and NGT have had to manage large numbers of business transformation projects. NGT's story is told throughout this and other chapters. Those of Boeing's non-production procurement department and ODOT are summarized in the "Window on the Real World: Client Stories" section at the end of this chapter. All these organizations had their hands full with daily operational responsibility for extremely high volumes of transactions — from monitoring natural gas levels to highway maintenance, vehicle registration and purchasing office supplies. In addition, they were engaged in major business process re-engineering, long-term change programs and software package implementations or assessments.

The challenge was to sort through all this activity to find the strategic guiding threads, and link those to major programs that would produce tangible business results. The Benefits Realization Approach helped managers to gain this bigger picture and then to manage better at the program and project level – dealing with such issues as competition for resources, overlaps among programs, interdependencies and the prioritization and sequencing of work.

Selecting and Managing Portfolios: Getting from Here to There

Having established the need for portfolio management, the central management question becomes: How do we go about assembling and managing a portfolio of blended investment programs? Unfortunately, given the complexities of business reality, there is no easy answer to this question.

The challenge is too many choices chasing too few resources, as mentioned above. Organizations do not have the luxury of designing, say, 50 of the best of all possible programs on paper and then selecting the optimum portfolio. Rather, they start with the practical challenge of sorting though a grab bag of anywhere from 20 to 200 ongoing projects that were designed with an industrial-age mind-set.

The practical questions are: How do we sort this grab bag into programs? How do we select the programs that will deliver the most value? And, how do we adjust the composition of our portfolio over time? The following is a typical series of five concrete steps organizations can undertake, with the aid of the Results Chain technique, to design and manage a portfolio of blended investment programs:

1. Categorize Programs.
2. Prepare Value Cases for Business Opportunity programs.
3. Manage Risk to Increase Value.
4. Manage and Leverage Program Interdependencies.
5. Adjust Portfolio Composition.

Let us review each of the steps in turn.

1. Categorize Programs

Many experts claim to have found the perfect method — in theory — for portfolio selection. The problem is that these methods lack common sense. They do not easily make the jump from theory to practical business reality. A major weakness is that they fail to take into account the real "degrees of freedom" of investment decision makers. Many projects and initiatives in the grab bag are not optional. A few strategic initiatives are. How do you identify and sort through your real options?

A typical practitioner's criticism of existing selection methods is: "This recommendation doesn't make sense. It's obvious that this project is needed, but the criteria rank it low. The process is clearly flawed!" Another criticism is: "It's too complicated and takes far too much effort to assess all these opportunities. Let's do something simpler. We know what we have to do in most cases anyway." Are these naysayers wrong? Unfortunately, often they are not. What can be done to make the problem of selection manageable and justifiable?

Too often overlooked is the fact that is that all programs are not created equal. Ranking approaches that ignore this do so at their peril. Consider two simple examples of programs whose value to the organization is relatively easy to determine.

Legally Mandated Programs. It doesn't make sense to treat programs that are legally required the same way as a pure business opportunity. Why attempt to measure benefits for the legally mandated program? The benefit is well known to start with: the company remains in business and the officers stay out of jail!

Asset Maintenance and Preservation. Investment programs are needed to maintain the capability of an information system, or other information-knowledge assets, at the level needed for effective service delivery. The benefit here is also obvious at the outset. It is to continue as a going concern. The real business decision is not whether to undertake the program or not, but rather to select the optimum maintenance policies that maximize the return on the original investment.

A massive amount of work — costly work — is required to treat all programs the same way, at the most intensive level of analysis. Such an approach is both unhelpful to making good decisions and very frustrating for all involved. The obvious alternative is to find a way to address programs differently according to what we call the degrees of freedom of management to make meaningful business decisions, and the nature of the programs in question. Effective portfolio management

TABLE 4-1
Example of Program Categorization

Category	Definition	Examples of work
Mandatory	Legal requirement (compliance, legislation, regulation, code changes)	Change in regulator's financial reporting requirements
Nova-initiated	Mandated by the parent company Nova, agreed by executive of NGT	Corporate Human Resources system
Sustain	Renewal of obsolete infrastructure (e.g., PCs, network elements, facility equipment) that is required to continue to supply the equivalent capability	Fleet replacement, building renovations, PC replacement
Growth of Existing Services	New assets required to cope with business generated increases in transaction volumes, data storage, gas volumes etc.	More customer contracts leading to larger computer
Development	Capital work needed to test and develop capabilities (e.g., in the information management group), not justified on immediate business benefits (but with expectation of benefits on roll-out, if successful)	First implementation of "object-oriented" programming techniques on a minor project to establish cost/benefit estimates of broad adoption
Facility and Information Management Infrastructure	Work intended to put infrastructure (i.e., common, shared assets) in place to implement aspects of a target architecture, and approved by the "owner" of this future asset	Compressor platforms work, office building telecommunications backbone
Business Opportunity	Programs aimed at realizing a business opportunity that will cause measurable business benefits	Desktop rationalization program, enterprise resource system

categorizes programs according to the types of decision that the port-folio managers can make and the nature of the investment. It allocates scarce resources to each category and then manages allocations to each program within the category.

NGT uses a set of seven primary categories to manage their port-folio of business opportunities, as shown in Table 4-1.

Of all the categories, only the last, "business opportunity," requires a full analysis of the prospective programs' value to support a portfolio decision. The level of portfolio management required in decisions about other categories is based on the value that it can add. In the "sustain" cat-egory, for example, the role of portfolio management is primarily to help define sound policies for maintenance and life cycle management.

2. Prepare Value Cases for Business Opportunity Programs

Value cases must be prepared to assess programs in the business oppor-tunity category. They include answers to the four "ares" questions based on relevant, business-focused information about the prospective pro-grams. The value case presents information in a concise, consistent form. It summarizes the work done to date in exploring the potential pro-gram and provides answers to the following version of the four "ares":

- *Are 1: Are we doing the right things?* What is proposed, for what business outcome and how do the projects contribute? The latter question is answered through a summary Results Chain of the pro-gram.
- *Are 2: Are we doing them the right way?* How will the work be done, and what is being done to ensure that it will fit with other current or future capabilities?
- *Are 3: Are we getting them done well?* What is the plan for doing the work, and what resources and funds are needed?
- *Are 4: Are we getting the benefits?* How will the benefits be delivered? What is the value of the program (financial worth, alignment and value risk)?

Unlike traditional one-off business cases, the value case is revis-ited as the program work progresses. It is used, with the underlying detailed information, to actively manage the benefits realization process. As explained in Chapter 3, answers to the four "ares" need to be normalized so that they can be compared across programs. To do this, we use three measurement dimensions: alignment, financial worth and risk. These are reviewed in detail below.

Alignment. The world is not as blessed with instruments to measure alignment as it is with measures of ROI and financial returns. You will undoubtedly need to develop a customized instrument. There are three main types of contribution a program can make:

- *Contribution to the current objectives and priorities of the organization:* This might be measured by reference to the impacts that the program will have on measures derived from an organization's balanced scorecard or similar directional goals as discussed in Chapter 3. Another measure might look at the impact of the program on key issues that the organization is currently facing.
- *Contribution to the objectives of a parent company or larger context within which the organization is operating:* This measure reflects the reality that organizations often need to adjust their plans to align with those of a parent and that programs that support these intents should score points for this contribution.
- *Contribution to the achievement of a desired future state or business vision:* This measure captures the contributions of truly transformational programs that are necessary to the long-term survival of the organization, but which don't have an immediate positive impact. As a result, they could get ignored, to the detriment of the organization. This type of contribution might be measured by assessing how, and to what extent, the program helps create some crucial elements of the vision.

Financial Worth. The issue of gauging and measuring benefits using the four "ares" has been discussed at length in Chapters 2 and 3. Suffice it to say that financial worth can be measured using the standard financial tools that your organization accepts as a valid measure of investment return. In doing the calculations, however, there are some key issues to be addressed within the new conceptual framework of programs and portfolios. Most have to do with accurately gauging costs over lengthy program life cycles that extend from concept to cash.

In this regard, you need a comprehensive view of both the up-front costs of the initial investment and the "all-in" costs of reaping the benefits stream and operating the asset. You need to make sure you accurately cost the full program. This requires that you establish the probable lifespan of the new organizational capabilities that the program will deliver, and include all the operating costs of the new organizational capabilities, as well as any sustaining investments necessary to continue delivering benefits over their full lifespan. Finally, it is important to allow for the time lags in benefits delivery — one element of the time dimension noted in Chapter 2.

Risk. The two components described above contribute directly to the value of the program. Why do we also need to look at risk? Not all programs are equal when it comes to the likelihood of their delivering the benefits they so proudly claim at initiation, or the probability they will meet cost and time targets. Two programs with the same expected ROI, the same costs and the same impact on alignment issues may have quite different risk characteristics. For example, renegade technical solutions often work right away but stand alone, like an Internet Web site that is built quickly. As a result, they are unable to integrate with other capabilities down the road; and may also require more skilled staff to deliver than the organization can easily assemble.

In contrast, more conventional solutions such as enhancements to customer information systems (CIS) may take longer to develop but integrate more easily with legacy systems. They often involve quite standard sets of work, with no need for especially skilled deliverers. Are these of equal value to the organization when making investment choices? Clearly not. Assessing risk allows you to take this difference between the programs into account.

The delivery of value must be the focus of risk assessment. There are many elements of risk with respect to delivering value related to the Results Chain for the program and the accountabilities associated with these elements. Once again, we find it helpful to group these risk dimensions under the four "ares" question headings:

- *Are 1: Are we doing the right things?* This question focuses attention on the risk of error or lack of clarity in business judgments in a changing environment.
- *Are 2: Are we doing them the right way?* This question focuses attention on the risk of inconsistency with other current or potential programs and with existing capabilities.

- *Are 3: Are we getting them done well?* This question focuses attention on conventional project risk — budgets, timetables, execution to agreed specifications and quality standards.

- *Are 4: Are we getting the benefits?* This question focuses attention on the risks around having the right business environment to be realistically able to harvest benefits.

The degree of risk along these dimensions can be measured, or at least assessed, using questionnaires, surveys and Delphi analysis techniques. A standardized questionnaire can be used to provide the structure for gathering the risk scores. Scores can be normalized by comparison with agreed scores for benchmark programs. The individual scores are weighted, according to the consensus management view of the relative importance of the risk element, to provide a score for each of the four "ares." These scores are then reweighted, according to the perceived relevance of each topic to the organization at its current point of evolution. Organizations that have difficulty with consistent project delivery might weight "Are we getting them done well?" risks higher than one that has this under control. Figure 4-1 illustrates the scoring process.

This exercise produces a lot of numbers, which, in their raw state, are not the best medium to help managers make decisions about the portfolio. The most useful approach is to present the information with judicious use of graphical aids to people who know the business. One approach is to prepare two plots of elements of value (alignment, financial worth and risk) for proposed new and benchmark programs.

One plot shows financial returns against an overall risk score; the other shows the alignment scores against financial value. For the first plot, we have found it most helpful to plot the programs using a four-quartile icon as shown in Figure 4-2. Each of the quadrants of the icon corresponds to the risk for the associated four "ares" question. We use a traffic light color code: Green for low risk, amber for cautionary scores and red for "There's a problem here." With this simple coding, executives are able to see under the covers of the overall risk score into the characteristics of the risk profile.

These value plots are superb aids to spark management discussion about the composition (graphical shape) of the desired portfolio and the actions to take in ongoing portfolio management. A sample plot, as developed by NGT, is shown in Figure 4-3. This gives a graphical representation of financial worth versus risk, and was one of two used to

FIGURE 4-1 The Scoring Process

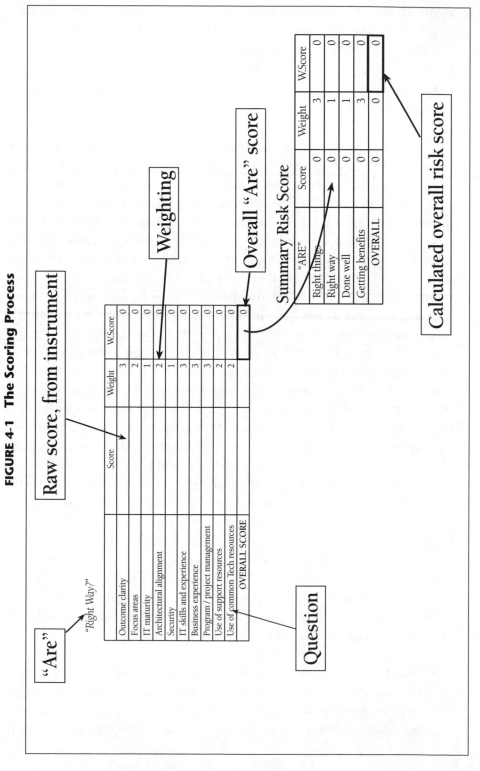

"Are"

"Right Way?"

Raw score, from instrument

Weighting

Overall "Are" score

Question

	Score	Weight	W.Score
Outcome clarity		3	0
Focus areas		2	0
IT maturity		1	0
Architectural alignment		2	0
Security		1	0
IT skills and experience		3	0
Business experience		3	0
Program / project management		3	0
Use of support resources		2	0
Use of common Tech resources		2	0
OVERALL SCORE			0

Summary Risk Score

"ARE"	Score	Weight	W.Score
Right things	0	3	0
Right way	0	1	0
Done well	0	1	0
Getting benefits	0	3	0
OVERALL	0	0	0

Calculated overall risk score

support selection of their portfolio. The second (which is not shown) plotted financial worth versus strategic alignment. Programs are clustered into high, medium and low bands, representing their potential to be selected for inclusion in the portfolio. The position of programs on the plot represents the result of considerable review and discussion of the value cases.

Value plots provide one piece of a value case. The next chapter discusses how value cases are used in the governance of programs and portfolios.

FIGURE 4-2
The Coding System

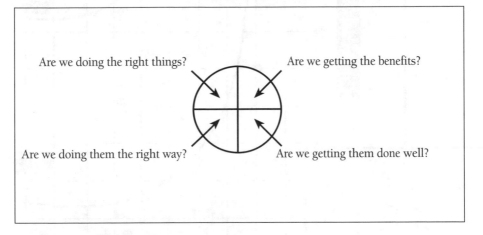

3. Manage Risk to Increase Value

Once you have assessed the value and risk for business opportunity programs, what do you do about it? Should you simply avoid risk, or at least throw out the programs with the higher risk rankings? The short answer is no. Total risk avoidance will not produce better results than silver bullet thinking. While risk is not to be courted, it should be expected in virtually every blended investment program that extends over any period of time. And, it should be actively managed so that you don't make the mistake of automatically avoiding risky programs that could generate major benefits if executed successfully.

Effective risk management is one of the most powerful applications of the portfolio concept. Risk is managed relative to potential returns and to the ability of the portfolio manager to diversify risk across a variety of investments, as it is in the world of finance. Clearly, packing the opportunity portfolio with risky programs, irrespective of the potential they

FIGURE 4-3
Value Plots
(Financial Worth vs. Risk)

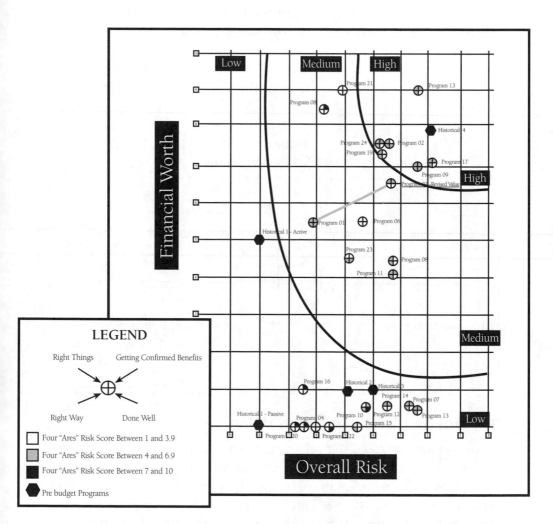

offered, would not be wise. There is room for higher risk investments as long as the potential reward is high enough. As in finance, portfolios should maximize expected benefits for any given level of average risk.

Organizations have varying propensities for tackling high-return, high-risk programs. Some very conservative organizations might largely avoid programs with a higher risk, while others, looking for major transformational opportunities, might accept the higher risk. When it comes to risk, your management group needs to look at itself in the mirror. When higher risk programs are included in the portfolio, they need special attention. If a program scores higher on the risk scale, the business sponsor and the portfolio management team need to ask two fundamental questions:

- Do the risks arise simply because we have not yet examined all the ways to reduce them?
- Are these risks inherent in the nature of the program and our knowledge about what is involved at this stage in the program life cycle?

In the former case, the program team should work to control and improve the program's risk profile. In the case of high inherent risk, the program needs to be monitored carefully and probably adjusted a number of times. In addition, the practice of progressive resource commitment, discussed at length in Chapter 5, becomes a potent risk management tool. Rather than risking the company (or the business unit) on a single investment program, progressive commitment breaks the program into stages, releasing the funds necessary to reach the next stage at various decision points. When there is little current knowledge and high risk, a relatively small amount of money should be committed, targeted at increasing the knowledge about the elements at risk. At the end of the stage, the prospective value (adjusted for risk) is reassessed before any further money is committed, and so on, and so on.

4. Manage and Leverage Program Interdependencies

One advantage of portfolio management is its ability to cut down on pointless inter-program competition for resources and, beyond that, to turn program overlaps into productive interdependencies. Any organization is a system where changes in one area usually have ripple effects on others. Portfolio management looks at the interactions between current and potential investment programs. When they are managed and leveraged properly, it views program interdependencies as a source of opportunity. In effect, they become the raw material for creative solutions to the problem of resource scarcity.

It helps to look at four distinct types of interactions between programs:

- Sequential Dependencies
- Overlapping Outcomes
- Competition for Scarce Resources
- Change Bottlenecks.

Sequential Dependencies. These are cases where Program A depends on Program B. If Program A is to go ahead, it will be necessary to implement Program B first, since A relies on some organizational capability introduced by B.

Using the Results Chain technique helps to identify hidden dependencies between programs. In many instances, such an analysis will reveal that the dependent program should be built into the first program. An example might be a program that introduces data mining capabilities. If the underlying systems to capture data are not in place, the data mining application won't create much value for the organization since it will be too limited in scope.

Many CIOs are familiar with another common dependency: to realize a business opportunity, such as electronic commerce, in the most effective manner a program will often need IT infrastructure support. This linkage to business benefits provides a criterion for ranking the infrastructure program ahead of other possible infrastructure work: all of it may have to be done sometime, but early wins have higher value.

Overlapping Outcomes. These are cases where Programs A and B are designed to produce overlapping outcomes. It is not unusual for more than one program to target the same set of benefits: revenue growth in a single product line, market share, dollar cost reductions or fuel economy for company cars.

Of course, the benefits do not keep adding up indefinitely. That would provide such wonders as market shares of 60 percent, a no-cost workforce and cars that actually produce fuel instead of consuming it. In such cases, benefits projections need to be reviewed and adjusted. Care must be taken to identify the essential assumptions and linkages underlying the transformation of organizational capabilities into benefits. Here again, developing Results Chains for the programs is a powerful tool for understanding the true impacts.

Competition for Scarce Resources. These are cases where Programs A and B require the same skilled people. As organizations move aggressively into adoption of new technologies such as electronic commerce and network computing, this phenomenon will become increasingly common. It's not that the gross numbers of people the programs demand are too great; it's that there isn't a cloning machine for some of the key contributors.

Individually, each program may be able to succeed, but collectively, there aren't enough of the critical resources. The resulting competition can quickly hold up a series of projects. Good portfolio management identifies the resource needs and profile of use over time for each possible program, and ensures that the selected set of active programs is indeed executable. Current areas of scarcity might include skilled Web application developers, database administrators or people with knowledge of the existing systems with which the new ones have to integrate.

Change Bottlenecks. These are cases where Programs A and B both require much organizational change and learning. They happen to hit the same business area. How much change can this area handle in a short time? It may not be practical to deliver all of the promised benefits from both programs.

The capacity for people to change is limited. It must be viewed as another scarce resource. Change bottlenecks can develop if there are too many hits on the same work group. This often occurs where an organization gets a clear focus for change (for example, a major new thrust of improved customer service). Naturally, there are many opportunities to do good things in the customer contact area, but the people in this area can get overwhelmed with the degree of change required.

In making portfolio decisions, it is important to ensure that the desires of various business units are being addressed in line with their potential for contribution to the organization as a whole. It is therefore necessary to temper any simple analysis of value with a cross check on the portfolio coverage of key business functions. Even with this check, multiple programs may be targeted at the same area. In such cases, portfolio management needs to push the issue of benefits delivery back to the business sponsors, the people who are signing up to deliver the results. They are the people who need to understand what is involved since they are the ones you will count on to live up to the commitment.

Sorting out all these interactions is difficult enough as a one-time activity. Unfortunately, the environment of portfolio management is dynamic and changing. This brings us to our next step in designing and managing a portfolio of blended investment programs.

5.   Adjust Portfolio Composition

Portfolio management starts with the selection process, but that is just the launch pad. An equally important role is to adjust portfolio composition over time to reflect changing conditions in the business environment. Although some accountants prefer to settle everything once a year, at budget time, the real world is trickier. Real-life portfolio management needs to deal with new ideas as they arise, evolving knowledge of the value of programs and changes in the organization and marketplace, whenever these happen. The composition of the portfolio, and the allocation of resources to the component programs, need to be adjusted to answer the following essential questions:

- *What do we do about over and under expenditure within the categories?* Degrees of freedom provide guidance here. If categories with smaller degrees of freedom such as mandatory or sustaining come in over budget (perhaps a major failure requires replacement of an expensive asset), the resources must come from the more discretionary categories such as business opportunities. This might mean delaying the launch of a high-value strategic initiative, or changing the delivery timetable of an ongoing program, bearing in mind the impacts on the benefits stream.

- *What do we do about programs that diminish in value?* Portfolio management, at heart, works on the view that no work is sacrosanct (unless legally required). If the prospective value of a program is found to diminish significantly as it moves forward, (whether due to changes in the environment, cost overruns or projected benefits shortfalls), you must stop throwing good money after bad. A program that focuses on benefits in a regulated environment may have significantly less value when the rules change and the industry becomes deregulated, and so might best be stopped in mid-execution. This frees scarce investment resources for other programs. Good portfolio management always has a "waiting list" of valued opportunities ready to take up resources as they become available.

- *What do we do when new opportunities arise?* The rapid pace of change in the world means that new opportunities, not identified in the original plan, may arise at any time. Some of these may be of very high value, indeed, while others may be mandatory. An example might be the introduction of new safety legislation that requires new employee records to be kept. The portfolio must adjust flexibly to such events, potentially by holding back some of the future resources from commitment, or by "bumping" or stretching already committed programs.

In practical terms, answering these questions is what we mean by monitoring portfolio performance, ensuring that we keep picking winners as time goes on.

Window on the Real World: Client Stories

This chapter opened with the story of Nova Gas Transmission (NGT), which faced requests for many more capital projects than it had the capacity to deliver. Portfolio management methods were developed to help its executives select the right programs.

The initial challenge was somewhat different in the cases of the Oregon Department of Transportation (ODOT) and a large-scale purchasing group in The Boeing Company, whose stories also appear below. They were less concerned with selecting programs than with managing an overload of major change programs all of which were judged valuable. The immediate problem was the prioritization, sequencing and queuing of project work.

Both organizations experienced a common core of implementation problems, including:

- Resource competition, change bottlenecks and overlaps holding up major programs

- Managers faced the challenge of managing complex ongoing operations while managing major business process redesigns at the same time

- Many work units were involved, but there was no shared vision of where they all fit in.

Benefits Realization Process

NGT recognized the strategic need to change the nature of the selection process itself. Accordingly, it adopted a full-scale portfolio management approach. ODOT and Boeing SSG Supplier Management & Procurement adopted a more operational focus. They built a high-level Results Chain model of all major change programs based on interviews with a cross section of senior and middle managers. Although their approaches differed somewhat, both organizations used the model to deal with the following issues:

- Map linkages among *initiatives, contributions, assumptions, intermediate outcomes* and *ultimate outcomes.*

- Understand resource limitations and program interdependencies, including overlaps, bottlenecks, resource competition and mutual reinforcement.

■ Group projects and programs according to the high-level outcomes they were designed to achieve.

Results

The Results Chain models provided a new big picture — a true strategic overview of all the change and business process redesign programs. It depicted how they related to each other and to high-level business objectives. This overview proved valuable both to guide management decisions and to communicate with all work groups.

At the project management level, the results were tangible:

■ Better definition and sequencing of programs and major projects
■ Firmer agreements on priorities and resource allocations
■ Realistic time estimates to complete programs and realize benefits.

The management group was able to move beyond making the "best decision" for each individual project to optimizing program decisions for the organization as a whole. Results Chain models also proved – once again – to be powerful communications tools. They were used to help work groups gain a better understanding of where they fit in the change programs, and what they contributed to the change initiatives. In the case of Boeing, the big picture was used in employee meetings and put up for all to see in a busy hallway, on what was called the Visibility Wall.

Transportation Development and Operations Branch, Oregon Department of Transportation (ODOT)

Presenting a unified program view — with projects grouped under multiyear work plans — to senior management was widely viewed as a major turning point in the BPR and change effort.

The Oregon Department of Transportation (ODOT) is a government agency in the United States, responsible for supplying services to the community in a wide range of areas — from driver and vehicle licensing to setting transportation policies to maintenance of all state transportation infrastructure. Managers at the Transportation Development and Operations Branch of ODOT had their hands full with daily operational responsibility for everything from highway maintenance to vehicle registration, combined with no less than seven major change and core process re-engineering programs.

The branch was seeking solutions that achieved multiple public policy objectives: rigorous environmental protection (in compliance with new standards and land-use restrictions), doing more with less in its core operations, serving customers better when they applied for vehicle licenses and registrations, and improving the "total transportation experience" and "community liveability" for a clientele that included almost every adult Oregonian.

The turning point in its change effort came when the branch began to re-engineer its project selection and design (PS&D) process. This was a core process that went to the heart of a major "line of business": maintenance and construction of all state-owned transportation infrastructure. It was a process that also intersected many other major policy and BPR initiatives. A few months into the PS&D program, the implementation team began to experience the classic symptoms of project overload. There was competition for resources among the seven major programs and initiatives, overlaps among many programs and interdependencies that were not understood. And prioritizing and sequencing work was a major problem for program decision makers and managers in the field.

"We were in a situation probably experienced by most organizations during major BPR efforts," recalls Tom Lulay, deputy director. "On one side, we had the BPR team leading the charge and on the other side we had some people showing reluctance to change. Some of the learning curves were pretty steep."

The branch put the PS&D program on hold and used Results Chain modeling to prepare a high-level road map of initiatives that would directly address the overload issues. Initiatives were organized into five multiyear "work plans" or programs which together, formed a "unified work program" or portfolio. Presenting a unified program view to senior management was widely viewed as a major turning point in the BPR and change effort. The change in perspective was radical, grouping major programs based on their strategic business outcomes rather than the traditional engineering view of delivery. The high level Results Chain is shown in Figure 4-4.

"The Results Chain made it easier for senior management to understand the change program, decide which change initiatives to start with and determine the order," says Lulay. "We used it as a road map to follow our progress, measure it and compare it to plan." Jay McRae, re-engineering implementation manager, says that the new road map began to pay off in practical ways. A cross-functional team of people from planning, engineering and maintenance was able to identify and eliminate project overlaps. Bridges were built between interdependent programs and projects. Implementation was wrapped into a single work program, with all teams sharing a common language and perspective focused on results.

The unified work program produced results that are typical of portfolio management. Resource commitments were prioritized based on the high-level program outcomes. Project work was scaled

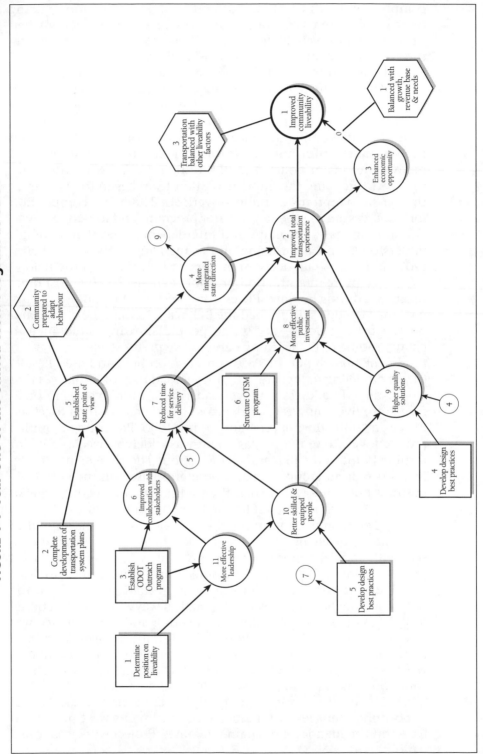

FIGURE 4-4 Year One of the Unified Work Program at ODOT

so that implementation could be broken into small pieces, resources committed gradually, and the "highest benefit" projects phased in first. Project and program work was packaged so decision makers could see the targeted benefits in relation to the costs, availability of scarce human resources and the ability of the organization to absorb the required change.

Lulay says the Results Chain was used widely to communicate the vision and overcome resistance to change. "The benefits approach allowed us to get people's buy-in to these changes and get specific commitments to deliver results from key stakeholders." Different views of the Results Chain were used with different stakeholder groups: an overall business view for decision makers; specialized views for project and change delivery teams; and a general view of the outcomes and essential programs for external stakeholders, including state politicians and advocacy groups.

The result was a major cultural change. The traditional approach was to take "an engineering view of success," Lulay says, and drive for quick project implementation. The resulting pace of change was unrealistic and disguised high resistance to change. Using the Results Chain helped to instill a "business change view of success," he says, where benefits were measured incrementally as the organization changed. Change and BPR targets were more realistic, increasing the chances of success for individual programs and of achieving the desired high-level outcomes.

Boeing Shared Services Group, Supplier Management & Procurement

A big picture emerged that helped to identify the three high-level business outcomes targeted by the 18 programs and select the key projects.

Boeing SSG Supplier Management & Procurement is responsible for purchasing "non-fly-away" materials for The Boeing Company of Seattle, Washington, a corporation with approximately 235 000 employees. It is nothing less than a business within a business. Purchasing nonproduction supplies — from pencils to personal computers to vendor services — the group manages purchase commitments of more than two billion dollars. Its activities have a significant, visible impact on Boeing's bottom line.

SSG Supplier Management & Procurement updates its strategic plan annually to identify priority actions for the year. When it made the decision to use benefits realization, a total of 18 programs already had been identified, including major initiatives such as re-engineering its core business process (called "order-acquire-pay") and revamping the supporting software package. There were also a number of employee satisfaction and training initiatives, and new undertakings like the creation of a Web site and an intranet.

With such a crowded agenda, seat-of-the-pants prioritization just could not cut it. A more systematic project selection method was needed. As well, the group's 280 employees and numerous work groups needed a coherent big picture of what was happening, given the large weekly load of change, re-engineering and operational problems they were being asked to solve.

"We were often making independent project decisions without considering the interactions among all projects," explains Candace Ismael, director of Supplier Management & Procurement. "We could end up making optimal independent project decisions that resulted in a suboptimal overall decision." There were two pressing questions, she says: "How do we select the choice projects that will have maximum business impacts?" and "How do we get a clear picture of project accountabilities?"

The group was ripe for the Benefits Realization Approach. It used the Results Chain technique to map the key programs and interdependencies between them. A big picture emerged that helped to:

- Identify the three high-level business outcomes targeted by the 18 programs.
- Select the key projects.
- Plan optimal resource commitments.
- Design individual programs with strong links to benefits.
- Reassess resource requirements to support the re-engineered business process.

The Results Chain had a direct impact on investment decision making and program management methods in the purchasing group. It was a guide to evaluate proposed new initiatives. It also provided a key communication, internal sales and leadership tool, widely used by work groups and employees to orient themselves in the universe of change programs. According to Michael Holser, senior manager of procurement systems and administration, the Results Chain has helped the group get commitment from key stakeholders and the leadership team. It has become "a perspective tool, a communications tool and a leadership/ownership tool," he says.

The Results Chain model was used at the spring employee meeting so the entire department could see what the targeted results were and where they were going. After that, it became even more visible. A large version was posted on SSG Supplier Management & Procurement's visibility wall, in a busy hallway, for all to see and discuss.

Summary

Now, more than ever, organizations have to face the problem of too many choices and too few resources. You need to pick the right set of programs that promise to deliver the best outcomes for the business, and you need to review those choices frequently, as the world evolves, and as benefits emerge and submerge faster and faster.

The lack of holistic attention to program selection and management is a serious problem for organizations today, and a root cause of the Information Paradox. As we move from IT being used for automation of work, where the issues were less complex and implications of failure limited, through information management to business transformation, where the impacts can be enormous, we are reaching the point where selection becomes a bet-the-business issue.

To address this problem, organizations must build upon the concept of blended investment programs and embrace the portfolio management approach. Portfolio management is not just a new name for the traditional ad hoc budget-time ritual. It is the intelligent alternative to the free-for-all competition for scarce resources that prevails in many organizations, a style of competition that displaces the required management focus on getting the best business outcomes from the resource pool available.

Portfolio management refocuses decision makers on the key issue of managing risk/reward relationships and offers them a rational approach to program selection, similar to financial portfolio management. Adopting this new approach generally involves taking the five practical steps described in this chapter:

1. Categorize programs to clear the decision field of clutter by ensuring that all programs are *not* treated as equals. A sound system for categorizing programs lets management focus on the key business decisions they need to make, in particular those involving major business opportunities.

2. Prepare value cases for the true business opportunity category of programs that merit detailed assessment in the competition for scarce resources. Value cases focus on much more than financial criteria. They employ the Results Chain and the four "ares" questions to develop broader investment criteria, including the alignment of programs with business strategies, the degree of risk around delivery of benefits and interdependencies between programs.

3. Manage risk systematically both by diversifying the portfolio across varied investment programs and by improving the risk profile of each program.

4. Manage program interdependencies with a focus on the four central issues of sequencing, overlaps, resource competition and change bottle-necks. The objective is to turn potential conflicts into mutual reinforcement so that programs leverage each other whenever possible.

5. Adjust portfolio composition as programs are completed, new ones are selected and priorities change to reflect shifts in the business environment. This process must be continuous, not another annual budget ritual.

By taking these five steps, your organization can ensure that portfolio management becomes an integral part of the ongoing, proactive benefits realization process to generate the most value for the investment dollar. This cannot be considered as a purely analytical process. Our approach requires the delicate balancing of many factors. While it serves as a powerful tool to support informed business decision making, it cannot be a substitute for business judgment.

****

Both portfolio management and its sibling, program management, are powerful tools to help organizations make sound business decisions. For these tools to be effective, they must be incorporated in an overall management process. In Chapter 5, we propose such a process, full cycle governance. We build further on value cases as a replacement for business cases, and introduce stage gates, a tool for progressive resource commitment. We discuss portfolio composition, and suggest an organization structure to support decision making.

5
THIRD FUNDAMENTAL: FULL CYCLE GOVERNANCE

The problem which Nova Gas Transmission (NGT), one of North America's largest natural gas pipeline companies, experienced when it faced the challenge of selecting from among 168 capital projects several years ago had important implications for day-to-day operational management. Because of the pressures described in Chapter 4, NGT tended to accept too many projects at once and then experienced problems scheduling and prioritizing the workload. The problem of too many choices chasing too few resources persisted long after initial project selection.

Full cycle governance was developed at NGT to deal with this project management overload. It operationalizes the principles of program and portfolio management. It represents a major change in the industrial-age project management methods discussed in previous chapters. These methods are inadequate to the challenges of designing blended investment programs to support IT-enabled business transformation. They are equally inadequate in selecting diversified portfolios of such programs. Not surprisingly, they are also inadequate to handle the everyday tracking and monitoring of project activity — often across dozens of major programs. Let's look briefly at the impacts of industrial-age project tracking and management systems.

Most organizations are tracking their project activity primarily on an individual-project basis. The problem starts with the one-off business cases, discussed in Chapter 1, that are used to launch the projects. Then comes the narrow focus on project delivery — rather than on the projects' contributions to business results. Organizationally, there are separate steering committees for each project that are not typically mandated to spend time reviewing project contributions to the overall goals of the organization. As a result, it is hard to get a comprehensive overview of all the projects: where they stand, how they are being managed and when they can realistically be expected to produce results. On the ground, it is ever harder to prioritize and re-prioritize programs as the inevitable changes occur. Over time, slowly but surely, the project grab bag described in Chapter 4 exacts a heavy toll in terms of the hidden costs of inefficient resource allocation, not to mention all those more visible cases of the Information Paradox.

The last two chapters have introduced fundamental concepts for responding effectively to the problem of too many choices and too few resources. Programs are designed to sort projects into the natural groupings that will produce key business results. Portfolio selection is then used to select and queue the programs. Full cycle governance operationalizes these concepts. This is a big job, involving a major change in management processes, organizational structures and most of all in attitudes.

Full cycle governance supports proactive management throughout the full cycle of project, program and portfolio management. It consists of a set of tools, processes and organizational structures needed to manage the benefits realization process every day — on the ground. Like the programs it is used to manage, full cycle governance radically extends the boundaries of project management, reaching beyond the myopic design-develop-test-deliver cycle of conventional projects. It truly means governance of the benefits realization process, from concept to cash, rather than management of an individual project.

The governance process helps you answer some of the critical questions that were so hard to answer in the midst of the project overload. These questions include:

- How do you go about ensuring that your portfolio actually delivers on its promises?
- While you are building the capabilities that will lead to benefits, how do you make sure that you are still on track?
- How do you control spending?
- How do you change course if circumstances change?
- What happens once the projects are delivered?
- Who manages all this activity?

Full cycle governance deals with the changes required to make an organization's blended investment programs successful. It brings about change by integrating today's advanced project management methods into the broader framework of programs and portfolios. It creates new decision-making processes and organization structures. Finally, it communicates and sells the new benefits mind-set to people, encouraging the development of new attitudes toward IT investments.

A Major Change in Management Processes, Structures and Attitudes: Practical Steps

Organizations need to implement four core components to establish full cycle governance and leave the industrial age behind. These components, which will be discussed in greater detail later in the chapter, will look familiar since they operationalize the key concepts of benefits management covered in Chapters 2 to 4:

1. *Value Cases:* Value cases replace conventional business cases to support the initial selection of individual programs and their ongoing management. These value cases capture the information which is the by-product of the program development process described in Chapter 3. They form a consistent basis for assessing program value using the four "ares" and allow a fair comparison of programs.

2. *Stage Gates and Progressive Resource Commitment:* Progressive commitment of resources is introduced for each project and program, as it is executed. As programs advance through their life cycles, knowledge is gained, which is used to update and enrich the value case. During this process of discovery and development, programs pass through a series of decision points which we refer to as stage gates. At each

Leaving the Industrial Age Behind

When full cycle governance is implemented, your organization begins to leave behind the industrial-age approach to project management and, by the same token, to manage the four dimensions of complexity more effectively.

- **Linkage:** Value cases pinpoint the benefits realization paths, using the Results Chain technique, leading from blended investment programs to end results. They give birth to programs that meet the risk/reward standards of the portfolio.

- **Reach:** The right people from all areas of the organization (both in the vertical chain of command and the horizontal chain of value) are selected to take part in all aspects of the full cycle governance process, including decisions at all stage gates. This encourages, and provides leadership for, participation by all key stakeholders.

- **People:** Full cycle governance focuses closely on all people and organization projects required to complete blended investment programs and produce benefits.

- **Time:** Full cycle governance allows organizations to take time and learn from their investments as they experiment with risky new technologies and work processes. This is known as progressive resource commitment or risking the company one step at a time. And it takes time. Time may be the most important dimension of the full cycle.

gate, programs can be assessed, modified or even cancelled. Progressive commitment replaces the all-or-nothing approaches towards new technologies with a pay-as-you-go method that allows for experimentation, testing and learning until the ultimate benefits are realized. It is an approach that attacks one of the biggest sources of the Information Paradox: silver bullet thinking.

3. *Program Decision Options and Portfolio Composition:* Decisions about individual programs are linked systematically to the process of adjusting overall portfolio composition. As programs progress through their life cycle, decisions about their disposition are linked to the higher level decisions about portfolio selection. Full cycle

governance processes ensure consistent linkage of program management with portfolio management — to meet overall risk/reward objectives.

4. *Organization Structure and Decision Making:* New organization structures are created to identify and empower key decision makers. Investment decision boards can be created to bring together senior decision makers from across the business to make key program and portfolio management decisions. Value management offices can be established to support the boards and program managers with information and advice.

Full cycle governance ensures that everyone concerned is reading from the same road map to benefits. It ensures, as well, that they all have the same landmarks in view, most notably the big picture made possible by blended investment programs and the even bigger picture of multiple-program portfolios.

Let us review each of the core components of full cycle governance, starting with program selection using value cases.

Value Cases

The traditional one-off business cases used to select projects are put together for the sole purpose of obtaining funding, as pointed out in Chapter 1. By more or less scientific means, the contenders for money are compared. These business cases are one-shot affairs — the project sponsors get the money for the duration of the project, or they don't get it and return to the drawing board. The cost, time and resource estimates are understood to be best guesses and their accuracy depends on the expertise and experience of the project planner.

The successful project candidates take on a life of their own. Although their spending and progress are usually — but not always — monitored, there is very little likelihood that they will stop until they arrive at their planned conclusion. If conditions change and progress does not match the original plan, you rely on the project manager's skill to manage the situation or obtain extraordinary funding. In essence, however, once the project is through the funding gate, it is like a runaway train that won't stop until it runs out of fuel, hits a wall or arrives at its destination. The business case itself gathers dust, somewhere on a shelf.

In this traditional view, the focus is only on, first, getting out of the gate, and second, project management. The approach to benefits realization, if considered at all, is strictly passive.

As a catalyst for promoting the change in viewpoint toward programs, you need a different form of business case. Rather than one that focuses purely on getting the money, value cases take a more holistic view. They seek to make explicit the linkages between the projects needed to bring about a particular business outcome. They encourage sponsors and other program team members to think about the reach of impact implicit in achieving these outcomes. They look at the changes needed to accommodate the effects of the program on people in the organization. They set out the picture over time of both the constituent projects and the benefits being sought.

Individual projects don't have business cases as such, just a statement of work that outlines what the project will achieve and how this relates to the overall program. Since they are already part of a program, they do not need to be justified separately.

At first glance, program value cases would appear to demand extra effort as a layer of justification is called for above that traditionally required for project business cases. To the extent this is true, there are major returns — in terms of benefits — on that effort. Also, the effort diminishes over time. With the knowledge gained as programs advance, the content of a value case is enriched. Thus the value case does not entail large amounts of additional work unless the value-related work, based on the four "ares," was not done in the first place. Rather, it represents the essence and level of accuracy of your current state of knowledge.

Stage Gates and Progressive Resource Commitment

The ability to progressively commit resources to programs doesn't just happen. Well-defined decision points must be established at the ends of defined stages in program development cycles. By establishing these stage gates organizations create opportunities to re-evaluate the program regularly. Program and project teams get clear targets to shoot for. At each stage gate, they commit only enough funding to reach the next gate. This limits risk while giving program teams an incentive to continuously improve the picture of the value they will achieve. With this framework, coming to the conclusion that a program should be discontinued, thereby releasing scarce resources to other programs, should be regarded as a success rather than a failure.

The progressive approach to resource commitment can be illustrated using a familiar example: home construction. Consider some of the basic questions you might ask as you proceed. Would you give all your money to the architect on the day he starts to design your house? Of course not. You spend some money to get the architect to propose a concept. How many stories will it be? How many bedrooms do you need? Is the garage built in or detached? How many cars should it accommodate? When the architect has satisfied you with the overall concept, you can go on to the next stage.

You get a builder to create detailed drawings which you check. Are the doors in the right place? Are the windows the right size? Is there room for appliances? Are all the sockets and switches in the right place? By this stage, you have a pretty good idea of how the house will actually look and feel.

When the drawings look right, you pay the builder the first installment in order to start the foundation. You pay more as building progresses, but you don't pay the final installment until you are satisfied that the last detail is complete.

What happens if the situation changes along the way? Say you don't get the bonus or contract you were after. Or perhaps you have the opportunity for a great new job in a different city. Maybe the builder can't finish the job as specified without further funding. Or, a new baby means that you need another bedroom. In any of these cases, you would consider revising the plan or selling your property to an interested buyer.

Complex development programs, with many phases and deliverables, are comparable to home construction projects. If you use the progressive approach to funding home construction, why would you consider approving all the money up front for a program that could cost millions of dollars to complete? Why not commit only the resources that match your current knowledge about the program and how it is advancing? As you gain knowledge about its potential value and risks, your confidence and the amount you commit to it will increase proportionately. Alternatively, your business environment may have changed so radically that you may abandon your investment altogether. How much better that you didn't spend all the money before finding that out!

Managers Must Make Tough Decisions Before It's Too Late. The progressive approach to resource commitment has proved useful for monitoring the progress and managing the risk of large projects. It also helps, as in the case of the sale of an uncompleted home, in making tough decisions about the projects that stop making business sense. The problems of implementing enterprise-wide application packages, mentioned in Chapter 1, provide an example. Such projects have encountered unexpected problems in part because they were not built into blended investment programs. Millions of dollars were often spent. The software had been ready for use as specified, but the business decided that it could not change its processes enough to use the system. No other projects had been organized to deal with this issue. In one such case, a $20 million software development was written off. While this was a bitter pill to swallow, how much worse would it have been if the business could not operate because the software system did not support its processes? Such a system could threaten the viability of the business. At least in this case, there was the opportunity to stop before disaster struck.

In another case, an entire program was cancelled much earlier in the game — to the surprise of the sponsor. "We've just spent a couple hundred thousand dollars and three months defining and refining the definition of the program," he said. "And now you say we can't have our funding to carry out the several million dollars of work in the program. That's crazy!" The primary issue, though, was not costs but benefits. The benefits uncovered during the process of defining the program were not nearly as great as everyone expected. In addition, several other programs with much better value had also come on the scene. The sponsor "knew" that his program was a good thing to do but the analysis showed that there were better programs to pursue at that time.

In implementing the Benefits Realization Approach we have found, over and over, an attitude of wanting to finish at all costs. But it is undesirable to sink money into undertakings that don't ultimately prove to be worth pursuing. And, it is certainly better discovering that at an early stage than after having spent all the money. By using full cycle governance to check for program value early and often, a lot of money that otherwise would be spent on low-value work becomes available for higher value programs. In this way, program stage gates reinforce the idea that program governance covers the full life cycle of the program and is not simply a hoop through which staff jump in order to acquire funding.

If you have succeeded in developing blended investment programs constructed using the big picture of benefits realization, you will have clear targets in mind. As you progress towards those targets, your understanding of their feasibility and desirability will increase. You still need to manage individual projects to produce their deliverables as planned. Solid project management is still required. What changes is how you monitor progress against objectives. You monitor not only in terms of managing the input factors such as time and money, but also in terms of your ability to achieve the targeted benefits. Your criteria for assessing the impacts of change are now focused on outcomes. This significantly changes the way you think about project and program delivery.

Overview of Stage Gates. Let's look at what program stage gates might look like in practice. There are four typical stage gates: program initiation; program commitment; program commissioning; and program completion. Figure 5-1 shows the gates and the activities that happen between them.

FIGURE 5-1
Program Stage Gates and Related Activities

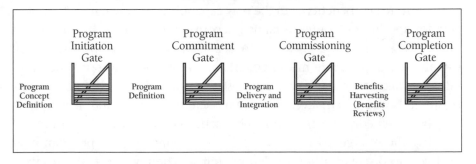

The first step (as explained in Chapter 3) is to come up with the concept for a program. At some point, this idea is articulated in more precise terms and tested for value relative to the other ideas and programs on the investment decision agenda. This testing can occur at the program initiation gate. This is also the point at which a high-level Results Chain would be produced to paint the big picture, identify the linkage, reach and people issues that will drive the need for key projects, and sketch the main benefits realization paths of the program. Once this is done, the program passes through the program initiation stage gate.

The process of developing a program happens frequently under full cycle governance. If the program shows sufficient promise and there are enough resources to develop it into something more concrete, it then needs to be defined to the point where it could be undertaken. This activity may include some small-scale testing of the idea such as a pilot project, or proof of concept. The Results Chain would be expanded to include a detailed view of all the projects, organizational capabilities and intermediate outcomes needed to achieve the program's benefits.

At this point, the program passes through the program commitment gate. If the program is still worth pursuing, the organization undertakes to carry it out and to deliver its benefits. Then, if funding is available and if there are no higher-value programs waiting, the program can be launched. Each individual project is launched when it makes the most sense and when the timing is right within the framework of the program and its Results Chain.

As each of the projects is completed, the organizational capabilities it delivers can be put into operation. At this program commissioning gate, each of the projects will be assessed to determine — on a go/no go basis — whether live operation begins. This is where the traditional project would end. However, when your focus is on achieving ultimate benefits from a program, a lot of hard work remains to be done, and another critical stage gate is on the horizon.

To realize benefits from the new capabilities, you will have to set targets for specific outcomes, establish accountabilities for achieving those targets over time and measure to see that you are achieving them. Establishing appropriate measurements, directly related to outcomes, and taking corrective action based on those measurements, is the key to successful full cycle governance. The program can be adjusted and new projects may be launched if targets are not being achieved or there are better ways of meeting those targets. In fact, the process of delivering the program may lead you to discover other ways to exploit it. The reviews at the relevant stage gates create opportunities to change or add to the program.

Eventually, after all the adjustments and corrections, the targeted benefits stream should begin flowing — and continue to flow. After more time passes, it will no longer be feasible to attribute a benefits stream to the program as conditions for fulfillment of the benefits change. At the program completion gate, all the players agree to retire the program, leaving the business areas affected by the changes to operate them autonomously.

These stage gates reflect the natural decision points in program development and project delivery cycles and let all parties know what to aim for. At each gate, they stop, look around, think and decide whether to continue, change or stop.

The Stage Gate Approval Process. The stage gate approval process provides program managers with a powerful approach to risk management. Each progressive approval is less risky. While it is important to estimate the upper and lower limits of the potential resource commitment over the life of the program, you commit only the resources needed to get to the next stage gate, just as you would in building the house mentioned earlier. In the early stages, we find managers can live with the uncertainty of inaccurate estimates. As the program progresses and the knowledge of the true costs and potential benefits increases, they find themselves in a better position to commit larger amounts of resources with confidence. To this end, we see the value case developing, evolving and supporting decisions at all stage gates throughout a program or project's life cycle.

Such incremental spending systems produce clear benefits when companies are assessing and introducing new technologies. Data warehousing, intranets, asynchronous transfer mode (ATM) and object-oriented programming are but a few of the technologies we hear about. Typically, IT professionals come back from a conference wanting to implement the latest wave of technological change. While tremendous benefits can be achieved, the Information Paradox indicates that such benefits are not inherent in the technologies. The level of benefit depends on how they are applied to *your* business.

The stage gate approval process helps to lower the risk of introducing such technologies in two ways. First, development of a program around the technology will help ensure that linkage, reach, people and time issues will be uncovered and understood. This forces hard questions to be answered around just what specific benefits an organization can achieve. In the end, the organization gets a much clearer idea about the elements of the technology that are actually needed and those that can be set aside.

Second, stage gates lead organizations to "try before they buy" through a pilot or proof of concept project, as part of the program design process. This lets them test the premise that the technology will deliver benefits. Only a fraction of the cost of a full implementation is committed to a small-scale test. Without betting the company, you get a chance to evaluate the real effects and benefits of the technology.

Redefining Project Management Success. Stage gates challenge people to develop new attitudes about what constitutes success when working on a project. Learning what works and what is valuable can be as helpful as successful delivery of a new information system. Releasing scarce resources by cancelling low-return projects should also be viewed as a success.

When stage gate approval processes are introduced, staff often view them in traditional terms as hurdles to be cleared to promote a winning project. Project champions still want their good ideas to be accepted and project teams still want to prove they are star performers. It is here that the concept of portfolio management plays an indispensable role. The issue is not whether an individual program or project team is doing good work, but whether their efforts are focusing on highest-value work. If not, they need to overcome their case of investment myopia and turn their attention to higher-value programs.

Stage gates impose a new decision-making process. To work effectively, this process requires new attitudes and perspectives about full cycle governance and the benefits realization process. For example:

- Program owners need to look continually for ways to improve potential benefits by modifying the program to achieve superior value, not just to defend their project at all costs.
- Project teams need to view stage gates as resting points where they are encouraged to take the time for critical self-examination.
- All players should work and think together to assess the current estimates of program value, relative to the costs and risks, in an objective manner.

Together program sponsors and project teams need to have a shared focus on risk/reward decisions. These attitude changes will mean a fundamental shift away from parochial interests towards a shared view of the interests of the organization as a whole. Bottom-line success needs to be redefined. It can mean working for a project team that delivers a new technology on time, on budget — in the classic way. It can also mean coaching users behind the scenes to help them adopt the technology faster. But success can also mean helping to stop a program in order to divert scarce resources to other programs of higher potential value or increasing the scope of the program to include projects which were not originally thought to have anything to do with the introduction of the technology.

Stage gates create many opportunities to creatively modify programs and value cases as the work proceeds. At Nova Gas Transmission, where a system of stage gating has been fully implemented, value cases can be thoroughly reworked at key gates. For example, a program sponsor was implementing a business change to reduce the costs of constructing new components of the gas pipeline by standardizing construction. To do this he needed to manage a large amount of information about pipeline component construction which was currently held in paper files. This included component specifications, maintenance profiles, and resource estimates. He determined that he needed a document management system to handle the information and began to put together a case for funding the implementation of such a system.

This turned out to be a difficult task. It was not at all clear what direct benefits a document management system would bring in and of itself. After a few rounds of trying, a new approach was proposed which built on the program concept. Instead of looking only at the technology, the sponsor and his team created a Results Chain which included all aspects of the business change and which put the technology in the context of its contribution to that business change. This turned out to be quite a revelation.

It was clear that the technology would help to enable the business change and indeed would significantly lower costs. But the real contribution was a new thinking process that was set off by taking a program view. The program was modified once it was discovered that the benefits of the change would not be achieved unless other information that was not originally in scope was also managed. Furthermore, they found that changes needed to be made to people management processes and to incentives in order to ensure that the new business processes would be used consistently. The technology itself was never an issue.

Project Management Stage Gates. Sound project management is still fundamental to full cycle governance, as explained in Chapters 3 and 4. It is one of the pillars of any good blended investment program. While the program defines the full package of work, the projects are where the bulk of the money gets spent. People spend time, things are bought and expenses are incurred within the projects. This requires different disciplines, closer to the traditional focus on delivery.

The focus of programs is on mapping benefits paths and handling the broad issues around achieving business benefits. These benefits come about because of the interaction of many projects. Each project, on the other hand, has a much narrower focus on delivering a product, be it a software system, training or a change in compensation policy. Because of this difference in focus and goals, it does not make sense to use the same criteria for judging the value of programs and projects.

The solution to this problem is to define a second set of stage gates specifically for projects. Initially, of course, projects are approved as part of an overall program. After that, each project passes through the project-specific gates at its own pace. All projects cannot be carried out at

FIGURE 5-2 Project Gates Relative to Program Gates

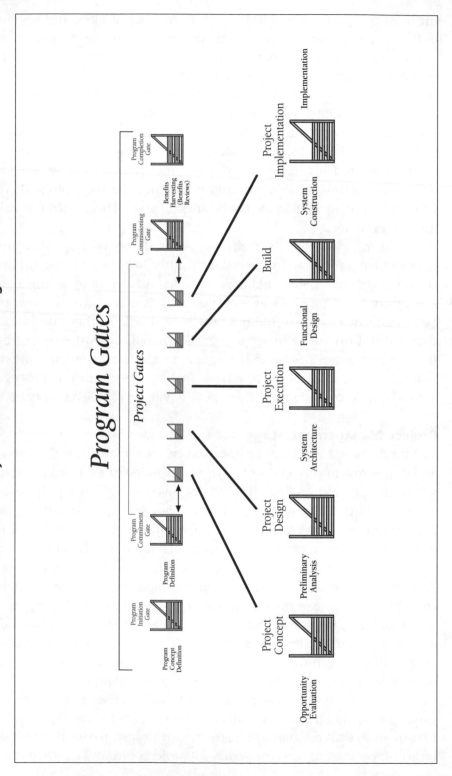

the same time. There are project interdependencies that dictate an implementation order.

Figure 5-2 gives an example of the project gates for a typical software development project and where they are positioned relative to the stage gates for the program.

The *project concept* gate is the point at which you validate whether the project is in line with the needs of the program. Further work is then required to develop a preliminary analysis with more refined cost and time estimates. At the *project design* gate, these estimates are reviewed in light of better information about the products and capabilities the project must deliver.

Each of the subsequent gates is designed to check whether the project is on track and to make adjustments that are necessary to keep it there. The architecture of the software design would be checked at the *project execution* gate. If you are contracting out completion of the project, this is the point where a fixed price bid for completion would be reasonable to ask for. The software would be accepted into service by the program sponsor at the *project implementation* gate. As with programs, your financial and other resource commitments only extend to the next stage gate.

The *project implementation* gate is the same as the *program commissioning* gate. At this point, the project's deliverables are complete and a decision is needed about whether to release them for live use. This is a program gate because the availability of other projects' deliverables plays a part in the decision.

Program Decision Options and Portfolio Composition

When programs and projects arrive at the stage gates, decisions must be made about how they will proceed. What are the main decision options? In the past, there were limited choices. You could stop or you could continue. You might need more funding or other resources. More often, these decisions were based on actual spending and project status relative to the plan. The focus was solely on project management issues, with little consideration given to wider program value issues.

With the viewpoint of programs and portfolios, we now have the tools to steer our investment programs more precisely toward the benefits we seek.

Program Decision Options. The structure of stage gates generates a much richer variety of decision options. This is because they incorporate a more complete assessment of the value cases as they are updated over time. The decision options include:

- *Stay the course:* If the program is on track and the next stage is adequately planned, proceed.
- *Modify the program:* If conditions change sufficiently, take the opportunity to reassess and adjust course appropriately. For example, if a program's alignment with business goals and strategic aims is not strong enough, the program can be redirected to better support the business.
- *Delay next stage:* When the requirements of the previous stage are not met, wait and see rather than carrying on, come what may. This does not mean hoping for a silver bullet but rather revisiting the value case for the program or project to determine if it is still worth pursuing.
- *Withdraw:* Change is the norm today. Sometimes conditions change so radically that the original benefits sought from a program are no longer achievable or desirable. In that case, just stop before you have spent all the money. There is no point in throwing good money after bad.

Where the option is selected to modify a program, there are a variety of actions that can be taken. Consider a few examples.

- If the program's risk profile becomes too high, corrective action can be taken.
- If the projected financial returns are too low, certain project deliverables can be scaled down to contain costs.
- If the time frame is too long, you can look for opportunities to accelerate the delivery of carefully selected benefits.

Modifying programs becomes a much richer option — a major source of benefits — in the cases of technology assessment and business program redesign mentioned above. In all cases, the benefits to be delivered are the major driver in investment decision making rather than input measures such as spending or time.

Portfolio Composition. Obviously, decisions to change resource commitments to programs have an impact on the portfolio. Stage gate decisions may deal with a variety of program interdependencies and portfolio management issues. For example, a delay in delivery of some IT infrastructure can hold up another program that is counting on that infrastructure to be in place. By linking program decisions to an understanding of the investment portfolio, decision makers are armed with the information and knowledge they need to make intelligent course corrections.

At the project level, decisions primarily focus on delivery, as before, but now within the broader program and portfolio context. If the plan for the project cannot be met, what do you do? You are, of course, tempted to get the project back on track, whatever it takes. However, you must also take into account the impacts such corrective measures may have on the overall program. Is there a significant change to the program costs? How are other projects in the program affected? Are the targeted benefits still achievable? If not, is the program still worth pursuing? Having developed the big picture of key benefits paths with a Results Chain model, you can assess such changes from a position of knowledge.

What happens if you cancel or delay a program? Potentially this could free up money for other work. What happens if an unforeseen and non-budgeted program arises? Where does the money come from? Decision makers face these real-life problems every day.

When practicing full cycle governance, they base their decisions not only on the prospective value of individual programs, but on the overall impacts on the investment portfolio. As explained in Chapter 4, there are a number of business investment categories — from mandatory and sustaining programs to strategic business opportunities and experimentation. It is the portfolio perspective that brings some clarity to the consequences of stopping a program, even if it doesn't make the decisions any easier.

The categories in the portfolio were devised because different types of programs offer different degrees of freedom to decision makers. If, for example, you are unable to carry out a sustaining program when planned, does this mean you have freed up money for some other program such as one for business improvement? As with many things in life, the answer is it depends.

You arrived at the mix of work in each category by setting policies on the amount that was needed and that you could afford to support your business. If not all of the work can be carried out as planned, it probably does not mean that the planned work will never be done. It just means that it will be deferred until later because it still needs to be done sometime.

The cases of unforeseen projects needing emergency funding demonstrate the clarity which the portfolio perspective gives to investment decision making. Nova Gas Transmission, for example, needed to rewrite its billing system. The old system had served the company well for many years. However, like many systems of its age, it was becoming more and more difficult to change without causing unexpected impacts in other parts of the system. A change in regulation was expected, but its exact nature had not yet been determined. By the time the exact change was defined, there would not be enough time to change the old system before the regulations took effect.

The decision was made to start developing a new system with a view to ensuring that it would be flexible enough to meet any likely changes within the required time frames. The problem was that there was no money in the budget at that time to carry out this work. Furthermore, in a regulated environment, there was nowhere to go for extra money. It appeared necessary to take money from other planned and in-progress projects.

The first thought was to take money from the sustaining budget. It was only the middle of the year and the year-long project to replace aging desktop computers had not spent all its funds, but the policy on sustaining the desktop environment had been set for very good reasons. It had been found that waiting longer than planned to replace the desktops involved significant extra support costs. It would also drive up the need for sustaining funds in the following year, further squeezing the money available for business improvement programs. For these reasons, the capital was sought in the business improvement category where schedules could be adjusted without such a significant impact on the business.

Organization Structure and Decision Making

Full cycle governance requires people to analyze information, decide on courses of action and set the policies that will drive governance of the investment portfolio. Who should make these decisions? Where does the decision-making authority lie? In answering these questions, it is important to recognize that blended investments in technology and other elements of the BTOPP business system are fundamentally business decisions. Just as war is too important to leave to the generals, decisions on blended investment programs and portfolio composition are too important to leave to technology experts. Clearly, it is the business leaders who need to be making critical decisions about the portfolio and its key programs.

"It's only a technology decision," many executives say. "We're not competent to judge the merits of the proposal. We can delegate that to the experts." Wrong! It is not only a technology decision, and what's more it never has been. Yes, there are technical elements of any blended investment proposal. But there are much more important business issues. The decisions you are making about IT are business decisions, decisions about the way you want to configure your business capabilities for the future. They are decisions about the tools people will use to get their jobs done. The options are not always easy. There will be tough decisions to be made. As Michael Porter says, "If you don't have to make trade-offs, you don't have a strategy." There will be individual winners and losers, but the main winner will be the organization. If you are delegating the decisions about these issues, you are not delegating...you are abdicating!

Delegating technology decisions to the experts is a management practice that dates from the automation era of IT applications. At that time, many IT projects stood alone and could be carried out in relative isolation from the rest of the business. This is no longer true of information management and business transformation programs which affect the entire BTOPP business system.

So, if these business decisions are the responsibility of senior management, where does the IT group fit? Aren't there decisions that they themselves can handle without dragging senior management into technical discussions? Yes, the IT group still has a role. The experts should rightly be deciding what the technology should be — what standards to adopt, what brand of computer to buy and so on. They need to provide expert opinion about the degree of adherence to standards, and the validity of the estimates of technical work. They also need to participate actively in the general management debate on business issues — the four "ares" questions which lie at the heart of portfolio management. In so doing, the IT group must participate on an equal footing with other groups, and should propose IT projects on the same equal footing as well. If the group wants, for example, to invest in a new network of PCs, their program should be treated in the same way as any other business program, and judged on the business value that it will deliver. The IT group's seat at the table is the same as that of any other business function.

We can illustrate the different roles of business management and the IT group by returning to the four "ares" framework (see Figure 5-3).

FIGURE 5-3
Management Roles Within the Four "Ares" Framework

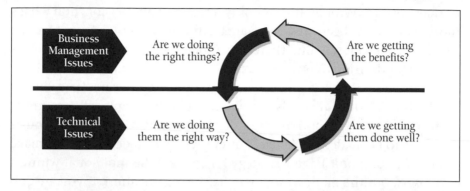

What the four "ares" framework shows is that full cycle governance won't work unless it is cross-functional, involving people from all areas of the business, including the IT group. The intent is to make the organization as a whole the winner. In all cases, making portfolio decisions should be about getting the best value for an organization from investments wherever they are made, rather than local optimization in any specific business area.

Investment Decision Board. Decisions about how to manage individual programs rest with the business sponsor, whose essential role is described in Chapter 3. This principle of program accountability is fundamental to full cycle governance; however, this level of accountability is necessary but not sufficient. Portfolio decisions must be made by decision makers representing all parts of the business. While decision-making authority could be vested in a single individual, it is rare for all business units to support and buy into key portfolio decisions without wider representation.

For this reason it is preferable to constitute a steering committee, or an investment decision board (IDB), on which all significant parts of the business are represented. This adds credibility to the decisions since all major business factors can be considered when issues arise. Board members can also individually promote the results of the decisions, covering all parts of the organization in the process. In this respect, the IT group is represented on the board alongside other business units. This ensures that both technology and business perspectives feed into the decision-making process.

The IDB concept can be taken a step further by introducing a value management office (VMO) to assist the decision board. The VMO's value analysts assess the value of business results, alignment, risk and return; monitor progress on benefits realization; and coach program staff on value concepts. In short, the VMO supports the decision board in bringing a sharper focus to portfolio management and the design of sound blended investment programs. The structure and roles of the IDB and the VMO are described in detail in Chapter 6.

Window on the Real World: Client Stories

The problems which Nova Gas Transmission (NGT) experienced with project overload described in Chapter 4 led this large natural gas pipeline company to implement full cycle governance completely. In the process, NGT has shaped development of this practical aspect of the Benefits Realization Approach. The NGT experience, summarized below, provides some vivid impressions of how full cycle governance actually looks and feels as investment decisions are made.

Nova Gas Transmission

NGT wanted to be more rigorous in the way it selected, funded and managed investments in IT-based business programs throughout the year — over the entire program life cycle.

> Nova Gas Transmission (NGT), one of North America's largest natural gas pipeline companies, has adopted the Benefits Realization Approach, and has, in fact, adapted it, improved upon it and institutionalized it under the name "Investment Value Management." NGT first implemented Investment Value Management (IVM) in the IT department, and plans to introduce the new approach to manage capital discretionary investments throughout the company.
>
> In the past, investment allocation at NGT was reserved for the last few months of the year. But too much was being played out in sudden-death play-offs. There were no round robin or regular season games. Everyone had to be ready when the whistle blew. Tom Whitehead, manager of planning and practices, says the process was like an annual sweepstakes. "Everybody would send their best man in with gloves on once a year to win some money. It would be a euphemism to say that it was somewhat heated. Not only was negotiation intense during the process, some decisions were being made based on issues such as equity and fairness, instead of the real issues: business objectives."
>
> NGT wanted to be more rigorous in the way it selected, funded and managed investment in IT-based business programs throughout the year. It was also concerned about harvesting bene-

fits over time. NGT developed extensive governance mechanisms, tools and techniques for benefits realization that are applied over the entire program life cycle. The results of this full cycle governance have been very positive. Whitehead says that institutionalizing IVM has allowed NGT to:

- Find the investments with the most value, that will generate the greatest benefits, while at the same time rigorously assessing risks.

- Do all the things that must get done to obtain results, whether they are related to IT or changes to the business itself.

- Engage the business units in the IT development of the company, and help all business users to work together.

- Receive higher value for dollars spent.

- Spend more time thinking about the right ideas for new investment opportunities.

The company has created two governance groups that are central to the process — the investment decision board and the value management office. A cross-functional team of senior business managers, the board meets regularly to allocate funds for all IT investments. It compares and evaluates and accepts or rejects them based on their relative value. The value management office acts as a secretariat to the board, coaches sponsors and staff in developing program proposals that are based on value and monitors spending and the status of available funds.

According to Bob Coote, manager of facilities provision and a member of the investment decision board, "People who submit programs for review certainly feel it is lengthier at the early stages of the process. However, they soon realize that the process leads them to better proposals, provides them with a better assurance that their program will deliver results and helps avoid costly routes. In fact, what is unique about the IVM process is its continuous nature. The investment decision board meets regularly, new programs are continually proposed, active programs are reviewed and understanding of the overall picture grows constantly — always with an eye on business benefits."

NGT has implemented a number of checkpoints in the program life cycle where a program's value is assessed relative to other investment opportunities before it is allowed to proceed. These stage gates — the program initiation gate, the program commitment gate, the program commissioning gate, benefits reviews and the program completion gate — are managed by the investment decision board.

Business cases are not simply reviewed by the board and OK'd or vetoed. At any given time, there are a number of active programs in different stages of development, and a queue of valued programs waiting for resources. At the first two gates, the board compares programs to select those that have the greatest value to the organization. At the following two gates, it monitors progress in delivering programs and realizing benefits. At the program completion gate — once all of the intended benefits mechanisms are in place and the program has reached a steady state in harvesting benefits — the board passes responsibility for ongoing benefits realization from the program sponsor to the business operation.

According to Bruce McNaught, vice president of internal resources, adopting full cycle governance has made a huge difference at NGT. "The priorities are clear and everyone knows what must be done. The IT people are not tempted to tease out the benefits of a pet project. They can see and understand why we need to do certain projects and not others. They are confident that the decisions were made for all the right reasons. And since the IVM process is continuous, sponsors know that a better, more disciplined business case could get them in the queue."

Summary

The shift from stand-alone project management to program and portfolio management creates the potential to harvest vastly increased benefits from IT-enabled business transformation initiatives. To realize that potential, you need to operationalize these key concepts with full cycle governance. Only then will you be able to measure the results of benefits realization.

In this chapter, we have reviewed the four core components required to establish full cycle governance as the new way of making major investment decisions and managing programs in your organization. These are: value cases, stage gates, portfolio composition and program decision options, and organization structure and decision making. Each of these components requires significant change in how people think, manage and act.

When value cases replace conventional business cases to support program selection, your organization needs to embrace a new multidimensional view of business value. ROI remains important, but is not in itself more important than strategic alignment with the corporate vision, or an assessment of the risk that the business environment could change. The all-or-nothing bet of traditional project approval must also be replaced with value cases that are designed to allow continuous monitoring of programs through their entire life cycles.

When progressive commitment of resources is introduced for each project and program, your people need to learn how to pilot their initiatives through a series of stage gates. At first, this may seem like extra work, until they understand that value is added at each gate. As they proceed, they will learn to think beyond the old go/no go project decisions to a far richer menu of options. This is a new world where a cancelled project is not a failure, but a source of information for management and of scarce resources for other higher-value programs. It is also a world where program and project managers are encouraged to modify their initiatives frequently in order to reduce risk and increase benefits.

Whenever critical program management decisions are made at the stage gates, your investment decision makers must get used to assessing the impacts on overall portfolio composition. Program and project managers need to share the bigger picture with the executives making portfolio selection decisions as the programs progress through their life cycles. A shared overview helps everyone handle overlaps, emergency funding requests and other special events more smoothly and effectively, to maximize benefits.

****

The introduction of the Benefits Realization Approach, and its operationalization through progressive resource commitment, and the stage gate approval processes, represents a significant change to organizations. It forces a change in the management mind-set that will challenge the way work is done and decisions are made today. More importantly, it may challenge your organization's formal and informal power structures. In Part III, we move on to discuss the three necessary conditions that articulate further organizational changes required for the approach to be successful. Accountability must be activist, and supported by new organization structures. Relevant measurements must be in place to support accountability, and the ongoing management of benefits realization. Proactive management of change is required, both to introduce the approach, and as an integral part of business programs.

While all this change is a lot to undertake, the potential benefits are major. Your organization will be able to transform itself and enter the Knowledge Economy by taking the necessary risks in a controlled way.

THREE NECESSARY CONDITIONS

In Part II, we discussed each of the three fundamentals of the Benefits Realization Approach: program management; portfolio management; and full cycle governance. Part III moves on to an in-depth discussion of each of the three necessary conditions of the approach: activist accountability; relevant measurement; and proactive management of change.

Chapter 6 introduces the concept of activist accountability and ownership. We present the seven plus one key conditions for activist accountability. We discuss the key roles of business sponsor, program manager and project manager, and their responsibilities. Finally, we describe two organizational entities that are required to support implementation of the Benefits Realization Approach, the investment decision board (IDB) and the value management office (VMO).

Chapter 7 takes accountability one step farther, in that there cannot be effective accountability without relevant measurement systems. We discuss the blind spots in today's measurement systems, and show how the Results Chain can be used to provide a unique perspective on measurement. This perspective lets you better manage those four dimensions of complexity: linkage; reach; people; and time by ensuring that: measures exist; you are measuring the right things; you are measuring things the right way; and measurements are guiding decisions and action.

Chapter 8 presents the case that results are the leverage point of change, and that change must be proactively managed if benefits are to be realized. Implementing the Benefits Realization Approach requires major changes in how people think, manage and act. These changes will not happen by themselves. Change management is the job of senior business management, not human resource experts or psychologists. Business sponsors, in particular, must take the lead in managing the process of change. Change initiatives must be built into business programs at the beginning, not bolted on after the fact. They must address all elements of the business system, with emphasis on the organization, process and people aspects.

6
FIRST NECESSARY CONDITION: ACTIVIST ACCOUNTABILITY

"The buck stops here," the famous slogan of Harry S. Truman, is a clear and succinct description of what is generally understood by the term accountability. This simple idea is the foundation of activist accountability, too often forgotten in the disputes between technology experts and business managers.

One of the most common reasons why even stand-alone projects don't deliver the intended business benefits is the failure to properly locate accountability up front, at the stage of program design. When people say things like "Everyone is accountable for the success of this project," it may be true as a general philosophy, but if everyone is accountable for everything, then in real terms, nobody is accountable for anything. In short, everyone loses sight of where the buck really stops.

Another common mistake is to adopt an overly passive, negative attitude towards accountability. For example, *Funk and Wagnall's* definitions of "accountable" include "liable to be called to account." This rather threatening definition is the way all too many organizations apply it. Some managers have been quite surprised to find themselves "accountable" after the event, sometimes with dramatic consequences.

The scapegoating of the IT group associated with silver bullet thinking is an example of this passive, negative attitude toward accountability.

A positive sense of accountability is required to support the benefits realization process. Instilling this sense will increase the odds that we can achieve the intended benefits of an investment program, and drive our success rates up toward the 80 to 90 percent we should be achieving with IT-enabled business transformation initiatives.

If the buck doesn't stop somewhere in a positive way, bucks are unlikely to start flowing. That's why our accountability motto is: "The bucks *start* here."

Three Routes to Activist Accountability

Full cycle governance requires changes in roles, attitudes and culture which must reinforce the emergence of projects, programs, portfolios and stage gates. Each organization starts with a unique set of initial conditions, so it is not advisable to define a generic approach to activist accountability in advance. Experience tells us, however, that there are three routes to changing any firm's accountability systems to support benefits realization. All these routes must be travelled in order to implement full cycle governance. We use the routes to activist accountability as guidelines for management action:

1. *Understand the Essence of Activist Accountability:* Ideas and mind-sets must change. Focus people's attention on how the concept differs from traditional passive approaches to business results still operating in many organizational cultures today. Explain why cultural and organizational change will be required to do a good job of benefits realization and program management.

2. *Introduce Seven Plus One Key Conditions of Activist Accountability:* Apply these practical conditions to the articulation of accountabilities for a specific blended investment program. Make each condition actionable so people learn by doing to every extent possible. Full cycle governance is operational, not theoretical.

3. *Introduce the Accountabilities Required for Full Cycle Governance:* Define new activist accountabilities for both program and portfolio management, usually (but not always) drawing on the experience gained with a single program. This will involve introducing permanent changes in organizational structures.

Each of these three routes to change will now be reviewed in detail.

Understand the Essence of Activist Accountability

To get the benefits, you not only define them and articulate a program to achieve them, you need to know who is going to make them happen. If the intended benefits are business benefits, then it is the business sponsor — a senior business manager or executive — who should own them and be held accountable for achieving them. This concept of business benefits ownership is central to benefits realization.

The accountability of the IT group is to be a partner in delivering the new technological and organizational capabilities that will support the achievement of benefits. But IT project teams are rarely, if ever, positioned to achieve the benefits themselves. Nor should they be expected to do so. It is the role of IT to deliver the technology and/or the applications that provide the capability that can support the business. Significant business benefits are only achieved through the process of business change, and it is the business itself that is ultimately accountable for that change.

With clearly defined roles, IT experts and business managers, as members of the program team, can actively accept, even embrace, their respective accountabilities. So how can accountability be defined in activist terms? Elliott Jaques and Stephen D. Clement, in their book *Executive Leadership: A Practical Guide To Managing Complexity,* describe the role of manager in terms of three critical accountabilities:

- For the outputs of employees
- For maintaining a team of employees who are capable of producing the outputs required
- For the leadership of employees so they can collaborate competently and with full commitment with the manager and with each other in pursuing the goals set.

Accordingly, they say managers require, at an "absolute minimum," the following four authorities:

- To veto an appointment
- To decide about task assignments
- To decide personal effectiveness appraisal and merit awards
- To decide to initiate a person's removal from a work role.

Theoretical definitions provide a useful starting point. When it comes to accountability, especially, it is important to phrase the changes you are looking for in terms that readily translate into actions. With this in mind the seven plus one key conditions for activist accountability have been developed.

Introduce Seven Plus One Key Conditions for Activist Accountability

Activist accountability is more than just being active. Too often being accountable is seen as a framework for blame. Since we cannot afford this traditional "passive-negative" approach to large-scale transformation programs, the seven plus one conditions were designed to create a framework for success.

Following is a practical checklist of seven key conditions to be applied when accountabilities for any given outcome or benefit are assigned and accepted. This list is particularly useful when applied to the design of the organization and people projects of a specific blended investment program.

Condition 1:   Clear mandate and scope

Condition 2:   Sufficient authority and latitude to act

Condition 3:   Requisite competence

Condition 4:   Commensurate resources

Condition 5:   Clear lines of accountability

Condition 6:   Understanding of rights and obligations

Condition 7:   Relevant performance measures

And, of course, there must be acceptance of accountability.

Accountabilities must be made specific. When the above conditions are in place, you have the parameters for the required accountabilities. Let's review each of these necessary conditions and illustrate how they create an environment for success. Often, these conditions are presented in the form of questions team members and executives must ask themselves, so they are phrased in fairly personal terms.

Condition 1: Clear Mandate and Scope. This condition addresses the question: "Accountability for what?" Am I accountable for the successful execution of a project on time and within budget, or am I accountable for the achievement of actual business benefits? If so, which benefits? The Results Chain model can be used to link accountability with specific results. Each member of a particular investment program should be able to describe his or her mandate in terms of one of more specific measurable results identified in the model — both business benefits and technology capabilities.

A second issue is the *scope* of your accountability. Does it match the task at hand? One of the reasons why so many BPR projects have come to grief has been the inability to get scope right. In some cases, the project scope was narrow, often because it was confined to a single department rather than an end-to-end process, such as order fulfillment. This kind of tinkering is frequently counterproductive, giving the illusion of improvement, while often merely moving a bottleneck somewhere else in the supply chain. On the other hand, if the scope is too wide the problem may be seen as unmanageable — to be admired rather than dealt with.

Defining the scope of accountability brings you face-to-face with Reach, one of the four critical dimensions of complexity. How far does the scope extend up and down the chain of command and laterally across the supply chain? Answers can be generated using the discipline of "systems thinking" identified by Peter Senge in his book *The Fifth Discipline* (which gives "system" a broader meaning than in common IT usage). Determination of scope requires decisions about the size of the system you have to manage.

As described in Chapter 2 and further illustrated in Chapter 3, the Results Chain technique allows you to build the working model of a system, to map the network of initiatives and intermediate outcomes that contribute to the desired outcomes. Programs and projects can be identified in terms of meaningful subsystems, corresponding to specific benefits realization paths, within the overall model. Their scope can be depicted by shaded areas, such as the one shown in Figure 6-1.

You can use this model to review the program in the context of the benefits framework over time as your understanding or the situation changes.

Condition 2: Sufficient Authority and Latitude to Act. If you are to accept accountability for achieving business benefits, does your span of control have the reach necessary to manage all the contributing initiatives? The projects (or Results Chain initiatives) required to make the programs successful frequently require the buy-in and commitment of the principal decision makers across the organization. As a rule of thumb, the business sponsor who accepts ownership of the expected benefits and accountability for achieving them must be a senior officer *and* have earned wide credibility within the organization. In other words, formal authority is important but is not enough alone to make complex blended investment programs a success. That authority must be boosted by the informal authority that comes through being able to influence other holders of authority at many levels.

What does "latitude to act" mean? Even though you appear to have sufficient authority, there can be other constraints. For example, we all know about the hidden power of corporate culture. The values and beliefs of the organization may not be open to change, whatever your vested authority. Many CEOs have been chewed up and spat out by organizations where they confused their formal authority with their real latitude to act. The degree of latitude exists at a point in time and may, of course, be expanded through achieving credible successes. When you assess your latitude to accept an accountability, you need a firm grasp on the reality of what you can change in what time frame.

Condition 3: Requisite Competence. Qualified people are needed to engineer business transformations because the changes go to the heart of

FIGURE 6-1
Scope of Subsystem on Benefits Realization Path

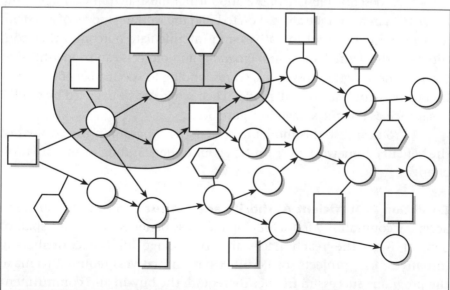

the business. This condition must therefore be highlighted — and insisted upon. Organizations are most successful when they put their most qualified people into the key positions of accountability for their critical investment programs and projects. Of course, this is easier said than done. In today's lean organizations, these people are in high demand. Their time is a scarce resource in the competitive free-for-all at budget time. However, the programs in question are often the fundamental change initiatives to assure the organization's future in the Knowledge Economy or a radically restructured industry. So, keep asking: "Are we really going to put less than our best people on this one?"

Condition 4: Commensurate Resources. Checking the true availability of resources imposes a reality check on the assignment of accountabilities. It comes back to the issue of scarce resources discussed in Chapter 4. Jaques and Clement in their book, *Executive Leadership,* give managers the authority to hire and fire and to muster the resources both human and otherwise that are necessary to get the job done. But formal authority does not create resources. Are they really available? Do they even exist today? Must they be purchased outside? And so on. If the necessary resources are not obtainable, you should think twice about whether you can solve the problem before accepting accountability.

This observation lies at the heart of the program selection decisions of portfolio management. And it raises the fundamental issue of understanding the difference between launching and landing major investment programs. The resource requirements are quite different in each case.

Condition 5: Clear Lines of Accountability. When considering this condition, you need to ask a simple question: "To whom am I accountable?" You probably know the answer today, but things can change fast. Full cycle governance embodies the concept of progressive resource commitment as a method of dealing with the realities of an everchanging environment. You can never know enough from a snapshot view to answer all the questions and predetermine all the decisions that will arise down the road. Accountability in these terms will involve dialogue and negotiation, and the lines of negotiation should be both clear and open.

Condition 6: Understanding of Rights and Obligations. It is important to make clear the rights and obligations of all parties. Accountability is more than the conferring of authority by one party on another. In the context of investment programs and projects, it requires that people accept commitments of scarce resources to, in effect, sign "contracts" to deliver — whether the deliverables are specific technologies, capabilities, intermediate outcomes or business benefits. These contracts define the rights and obligations of two parties, and at times many more than two parties. These rights and obligations must be made specific. Of course, they may be renegotiated over the term of the contract, but they should never be in doubt. In an environment of activist accountability, there should be common recognition that the success of each is in the success of all. Being accountable will mean going the extra mile to assist others, but never at the risk of failing to fulfil your own obligations.

Condition 7: Relevant Performance Measures. Measurement is what gives teeth, and life, to accountability. So, this condition is essential. There must be agreement about the measures and measurement systems that provide the yardstick of success for accountability. If you are accountable for achieving the business benefits, how will you know they have been achieved? The measures of your success must be directly tied to the measurable outcomes of the program. However, measures of performance must also take into account what must be done to bring about these outcomes, as is pointed out in Chapter 7.

The mere action of defining measures of success will change behavior positively or otherwise. When measures are set and understood, most people will begin to optimize their behavior. If new behaviors are necessary to achieve the desired results, then new measures will be needed, and they will need to be reset at each stage in the program.

Management must be consistent in adhering to the measures they define. For example, if they are measuring effective achievement of results rather than hours in the office, people cannot walk around glancing at their watches, mumbling about who is late.

One Additional Condition: Acceptance of Accountability. This is not so much a condition, as an absolute requirement. If accountability is contractual by nature, then activist accountability is about enabling successful delivery. Your accountability is inextricably linked to those of others. That means all parties must commit to the result, and act to make it happen. Later in the chapter, a high-level view of an accountability matrix, which is useful in defining the accountabilities of the various parties, will be discussed.

The new activist accountability agenda can be applied both to shape individual investment programs and the broader organizational structures supporting full cycle governance. This brings us to the third route to implementation of activist accountability: introducing the accountabilities required for full cycle governance.

Introduce the Accountabilities Required for Full Cycle Governance

Understanding and applying the seven plus one conditions of activist accountability is the first step many organizations will take to develop the new accountability systems and culture required for active benefits realization. The conditions apply most naturally to the design of an individual blended investment program.

However, activist accountability reaches beyond programs to decisions about the entire investment portfolio. Eventually, it must be embedded in all phases of full cycle governance. This presents some new, higher-level challenges, most notably the creation of shared accountability in the senior management group for program selection decisions and the related adjustments to portfolio composition, discussed in Chapters 4 and 5.

Make no mistake about it, some of these decisions can be the toughest that executives have to make. Some can involve difficult strategic trade-offs about the future direction of the company, including its Knowledge Economy initiatives. Making these trade-offs plays a central role in shaping a business strategy. Some decisions must be made in the context of fierce competition for scarce resources, driven by the problems of too many IT choices chasing too few resources discussed in Chapter 4.

To deal with these issues and challenges, implementation of full cycle governance must be carried out not only by applying new principles of activist accountability, but also by creating new organizational structures and decision processes. In this regard, organizations with significant portfolios of blended investment programs require an investment decision board supported by a value management office. Underneath this portfolio management layer are the investment programs themselves with structures appropriate to their stage in the life cycle. Of these multiple initiatives, some will be actively pursued as programs, while some will be waiting in the wings. The programs on the go will be at different stages with different objectives running to different time frames. Figure 6-2 shows an outline of such an organization. The structure for just one of the programs, involving three projects, is illustrated.

FIGURE 6-2
**The Value Management Office and
the Infrastructure for Full Cycle Governance**

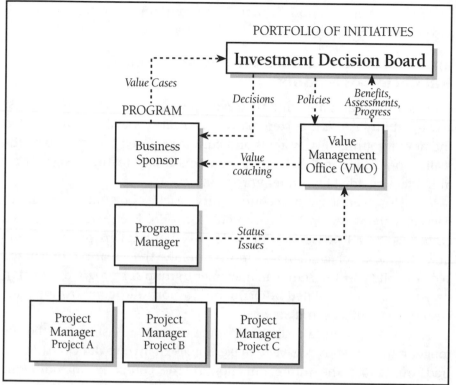

Nova Gas Transmission (NGT) provides one example of how this structure operates in practice and, in particular, how the new decision processes have helped the company sort through its project overload. This story is told in the "Window on the Real World" section at the end of this chapter.

Another case, that of a financial institution, illustrates how the full cycle governance approach can be applied to strategy development. Historically, the company had consisted of a collection of highly autonomous and diverse business units. Its business strategy called for developing a one-company approach to serve international markets by leveraging common strengths, while responding to necessary market and line-of-business differences.

Recognizing the magnitude of investments and the significant cultural changes implied by this direction, a "user council" was established by executives during the strategy project. The council had broad business head representation and these heads had to collectively decide upon enterprise-wide priorities — and not merely represent their distinct business areas. The culmination of the strategic planning exercise resulted in identification of a number of major enterprise program initiatives.

While focused on the future use of IT, all of these initiatives required significant business effort to achieve the identified business benefits. They were blended investment programs in all but name. Each of the active programs has a full-time business sponsor accountable to the council to deliver the benefits of the program. This user council has endured beyond the strategic planning project to become, essentially, the investment decision board for the ongoing programs. As such, it is accountable to the CEO and the board of directors for the achievement of the strategy.

With these real-life cases in mind, let's review the critical roles of the players leading the full cycle governance process, paying special attention, of course, to their principal accountabilities.

Investment Decision Board (IDB). The board is accountable to senior management and has broad representation from all groups, including IT. In some cases, it may be a senior management committee. The IDB is primarily accountable for managing the portfolio of blended investment programs, each identified and mapped using the Results Chain model. In a real sense, the board is the owner of the portfolio. In large organizations with multiple lines of business, the board will often have to manage the level of overall funding to provide the necessary balance between company-wide and specific line-of-business needs.

The specific accountabilities of the IDB are to:

- Review value cases for investment programs and the essential projects to accomplish them.
- Select the winners.
- Assign a committed business sponsor to each approved investment program.
- Review the status and direction of these approved programs and approve funding progressively as the various stage gates are reached.
- Be the arbiter of last resort for major program/project roadblocks or conflicts between programs and projects.

It is *not* the role of the IDB to:

- Provide detailed project management.
- Recommend or select specific technology solutions.
- Involve itself in any of the day-to-day management.

In short, the IDB leaves aside some of the old roles of championing specific technologies and projects. It focuses on overall portfolio management, defining value assessment criteria and establishing the ground rules for competition among program sponsors for scarce resources.

The IDB must have the clout to grant or withhold money and must be able to call program sponsors to account both for project delivery and for benefits realization. The type of representation needed on the board to achieve this depends largely on the culture and authority structure of the business. Since the decisions of this board have a significant effect on business direction, the ideal body is the senior management team. It has the necessary authority and stature to make credible decisions that will be followed. However, with today's flatter, empowered and networked organizations, the management team can invest decision-making authority in other levels of management.

The role of IDB members is to bring knowledge of different areas of the organization, and to act collectively to promote a company-wide view of business needs. The key to maintain the credibility of the board is to have members whose judgment is respected and who collectively span the main areas of the business.

Value Management Office (VMO). The value management office is accountable to the investment decision board. It is similar to the project management offices created in recent years to ensure that a central pool of experienced project managers apply their know-how to the effective delivery of projects. The project managers are assisted by a support office acting as a secretariat and back-up. This consolidated function allows managers to take an overall view of current and planned projects and to keep a close eye on project progress. This is intended to lower the delivery risks and to enable resources, particularly people, to be balanced across potential demands.

The VMO incorporates many of the project reporting functions of the project management office. However, the VMO extends them in some significant ways. First, its focus is on program value rather than strictly on project cost. This means that the VMO's value analysts also assess the value of business results, alignment, financial worth and risk.

Second, its monitoring activities include progress on benefits realization, not just project delivery. Third, it coaches program staff on value concepts. In this capacity, it acts as an advocate of change in the organization in the way people think about value. In short, the VMO supports the IDB in bringing a sharper focus on how to get the best value from blended investment programs.

The VMO is the day-to-day contact for business sponsors, program managers and others who are struggling to come to grips with a major shift in their perspective on value. Therefore, they are well placed to deliver the board's messages about the four "ares" approach to assessing value and the more active states of benefits realization. They also transfer the skills that are needed to deal with the new decision-making processes. In doing so, they are able to contribute to both the willingness and the ability of staff to move to a new way of thinking. The VMO's participation in this aspect of change management is vital to successful benefits realization.

The VMO's accountability is to track the various programs and initiatives and to support the program managers in developing value cases and recommendations for the IDB. The VMO will try to facilitate the resolution of program and project issues without passing them up to the board. In addition, the value management office maintains core competencies in the disciplines of benefits realization to support the various program areas.

Value analysts occupy a primary position in full cycle governance. They help business and technology teams to design programs that provide the best value to the business. They need to have both an appreciation of IT capabilities and an understanding of the key business drivers. Although there is a large degree of consulting skill involved in this job, it is vital that internal staff carry it out. Asking hired guns to impose new standards of value assessment and benefits — the standards used to pick winning programs — has proved counterproductive. It fails to bring about the fundamental change in thinking needed to realize benefits from blended investments.

Business Sponsor. As indicated in Chapter 3, the business sponsor has the *most* critical role in the benefits realization process. This is the individual who accepts accountability for delivering the benefits of investment programs to the organization.

There is a self-evident truth that "organizations don't do things, people do." The capability to achieve benefits can be knowingly or innocently hijacked if it is not actively managed. The distinction between the capability to achieve benefits, which is what projects have traditionally delivered, and the active harvesting of them as a distinct and overriding accountability, is what differentiates the Benefits Realization Approach. It is this latter accountability which defines the role of the business sponsor.

Every major initiative and program approved by the investment decision board requires a business sponsor. When you are dealing with programs in a benefits realization context, you are dealing with complex multimillion dollar, usually multiyear initiatives. The business sponsor must be a senior executive from within the fabric of the business, usually from the line organization, who accepts accountability for delivering the benefits to the whole organization, not just his or her own area.

Business sponsors are accountable to the chair of the IDB for the success of their programs. They are accountable to ensure that as elements of a program are achieved and implemented, the program continues to meet the overall goals of the business initiative. Their success is ultimately measured by the achievement of these measurable business benefits.

The successful business sponsor must practice the principles of activist accountability. This means more than applying the seven plus one basic conditions discussed above. It means accountability for leadership since business sponsors are probably the most visible individuals — day in, day out — in the entire full cycle governance process. The key behaviors of an activist business sponsor are: vision, commitment, persistence and communication.

- *Vision:* The business sponsor must provide a clear vision of the benefits sought by the initiative. The word *vision* is important. One of Senge's five disciplines is "shared vision." Since blended investment and business transformation programs are complex, the people involved need to understand and have a common view of the ultimate goal. The benefits identified in the Results Chain model are simply the starting point. The vision fills in the details and conveys the big picture of the benefits realization process from concept to cash, as discussed in Chapter 3. The vision also provides the clear picture of what the world in which these benefits are achieved will be like. The business sponsor must demonstrate a strong belief that change needs to occur — that the program is necessary — and provide strong leadership for the change process.

■ *Commitment:* The business sponsor needs to be committed to the real value of the program, to its achievability and to his or her own ability to make it happen. Jaques and Clement (cited earlier) question the idea of "a good manager, but not a leader." A manager who does not lead is a caretaker, not a manager. The business sponsor must be willing to lead. He or she must have a thorough understanding of the scope of the program and be willing to find the necessary resources to make it happen.

■ *Persistence:* One reason many projects have failed is a lack of real commitment to see the transformation initiative through to completion. In many BPR projects, for example, the participants get really fired up about the intellectual exercise of designing the new ways of doing things. The initial process redesign exercise goes well — on paper and flow charts — until people are faced with the reality of the changes they must make. For some, the changes may offer exciting new challenges, but for others, when faced with giving up "accustomed turf," they just bail out, quietly or loudly, as the case may be. It is the role of the sponsor to be persistent and to provide consistent, sustained support for the program. He or she also needs to challenge inconsistencies and overcome roadblocks.

■ *Communication:* One of the primary ways to reinforce vision, commitment and persistence is communication. A critical role of the business sponsor is to communicate the big picture of the overall change program, and its expected benefits, showing all key organizational units and work groups where they fit and the specific contributions each is making to the achievement of benefits. The business sponsor must also regularly communicate progress, and problems, to the program team, the IDB and the community at large. While communication experts may be able to support communications activities by providing advice and support tools, they should never be perceived as replacing the business sponsor. The communications process, like the benefits realization process it supports, must be continuous and flexible. It must also be two-way, with ample time left for dialogue and feedback. As illustrated by many of our client stories, Results Chain models can be a powerful tool to support this effort.

Program Manager. The program manager is accountable to the business sponsor for day-to-day management of the program. This role requires someone who is proactive with demonstrated leadership skills, who is highly organized and detail oriented, is an excellent communicator with good negotiation skills and good business sense. The program manager has two clear responsibilities: organizing projects within programs and controlling the program.

The responsibility for organizing projects within programs involves many initial steps, such as:

- Supporting the business sponsor and working with the VMO in building and presenting value cases for programs
- Negotiating assignment of available project managers with the appropriate skills to deliver planned projects
- Confirming project mandates
- Establishing program/project organization, and briefing all participants and key stakeholders
- Getting projects started.

Controlling the program, the second responsibility, means attending to many ongoing tasks, including:

- Ensuring the program and project plans and time reporting are in place and are adequate.
- Implementing appropriate progress, issue, change and quality control processes within current guidelines.
- Managing the program budget.
- Resolving or escalating all project issues.
- Providing progress reports, project reviews and status reports.
- Negotiating staffing issues with project managers and other program managers.
- Getting projects completed.

Project Manager. In organizations with a culture of high-quality and successful project management, the accountabilities in the value management model will not seem strange. The project manager is accountable to the program manager for the achievement of project objectives on time and within budget. He or she can also be considered accountable to the business sponsor for the quality of the deliverables and the related capabilities.

The Benefits Realization Approach provides a framework for ongoing evaluation of the progress of the project. It also applies to usefulness and continued relevance of its individual benefits realization paths and benefits streams. The project manager needs to design effective processes for change management and dynamic adjustments to the benefits realization paths.

If a project is cancelled or delayed because its objectives cease to be necessary to the company's goals, the project manager must ensure that the team does not see this as failure. A little groundwork in positioning the company's Benefits Realization Approach will make such an event less traumatic. We do not mean to imply that a high percentage of projects will be truncated, but change is likely, particularly in very dynamic environments.

The Accountability Web. Project managers play a critical role in the whole web of accountabilities involved in effective benefits realization. As stated earlier, the business sponsor is responsible for achieving business results. The program manager is responsible for coordinating the execution of the projects that together provide the capability to achieve those results. This is an essential role but, as we have said, providing the capability is necessary but not sufficient to ensure that benefits are achieved. In turn program managers can only succeed if they are supported by high quality project managers, each managing motivated teams to deliver their specific results. This accountability web is intricately woven. It involves both rights and obligations. One player can hardly succeed where the others fail.

To assist with the definition and documentation of the various functions and accountabilities, an accountability matrix has been developed. Table 6-1 provides a simplified example. This kind of matrix can be expanded beyond the main accountabilities to provide a comprehensive view of the rights and obligations of all parties to a specific program at each stage in its life cycle.

Succession Management

One of the fundamental issues around the role of business sponsor is the long-term nature of the role. Many programs last a number of years. The business sponsor may change roles, be promoted or leave the organization while the program lives on. This is an unavoidable reality. Clearly, the issue of succession management deserves attention.

TABLE 6-1
Accountability Matrix

Function	Decision Board	Value Management Office (VMO)	Business Sponsor	Program Manager	Project Managers/ Delivery Teams
	Accountable through portfolio management for the value of IT investments and the achievement of the associated business benefits	*Accountable for the progress of the initiatives through properly founded and funded programs*	*Accountable for the achievement of the agreed business benefits of the program*	*Accountable for overall program management and the combined results of the projects within the program*	*Accountable for timely delivery/ implementation of the agreed deliverables*
Portfolio Management	owns and manages the portfolio	provides planning and support to the IDB, business sponsors and the program managers	provides recommendations on the program provides status on achievement of benefits	has a consultation role provides program status and facts to VMO	N/A
Business Plans	sets annual planning guidelines approves annual plans	proposes and structures programs formulates value cases prepares annual plans	confirms program requirements negotiates priorities with IDB	prepares the program plan in support of program requirements	prepares project plans
Program Budgets/ Funding	approves the budgets and sources of funding for program commitments	facilitates the budget process prepares funding recommendations	confirms project benefits and costs for next commitment phase negotiates cost and time frames with program manager	prepares consolidated budgets for the projects allocates funding to projects	provides project schedule and cost information
Programs	monitors status and resolves major issues/conflicts recruits business sponsors	facilitates the value (business) cases monitors progress and budgets of programs	is the business owner of the program is responsible to IDB for the achievement of business benefits recruits program manager	directs and coordinates the program is responsible to the business sponsor for the success of the program recruits project managers	is accountable to the business sponsor for project deliverables is accountable to the program manager for project execution

How do you commission and decommission new business sponsors for an ongoing initiative in an orderly manner? One of the great strengths of benefits realization models built with the Results Chain is that it allows you to clearly identify and understand the intermediate outcomes that contribute to achieving the end benefits. A well-designed program will have a series of intermediate outcomes and a continuously flowing benefits stream. As part of the progressive value cases, the business sponsor will always have specific and measurable outcomes to achieve within the next stage of the program. A new business sponsor may have to take over in the middle of one of these stages, but will be actively working towards building commitment to the next stage.

Clearly, there are challenges to this transition, but there are also opportunities. There is a chance to bring in a new set of experiences and knowledge that may be more appropriate to the next stage of the program. There is also an opportunity for the new sponsor to take a 360-degree scan of all elements of the program with fresh eyes.

Window on the Real World: Client Stories

The biggest change in introducing full cycle governance is also the most obvious, in most cases. It is the idea of *business sponsorship* for major blended investment and business transformation programs. This is supported by the idea of the business sponsor's clear ownership, or activist accountability, for delivering business results. The Benefits Realization Approach helps to ensure that business units take ownership of benefits. Once again, Nova Gas Transmission provides the case in point.

Nova Gas Transmission

Grouping projects into programs with a definable business outcome lies at the heart of accountability. Programs are where value is measured.

> Nova Gas Transmission Ltd. (NGT), one of North America's largest natural gas pipeline companies, realized that IT investments must be linked to business programs, and that benefits can be harvested only if there are business users who are accountable for achieving them. Bruce McNaught, NGT's vice president of internal resources, says this represents a major change from previous business practice: "In our new environment, IT investments are not made unless there is a committed business-process sponsor with a well-defined benefits realization plan." No program proposal can be submitted

to the investment decision board without having at least one business sponsor.

NGT has found that grouping projects into programs with a definable business outcome lies at the heart of accountability. Programs are concerned with the business objectives, and they are where value is measured. "The project focus had to change," explains Bruce McNaught. "Such a focus made it possible for four or five different projects to be driving towards the same business unit in isolation. We switched to the idea of programs — the sum of the individual projects — because it only made sense to group projects according to the business result they were trying to achieve." A program originates with a sponsor, who submits a proposal and requests money to carry it out. The sponsor is then accountable for achieving the projected benefits.

The challenge is for sponsors to develop meaningful benefit plans, commit to making the required changes in the business and assume program accountability from concept to program completion. "Although IVM (investment value management) is an important evaluation tool, its own value is most recognized in its ability to discipline sponsors in their proposals," says McNaught. "They must think value all the time and be confident that their predictions hold up over time."

McNaught feels that, in hindsight, the IVM process would have helped NGT when it implemented its new enterprise information system. At the time, business units were still handing their IT work over the fence to the IT department, and then moving on to other issues. However, management discovered that one of the most important challenges was re-engineering their business processes to accommodate the new system. This would have been done from the outset, he says, if the company had been using the IVM framework. Now that IVM has been institutionalized, business processes are unavoidably linked to IT programs.

Summary

Without appropriate and clear accountability, full cycle governance will become no more than an experiment — and usually a short-lived one at that — which might take considerable time and effort, but will not result in the improvement in benefits realization that it was intended to provide. The industrial-age division of labor between technology experts and business managers creates a barrier to implementation of full cycle governance. What is required, as we pointed out in this chapter, is active dialogue between all the players contributing to blended investment programs. All must share a common understanding of how

IT enables business transformation across the business systems, and the pieces which each group must contribute. They must understand, in particular, that while the IT group may deliver exciting new technologies and capabilities, business groups will handle 80 to 95 percent of the work involved in most business transformation and advanced information management initiatives.

Activist accountability encompasses the measures that managers must take to create this positive environment for success in the new program universe. Its central assumptions are familiar. Business sponsors make the value cases for investment programs and lead those programs from concept to cash. They must therefore be held accountable for delivering the targeted business benefits. IT managers are held accountable for delivering the right tools and technological capabilities. Business managers are held accountable for delivering other capabilities. Each party to this set of linked transactions has an active sense of ownership, which includes a share of ownership in the program and clear ownership of specific initiatives and outcomes in the Results Chain model.

Building activist accountability across any organization is a big job. To succeed, you need to travel the three routes to implementation outlined in this chapter. Here is a brief recap.

Understanding the essence of activist accountability means changing people's industrial-age mind-sets and getting them to accept the new form of outcome ownership. It means leaving behind the traditional passive approaches to business results still operating in many organizational cultures today.

Introducing the seven plus one key conditions of activist accountability means translating the new mind-set into actionable terms within the context of specific investment programs. It means, for example, defining the scope of people's accountabilities, using the new shared understandings that grow around Results Chain models of the benefits realization process. It means making sure many people playing many roles have the authority, competence and resources they require to deliver their pieces of the program. Finally, introducing the seven plus one conditions means ensuring that all the players understand and accept their accountabilities, rights, obligations and performance objectives. All these conditions fit together into the human networks supporting all successful investment programs.

With activist accountability embedded at the program level, it becomes possible as well to *introduce the accountabilities required for full cycle governance.* This means building the new organizational units, the investment decision board and value management office that will monitor and adjust the portfolio as a whole as its multiple programs pass through the stage gate system. Business sponsors and their program managers remain on center stage throughout the process. Without their leadership, programs simply do not get off the ground.

Full cycle governance sets out a solid process for benefits realization. However, no amount of process will achieve results without the focused and committed efforts of competent people. Achieving real benefits is not easy. It is very challenging, but with clear objectives, the right resources and an environment for success, accepting and fulfilling activist accountabilities can be immensely rewarding, both for organizations and individuals.

****

For activist accountability to work, there must be a solid measurement system in place. It is certainly true that "if you can't measure it, you can't manage it." In Chapter 7, we explore the current blind spots, and discuss the need for measurement systems that: measure the right things; measure things the right way; and guide decisions and action.

7

SECOND NECESSARY CONDITION: RELEVANT MEASUREMENT

Source: DILBERT reprinted by permission of United Feature Syndicate, Inc.

The Benefits Realization Approach requires full cycle governance with activist and clear accountability. There must be ownership of business programs and projects. If such accountability is to work, there must be relevant, accurate and consistent measures of the performance of each blended investment program, and of the projects within them. As Kaplan and Norton say in *The Balanced Scorecard*: "An organization's measurement system strongly affects the behavior of people both inside and outside the organization. If companies are to survive and prosper in information age competition, they must use measurement and management systems derived from their strategies and capabilities."

Measurement information is a vital input to two backbone decision processes:

1. Progressive commitment of resources through the stage gate system to manage risks and rewards
2. Dynamic benefits path adjustment, to respond to a changing environment.

Without a strong measurement system, the basis for well informed decisions will erode, and the quality of decisions will be, at best, suspect.

The "New" Manager: Navigating in the Program Universe

As in other areas of benefits realization, the starting point in the field of measurement is a new mind-set. The new universe of blended investment programs demands new navigational instruments. It is clear that stand-alone project management methods — from the world of industrial-age projects — are not powerful enough for true program management. The measurement systems built into those methods are no exception.

Project-based measurement systems were designed for the purpose of monitoring industrial-age work automation projects through life cycles that ran from design to delivery. They are too narrowly focused to track the progress of information management and business transformation programs through life cycles that run from concept to cash. Project measurement systems also focus too narrowly on cost and time, and not enough on benefits. They were never designed to monitor activity along the complex benefits realization paths underlying major blended investment programs. So, it is not surprising they also suffer from investment myopia.

Benefits realization requires the accurate measurement of new domains of organizational performance. These domains are captured by the new benefits terminology presented in previous chapters (e.g., organizational capabilities, intermediate outcomes, alignment and time-based profiles of the benefit streams). As pointed out above, traditional project delivery is just one phase in a blended investment program.

Full cycle governance, which operationalizes program and portfolio management, is where the measurement rubber hits the road. To launch a program, as discussed in Chapters 3 to 5, you need a value case dealing with many types of benefit — from hard measures like ROI all the way to soft indicators of alignment with long-range corporate visions. These benefits are captured by the four "ares" framework and its three supporting measures: alignment, financial worth and risk. At each stage gate in the program delivery cycle, the value cases are updated and refined based on monitoring of the benefits realization process. The validity of the value cases will depend on the integrity and reliability of the measurement systems that are used do this monitoring.

The key, as we show in this chapter, is to anchor critical measurements firmly in the models of benefits realization developed using the Results Chain technique. Before demonstrating how to do this, we should take a second look at the initial state of measurement in many organizations today.

Four Measurement Blind Spots

The problem is that appropriate measurement systems do not exist in organizations that are implementing full cycle governance processes for the first time. In fact, we find that most of them quickly encounter some well-known measurement blind spots:

- *Financial systems* produce too much detailed data on past performance, which is difficult to use to identify the factors that drive future business performance. Often, financial information can only be used to identify a benefits problem or a case of the Information Paradox without suggesting any corrective action.

- *Operational systems* produce an abundance of data on core manufacturing, distribution, purchasing and other processes. The data is usually actionable but it cannot be linked easily to benefits. Quality management and BPR efforts often encounter similar measurement problems.

- *Project management systems* provide vitally important data on costs and other project inputs, such as person hours and capital spending. They integrate this data with advanced systems for tracking project activity and progress. As we know, however, these systems do not measure outcomes and benefits.

- *Human resource* and *marketing information systems* can also produce much useful information, when required, but they do not integrate naturally into a benefits realization framework.

In practical terms, it is fairly easy to find information on individual projects and the performance of business units. However, benefits realization and full cycle governance are essentially cross-functional processes. Current measurement systems are confined to silos that do not easily yield an integrated picture of such processes. Now, let's say you are managing a program composed of 10 to 15 major projects in various areas of the BTOPP business system. Conventional measurement systems could give you 10 to 15 sets of lenses — one for each project. But you do not have a single set of lenses to see how the family of projects fits together into a blended investment program, much less how programs form an investment portfolio.

Similar blind spots have been identified in a number of contexts, notably by Kaplan and Norton in *The Balanced Scorecard*. They advocate the integration of selected measures across functions and argue this is key to strategic performance management in any organization. Interestingly, their approach is easier to implement — as is full cycle governance — in organizations that have developed measurement systems for Total Quality Management, BPR and continuous improvement (CI) programs. We will explore the reasons for this after first looking at the essential areas where existing measurement systems can be modified and improved to support benefits realization.

Benefits Realization Approach to Measurement

To support implementation of program management and full cycle governance, the fundamental concepts of benefits realization help organizations deal effectively with measurement issues in four important ways:

- Identify the *outcomes* you need to measure, and when you need to measure them.
- Show the reasoning about the *linkages* relating blended investment programs and projects to outcomes, making it easier to understand what's going on.

- Make measurement come alive by tying executive *accountability* to measured results.

- Complement, extend and seamlessly integrate *measurement systems* with the widely used performance measurement approach of the balanced scorecard.

The key to this approach is not a frontal attack on your organization's existing measurement systems. Rather it is to refocus those systems on the significant dimensions of measurement required to proactively manage the benefits realization process. The first step is simply to gain a new perspective about how benefits are being realized and how they relate to investments. This means using the Results Chain to build a model of the benefits realization paths for a specific blended investment program, as explained in Chapter 3.

Results Chain Models: A Unique Perspective

The Results Chain model of an investment program precisely highlights the areas where measurements are needed. It allows you to articulate the chain of reasoning that links initiatives to results. The Results Chain for a specific, live program isn't an externally created piece of documentation. It is the end product of discussions and should articulate an emerging management consensus about the way the program will deliver results. You gain commitment to the outcomes displayed by the model. When you review the program status using the Results Chain model, you do two things:

1. Create a shared understanding of the linkages leading from investments in all elements of the BTOPP business system to management actions to predictable business outcomes over time.

2. Build organizational bridges that make those linkages a reality and deal with any major reach and people issues.

To illustrate these points, consider just one small fragment of a program model built using the Results Chain. It comes from the plan of a retail chain to replace its core sales forecasting, inventory tracking and replenishment systems. The purpose of these systems was to ensure a smooth flow of stock through the supply chain from manufacturer to the retail shelf, with optimal inventory levels. Forecasting and replenishment systems produce automated forecasts of retail sales by the stock-keeping unit (SKU), and make recommendations to merchants (the buyers) regarding purchase quantities for each SKU, and the optimal times at which to place orders. In addition, they provide a decision support component through which merchants can manually override the system recommendations after analysis of the sales history, forecast and so on.

Two projects were identified in this Results Chain. The first was to develop and install a new system. The second was to train the merchants in its use (see Figure 7-1):

FIGURE 7-1
Example Projects as Shown in a Results Chain Model

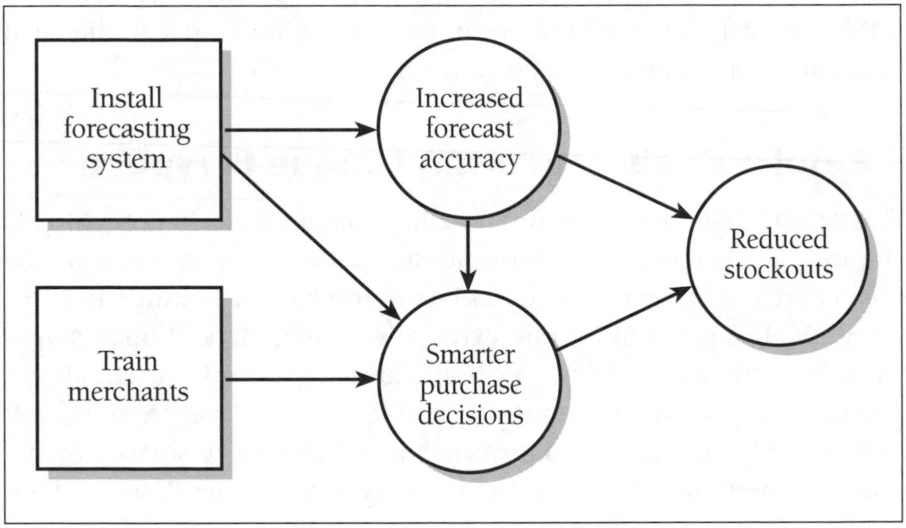

The final outcomes targeted by the firm were reduced stockouts (i.e., the number of times an item was not available when a customer requested it), combined with lower inventory levels. For simplicity's sake, we will focus on the outcome reduced stockouts. According to the Results Chain model, this outcome would result from increased forecast accuracy and better purchase decisions.

This model clearly identifies three areas for outcome measurement. In order to assess whether the new system was successful, the firm had to measure stock levels, but as the new system was implemented, it was also important to measure the intermediate outcomes of increased forecast accuracy and smarter purchase decisions. Then, if for some reason the final outcome was not being achieved, the chain of projects and outcomes could be followed backwards to see why not.

In this case, for example, the CIO could be held accountable for successful installation of the new system, but not for the business outcome, reduced stockouts. If the investment decisions were based on achieving this result, then the responsible business executive (e.g., the vice president, logistics) should have accepted the implicit reasoning around the results, committed to a quantified goal and have been told to achieve it. Then, as the program advanced, regular reports would have revealed how well the objective was being met. As long as the performance of the vice president, logistics was tied to the objective, the measurement system would become an instrument supporting active benefits realization, and much more than just a passive recording of results. The implication is that for any results measured, there must be some manager with accountability for that result, and the know-how, information, skills and authority to initiate action as necessary. (The power of the Results Chain in establishing accountability was described in Chapter 6.)

The Results Chain itself can be used to form an integrated scorecard for the program's success at any point in time. Suppose we shade each initiative in the Results Chain to illustrate the extent to which it has been *implemented,* and shade each outcome to show the extent to which that it has been *achieved.* Then the scorecard at some point might look like this (see Figure 7-2):

FIGURE 7-2
Results Chain as Scorecard

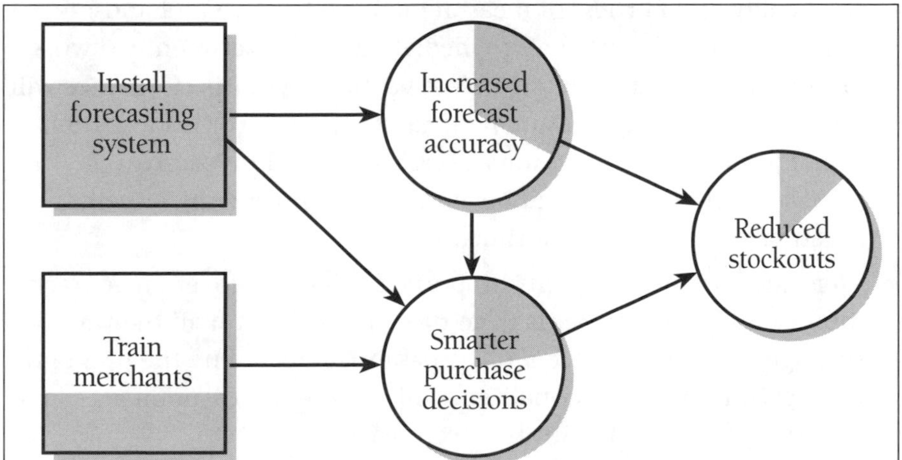

With an investment program model constructed using the Results Chain, your organization can then proceed to design a measurement system that will support the benefits realization paths depicted in the model. In many cases, you can adapt existing measures for this purpose, introducing evolutionary change into your measurement systems. You can also relate the approach to complementary approaches to measurement, in particular, Kaplan and Norton's balanced scorecard.

Managing the Four Dimensions of Complexity with Good Measurement Systems

New measurement systems help full cycle governance do its job of managing the four dimensions of complexity discussed in Chapter 1, which are so important to successful information and IT-enabled business transformation programs.

- *Linkage:* Good measurement systems can create precise understandings of linkages. They show the contribution of good program management and ensure it is tracked and visible to the team at all times. They also track external conditions that can affect performance and benefits realization.

- *Reach:* The consistent measurement of outcomes and contributions creates an information base that can be shared by all key players in the vertical chain of command and the horizontal supply/value chain.

- *People:* Good measurement is a necessary condition for true accountability and motivation in highly demanding change programs. Conversely, clear identification of accountability forces attention on the quality and fairness of measurement, so the two go hand-in-hand. Anyone who has had to mediate disputes between two work groups in the absence of any objective measures of performance will recognize that good measurement can also support the cross-functional teamwork required for successful blended investment programs, where the IT and business groups must work closely together, often for the first time.

- *Time:* Measurement systems supporting full cycle governance track forecast and actual benefits from program definition all the way through to the point where the capabilities created by the program have been fully institutionalized. Only through measurement can you know when this point has been reached.

Designing a Measurement System

You want to determine what to measure and when to measure it. This approach supports at every stage of the investment cycle the design of an effective measurement system, from the outset, when you create the Results Chain program model, through the planning stage and throughout program implementation.

The criteria for designing effective measurement systems are:

- Make sure measures exist.
- Measure the right things.
- Measure things the right way.
- Make sure measurement systems guide decisions and action.

Each of these criteria is described more fully below.

Make Sure Measures Exist

The first criterion for an effective measurement system is that measures exist in the first place. This may seem like a no-brainer, but experience shows that the point is worth making. Traditional measurement systems, built around silo or stove-pipe functional organization structures, simply don't cut it in a world of business transformation — a world where massive BPR, quality management and CI are becoming standard operating procedure.

Traditional measurement systems are quite effective at measuring inputs, such as dollars and staff hours spent on a project. These measures are the natural outputs of any decent accounting and human resource systems. But when these are coupled with existing project management systems, they give an organization a good handle on whether major projects are coming in on time and on budget. When a project runs into trouble, from a time and dollars perspective, these systems can help put it back on the rails. They can be readily adapted to support blended investment programs, but only for measuring the inputs.

Existing systems also do a good job of measuring the costs of continuing services, such as applications maintenance, where determining the value of outputs is not usually a major issue. For example, the CIO can normally tell you how many staff are working on network support or how much money is spent per workstation on regular maintenance.

The difficulty is that inputs aren't the same as outputs. That's true whether you are measuring end results such as revenues and market share, or intermediate outcomes like the number of new customers each month or improvements in service quality. Huge strides have been made in this area through the contribution of approaches, like Total Quality Management and BPR, which focus on processes rather than individual functions. Nevertheless, we still find many organizations neglecting to measure outputs in a sensible way, especially when attempting to implement large-scale blended investment programs. These are accompanied inevitably by organizational changes, which, in turn, demand new measurement systems.

When you build a Results Chain to describe the benefits realization process for one of these programs, you follow this modeling rule (one of a small number of useful rules): "Every initiative must be followed by an outcome." (See Figure 7-3.)

FIGURE 7-3
Results Chain Modeling Rule

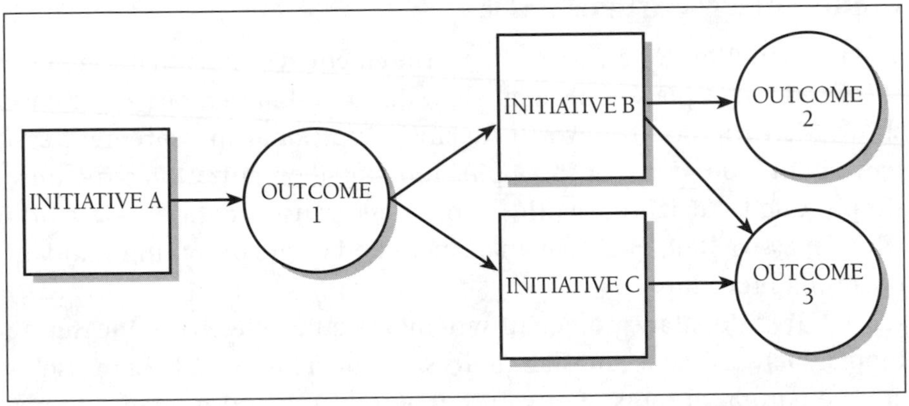

This simple rule forces measurement into the picture right at the start. Whenever you want to add an initiative — an IT project, a training effort, a process redesign — you have to consider what measurable outcome it will contribute to, and how it will contribute. So the measurement system is being designed naturally, along with the program.

Measure the Right Things

The second criterion for an effective measurement system is that it measures the right things — and nothing else. The key to finding these right things is *alignment*. The program must be delivering benefits that are aligned with the strategic direction of the enterprise. This means that the measurement system has to measure results aligned with what have variously been called strategic drivers, critical success factors and performance drivers.

Here is how the Results Chain technique ensures alignment. Every Results Chain model must terminate in final outcomes — the benefits being sought from an investment program. These are the outcomes that most closely relate to the strategic drivers of the organization and its critical success factors.

For example, suppose the strategic posture of a retailer depends on good customer service and everyday low prices. We may then select the final outcomes of increased service levels and increased competitiveness. These form the end points of the Results Chain, as depicted in Figure 7-4.

FIGURE 7-4
Results Chain End Points

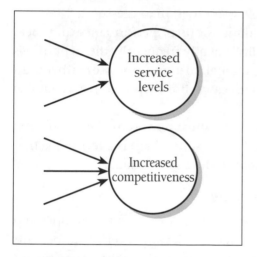

As you move left along the Results Chain, you expand the set of intermediate outcomes that are aligned with, and contribute to, the final outcomes. (These intermediate outcomes are similar to the performance drivers of the balanced scorecard approach.) For example, expanding the service level outcome, we might decide that the key intermediate outcomes driving increased service are the quality of forecasts and the quality of purchasing decisions, as depicted in Figure 7-5.

FIGURE 7-5
Key Intermediate Outcomes

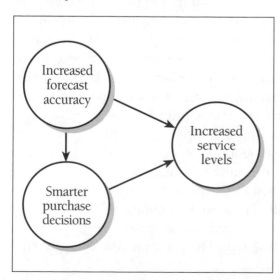

The measurement system defined by this simple model will be closely aligned with the strategic objectives of the enterprise: it is measuring things that matter. If it forms the basis of the reward-punishment system, it supports what organizational theorists call goal congruence, that is, what we have described as blended investment programs where everyone is reading the same benefits realization road map.

These two examples show how the Results Chain helps you build models of the way initiatives combine to produce benefits for the enterprise. Like all truly useful management techniques, it is deceptively simple. Deceptive, because the simplicity masks sophisticated thinking about what makes for effective models and the experience gained from dozens of applications of the technique through which it became refined. It is when you get into the details of designing complex blended investment programs and the supporting measurement systems that some of the sophistication becomes more apparent. These are the situations — major business transformation and Knowledge Economy investments for example — when a good road map is essential.

Frequently, the big three dimensions of performance and measurement are: cost, speed and quality. Equally frequently, the right things to measure are related to cross-functional business processes rather than an isolated business function. In both cases, it is helpful to have a kit-bag of useful ways to measure.

Earlier chapters stressed that you must rely on informed business judgment, not abdicate to analysis. The Results Chain is a technique that supports enabled business judgment. It does not replace it.

Measure Things the Right Way

This isn't a textbook on measurement. Measurement is a tough topic, and this book only touches on issues directly relevant to effective benefits realization. Many organizations haven't stepped up to the measurement challenge because they fall back on bad, but available measures. For example, a project to improve product quality might report an easy-to-measure indicator of outgoing product quality (e.g., "fraction defective") rather than harder-to-measure indicators of customer perceptions of quality. Conversely, organizations are often prepared to live with (even embrace) unquantified and vague objectives, where a more tough-minded approach would force accountability for results. For example, one organization targeted the nebulous "customer intimacy" as a key strategic driver, but failed to measure quantified components of this variable, such as the ability of customer service representatives to access customer files quickly from the database of a customer information system.

Again, we turn to the Results Chain as the integrating technique in this approach. A simple rule is that each outcome in a Results Chain must be described in a way that forces measurement, using a phrase containing relatively precise language. The acronym MEDIC represents the following:

- M : a level of service Maintained
- E : a function Eliminated
- D : turnaround time Decreased
- I : revenue Increased
- C : a certain capability Created.

These terms are preferable to the more vague improved, better and enhanced — the famed weasel words of performance management. If it isn't measurable, then you can't know if it has been achieved. The essential point about measurement is that, by definition, it involves quantification in some form. There are, however, levels of quantification. There are simple binary measures (0/1, present/absent). There are ordinal measures, which allow you to rank outcomes from bad to good. Finally, there are more precise numeric measures of relative quantities (e.g., how much profit was made last month).

In two of the above cases, "Created" and "Eliminated," a binary (0/1) measure is usually employed: either the capability exists or it does not; either the function has been eliminated or it has not; either the new information system has been delivered or it has not. The remaining three cases invite more "granular" quantification. At best, this is based on countable objects like dollars, or items produced or people employed. Sometimes this is not possible. There is no way, for example, to count customer satisfaction directly. In such cases, a measure must be based on the quantified judgment of people, be they experts or customers answering an opinion survey.

It is important not to endow a measure with greater strength than it inherently possesses just because it is convenient. It is common practice, for example, to measure customer satisfaction with a questionnaire which might contain, say, 10 questions, each of which asks the customer to rank some dimension of a service on a five-point scale, (e.g., from "violently disagree" to "strongly agree"). Then an overall numeric total is computed.

The danger of this approach is that you might forget the vague, subjective nature of the underlying components being "quantified." You might then begin to think of the numeric score as being somehow more accurate than it really is. Then, measurement myopia may set in, leading to distorted business judgment.

The Results Chain model from the retail firm, cited above, can be used to show these ideas in action. Three outcomes are shown in the model:

- Increased forecast accuracy
- Increased service levels
- Smarter purchase decisions.

The first outcome (increased forecast accuracy) is readily measured by comparing the forecast sales volume with actual sales volume and constructing a summary measure of the difference, such as its standard deviation.

The second outcome (increased service) is harder to measure because, unless a customer actually asks for an item in a retail store and you can't provide it, we don't really know if we have lost a sale. And we certainly don't know if the customer walking out of the store in a hurry feels poorly served, or forgot a credit card at home. In this case, the measurement of a seemingly obvious quantity, conceptually, is quite complicated in practice. Perhaps the best thing to do is administer a periodic survey of customer perception of service levels, to supplement indirect numerical indicators such as the number of stockouts.

The third outcome (smarter decisions) is hard to describe. Conceptually, we seek smarter purchase decisions, but unless we attempt a more concrete definition of what this means using the more precise MEDIC terminology, we will be unable to see whether our training program had any effect. This blind spot in the measurement system must be noted. To a degree, it may be possible to correct for it through regular group discussions or private discussions with purchasing managers about their recent judgment calls.

Managers Must Make Sure Measurement Systems Guide Decisions and Action

A conventional project management system tells you when a project is going off the rails, from a *delivery* perspective. At a high level, it can track overall project expenditure and relate this to overall project completion. When these diverge, a big red flag is hoisted, and the manager's job is to figure out what's going on. A decent project management system will be able to untangle the low-level detail and pinpoint which activities slipped in terms of schedule, and which activities overran their budget. This information, coupled with the project network, is sufficient to understand what happened.

Of course, this project information is not enough — certainly not to track a major blended investment program that includes say, 20 projects of varying scope in all areas of the BTOPP business system. The key issue is not just whether a program is being delivered on time and on budget, but whether it is delivering results. This is not an easy question to answer. Even though most business executives aren't academics, they still require a level of proof or rigor in their thinking to be convinced that their shareholders are getting value for money. This issue goes beyond simple measurement to encompass models of how a firm makes money, or, more generally, how an organization succeeds. This is precisely what a Results Chain provides in the case of an investment program. Without such a framework you just can't know the answers to these questions.

Consider what happens if a program is actually failing to deliver the results it promised. First of all, the project management system won't recognize this is happening on its own, and second, it can't tell you why, precisely, because it doesn't incorporate any model of how projects combine to produce intermediate outcomes and benefits. What the manager needs is a measurement system with the smarts to provide the same kind of analysis of the benefits that a project management system provides in the activities and tasks. What is required is a measurement system that is designed for the program universe, not just the project world.

The Results Chain holds the key to such a smart measurement system. It illustrates the chain of reasoning about the linkages leading along the chain to end results. To find out why a particular result is not being achieved, you backtrack along the Results Chain to examine the state of contributory projects and intermediate outcomes, especially those that have been identified as the most important. Up-to-date information on each project, and the extent to which each important outcome has been achieved, will be available through the measurement system.

When you design a blended investment program, you not only design the BTOPP projects that will be carried out. You also use the Results Chain to map benefits realization paths — including implementation sequences for the projects — that optimize the benefits stream. A proactive program, as mentioned in Chapter 3, will include proposals for capturing emerging benefits at the appropriate time. The program will incorporate, therefore, a benefits realization plan, including a concrete timetable which gives the expected time-based profile of each benefit. Figure 7-6 illustrates how a benefits realization plan, a program plan and the Results Chain are three different but coherent views of the same program.

FIGURE 7-6
Three Views of the Same Program

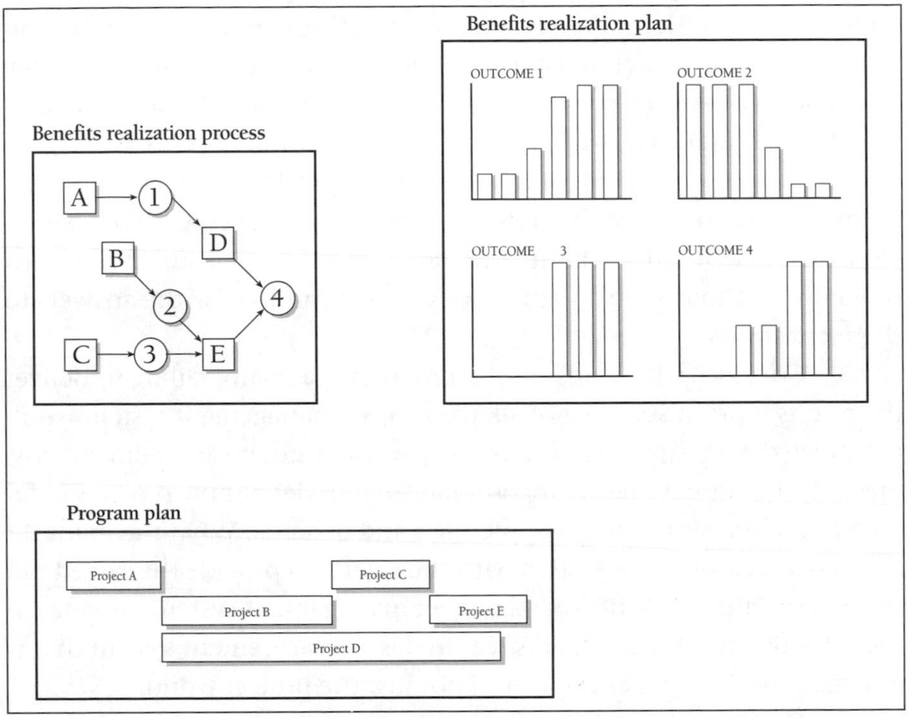

Benefits realization plan

Benefits realization process

A → ① → D

B → ②

C → ③ → E → ④

OUTCOME 1

OUTCOME 2

OUTCOME 3

OUTCOME 4

Program plan

Project A

Project C

Project B

Project E

Project D

These program planning tools provide a way of identifying problems with benefits realization and finding the persons or work groups who can take informed action to correct the problem.

Frequently, program management is supported with an active benefits register. This is a repository of expected and actual outcomes, linked to existing measurement systems, which provide its data. There are defined accountabilities for each outcome. The benefits register is a computer system to assemble program data, coupled with analysis and reporting tools to support a structured program review process (see Figure 7-7).

In such a process, the key program stakeholders conduct a systematic review of benefits achieved versus benefits expected, and identify problems and opportunities.

Benefits Realization and Other Measurement Approaches

Any organization that is devoted to quality, and is following the prescriptions of any of the well-known quality gurus (Juran, Deming, Crosby, et al.), is much more likely to pay attention to visible displays of measured results. It might be "fraction defective" for product quality, or order processing time, or machine set-up times, or percentage of calls answered within four rings. Graphs are everywhere. Continuous process improvement (CI) is, of course, totally dependent on exhaustive, sustained measurement.

FIGURE 7-7
Benefits Register

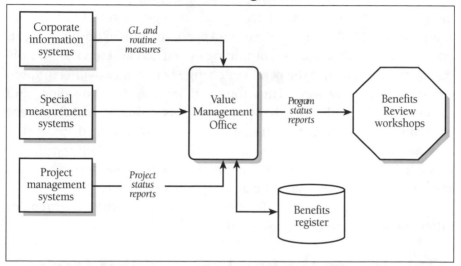

When the ideas of Total Quality Management (TQM) filtered into the white-collar world and became combined with the ideas of business process re-engineering, the primacy of measurement was retained. There was a strong focus on the measurement of previously unmeasured, but critical, domains — the domain of the "white spaces" in the organization chart, and the domain of process, as opposed to function. There is a similar challenge associated with benefits realization and implementation of full cycle governance. Most of these measurement approaches are applied at the operational level.

At senior management levels, the need is not for exhaustive measurement, but for focused, filtered measurement, drawing on the rich measurement infrastructure that the TQM and BPR approaches created. Information system designers have long been aware of the need to measure and report on critical success factors (measures of strategically important factors). The more recent work of Kaplan and Norton demonstrates how to create a balanced scorecard, to measure the factors that create and sustain value in the enterprise. In this approach, the underlying model is explicit, just as it is with the Results Chain.

What this means to the creation of an effective Benefits Realization Approach is that an organization that has embraced TQM or CI is much more likely to have the necessary basic measurement infrastructure. Similarly, an organization that has adopted a balanced scorecard is much more likely to have developed a shared understanding at the executive level around the major models and linkages leading to strategic business success.

These two methods, one at the operational level of measurement, and the other working at a strategic level, bracket and complement the Benefits Realization Approach. Where both fall short, however, is that they address continuing operations and services, not the transient program, and the period of change between two different periods of stable operations. Thus they can provide baseline data, and guidance in the high-level shape of a Results Chain. But as investment programs are implemented, the organization will still need to develop new measurement systems and new thinking to articulate the logical reasoning about how each specific program will create business value, and to monitor and manage the delivery of that value.

Over time, all these efforts combine to shape the measurement infrastructure of full cycle governance.

Window on the Real World: Client Stories

Measuring value was one of the main challenges confronting the natural gas pipeline company, Nova Gas Transmission (NGT), when it implemented full cycle governance. There needed to be a consistent standard for comparing the value of programs competing for scarce resources before the investment decision board. As explained below, NGT uses the Results Chain to define each program and a benefits realization plan to identify the accountability and time line for achieving benefits. The supporting business case specifies the value of the program using instruments that measure risk, alignment and financial worth.

Nova Gas Transmission

With Benefits Realization, the company can assess the value of 50 programs and surface the top 10.

> Nova Gas Transmission Ltd. (NGT), one of North America's largest natural gas pipeline companies, has found that one of the key benefits of Investment Value Management (IVM) has been that it provides a better way of measuring the value of IT investments.

"We went through the usual benchmarking exercises," says Tom Whitehead, manager of planning and practices, but were dissatisfied with them. We couldn't find an envelope that covered all measures. And once the data was normalized, we couldn't get much out of it. There was no way to know whether we were comparing apples to apples, or apples to oranges."

The benchmarking efforts, which largely took place in 1995, did indicate that the company was spending more — or less — than other companies on particular projects, but didn't answer a number of essential questions: Was the amount invested in the project justified? Was spending more money necessarily bad? Was spending less money necessarily good? Benchmarking concentrated on inputs, not outputs. It didn't take into account the organization's objectives, and it didn't measure the true value of investments.

Now, with IVM, each program is defined by a Results Chain that identifies all of the required technology and organizational change projects and specifies the sequence of events that produces each outcome. A Benefits Realization Plan identifies each benefit to be achieved, and the mechanism, accountability and time line for achieving it. The supporting business case specifies the value of the program using instruments that measure risk, alignment and financial worth. The investment decision board compares the relative value of programs based on the resulting scores.

Financial worth is calculated using traditional accounting methods. Strategic alignment determines how well the program contributes to current business objectives, to achieving the future strategic vision of the company and to supporting the goals of the parent organization. Program risk is measured with respect to the four "ares" questions:

- Are we doing the right things?
- Are we doing them the right way?
- Are we getting them done well?
- Are we getting the benefits?

NGT plots the resulting value scores to see the position of programs at a glance. The investment decision board uses two plots for program selection: one of financial worth versus risk, and the other of financial worth versus strategic alignment (see Figure 4-3 in Chapter 4). The plots have also proven to be helpful to sponsors in understanding how their program is positioned. Based on this information, they may decide to combine programs or to find other ways to enhance program value.

Measuring value has made decision making more objective. It's worth the extra effort, Whitehead says. "Investing is always a gamble, whether it be stocks, mutual funds or information technology. But we are now hedging our bets by investing quality time and analysis into our decision-making process, and by raising the bar for proposals."

An ancillary benefit of measuring value is that it sets priorities for using IT resources. Prior to adopting IVM, NGT's IT department would try to work on 50 projects at the same time. The tendency was to say "yes" to anyone proposing change. Inevitably, the department accepted too much work. It now dedicates its resources to a fixed number of programs and adds new ones based on the queue established by the investment decision board.

"With IVM, we can assess the value of 50 programs and surface the top 10," says Bruce McNaught, NGT's vice president of internal resources. "This year, we have already scrapped a dozen and kept about 10 to 15 good programs worth about $20 million in the queue, and they will be carried out once the resources become available."

Summary

As we said earlier, "If you can't measure it, you can't manage it." Without an appropriate measurement system, full cycle governance, portfolio management, program management and, as a result, benefits realization, will be no more than a pipe dream.

Traditional measurement systems were never designed to measure key linkages in a benefits realization process leading from concept to cash. They do not capture organizational capabilities, intermediate outcomes, some of the softer end benefits and benefits streams. Traditional measurement systems do not link naturally to value cases, programs and all the stage gates of full cycle governance. As we have seen, models constructed using the Results Chain provide a key for building — and adapting — the measurement systems that do support the decision and management processes of benefits realization.

The information requirements of benefits realization form an ascending hierarchy, starting with basic measurement of outcomes, to interpretation of linkages in the Results Chain models, to high-level decision support on program selection. These requirements must be met in order for program and portfolio management to be effective. A solid measurement and management information base for each individual blended investment program is one of the foundations on which full cycle governance is built.

To build powerful measurement systems, you must:

■ Make sure measures exist.

■ Measure the right things.

■ Measure things the right way.

■ Make sure measurement systems guide decisions and action.

Of course, measurements will only guide corrective action if there is clear and appropriate accountability for both programs and the investment portfolio. This is why activist accountability, discussed in the previous chapter, and measurement are naturally linked as two of the necessary conditions for the successful implementation of the Benefits Realization Approach.

****

Program management and portfolio management, their operationalization through full cycle governance, and the need for clear and activist accountability, supported by relevant and actionable measurements represents a significant amount of change for most organizations. In Chapter 8 we propose that results must be the leverage point of change. In order to manage the key dimensions of complexity — linkage, reach, people and time — change initiatives must be built into business programs from the beginning. The process of change must be proactively managed. It is this proactive management of change that will ultimately determine the success of benefits realization in your organization.

THIRD NECESSARY CONDITION: PROACTIVE MANAGEMENT OF CHANGE

Source: DILBERT reprinted by permission of United Feature Syndicate, Inc.

Making Results the Leverage Point of Change

It is a central tenet of the Benefits Realization Approach that benefits come only with change and, equally, change must be sustained by benefits. People must change how they think, manage and act in order to implement the Benefits Realization Approach, as pointed out in Chapter 2. These changes will be difficult and often painful, and they will not happen by themselves. They must be planned and managed. That is why managing change is an essential enabling condition for implementing benefits realization.

As mentioned earlier, IT is not just about installing hardware or software. It is a package of ideas about how people should work differently. This implies change — often massive change. Change is a major component of any blended investment program. As with accountability, an activist approach to managing change is required if organizations are to take charge of the benefits realization process.

Managing change includes defining where you want to be and how you are going to get there. We have shown in previous chapters how the Results Chain and blended investment programs help to define goals and map paths to change. But, managing change also includes managing the transition from where you are to where you want to be. That is the hardest part of all. Not only do you have to get from here to there, you have to do it while still running a business. It is like changing the engines on a plane while flying at 600 mph, at 37 000 feet, with 400 passengers on board.

Proactive management of change is not just a cosmetic exercise, providing touchy-feely support so that people will feel good about what is happening to them. Rather, it is about involving people in the process of change. It is about giving them the tools — and the working environment — to bring about the change and reap the benefits as immediately and visibly as possible. It is about managing the process of change.

Unfortunately, many current approaches to managing change are far from proactive. The specialist discipline of change management is too often viewed by line managers as offering help to the wounded, after the onslaught of change, or counseling to make people feel better about changes being imposed on them. Sometimes, change management is presented as a social responsibility of business. These managers believe that change management can be delegated to the human resource experts and psychologists.

Business Sponsor Responsibility

These approaches miss the essential point about the role of change in the benefits realization process. Managing change must be a general management responsibility. In a blended investment program, management of change is a core responsibility of the business sponsor. With managing change, as with accountability, the language and idea of ownership is appropriate. Business sponsors must take ownership of the process of managing change. This is not a responsibility that should be taken lightly.

Business sponsors must actively structure, and visibly lead, the major benefits realization processes embedded in their blended investment programs. Their leadership role must be shared with program and project managers. The investment portfolio managers in executive management need to create the vision and environment that allow people to work together to guide major changes in how they work. Through all these initiatives, change management must literally be built into each stage gate of the full cycle governance process.

Resistance to change, whether crassly calculated or fervently emotional, is a problem both for individuals and work groups. People question why change is necessary and wonder whether it will hurt them, or how they can gain an advantage from it. As such, change is also a significant problem for major investment programs that depend on people's ability and willingness to change. The dilemma was summed up by a business and technological innovator, Charles F. Kettering, the automotive engineer who invented the electric starter and helped Alfred Sloan build General Motors. He observed: "The world hates change, but it is the only thing that has brought progress."

Only the Business Application of Technology Can Deliver Value

The most convincing proof that change is a necessary condition for benefits realization, unfortunately, comes in the form of the high IT project failure rates underlying the Information Paradox. There are some very embarrassing and costly runaways and white elephants that make the point tellingly. Consider this well-known example.

London Stock Exchange/Taurus: After five years, and millions down the drain, the London Stock Exchange gave up on a new electronic securities registration and transfer system in 1993. There were major technology and systems design problems, but some observers have concluded that the critical distress factors were organizational and people issues. A postmortem analysis shows, for example, that a number of stakeholder groups — including securities registrars — were opposed to the plan. Certain government departments became concerned about financial industry and legal issues. A complex series of committees failed to resolve the differences of opinion. Communications were inconsistent. In the end, the committees did not create a unified vision, supported by all the interest groups in the City of London. Nevertheless, an expensive software package was acquired — in a classic example of leading a desired change with new IT — and work began on customization to the specific circumstances of the LSE. The problem was that the lack of organizational cohesion showed up on the technology side of the project. The central blueprint of the system kept changing. Millions of pounds were spent customizing and rewriting the software. Requirements changed. It was discovered in midstream that large parts of critical business processes had been omitted from the project. All the typical symptoms were present: delay, project management problems and weak quality control. Taurus was finally branded a runaway project and cancelled. It was a classic case of silver bullet thinking, with new technology alone being expected to bring about changes that key organizations and people were not prepared to support.

The importance of good change management is also proved, though less often perhaps, by the successes that depend more on people's winning attitudes to change and strong organization than on technological silver bullets. Here are two examples.

New York Stock Exchange: Consider the accelerated upgrade in the early 1990s of the four primary computer systems used by stock specialists on the trading floor of the NYSE. Growth in market volumes was overwhelming the exchange's vintage 1987 software and the volume was threatening to choke the system (as had appeared to be the case in London when Taurus was launched). With heavy deadline pressure hanging over the project, systems designers started not by writing software code, but by spending a full six months observing traders on the exchange floor and modeling how they worked, and how they saw their work. People — the traders themselves — were very much in the loop. In fact they were at the heart of the development process, constantly testing prototypes and asking for redesigns that reflected how the tool would actually be used on the floor. While the frequent redesigns frustrated software experts, because their specifications kept changing, the end results were impressive. The upgrade took two years to complete, compared to six years in previous cases. The traders got convenient hand-held computers which they could quickly learn to use, and put to work right away. A major business problem was solved, with system productivity and capacity growing quickly and error rates falling by a factor of 10.

Singapore TradeNet: This is another success story that, in many ways, was the mirror image — in reverse — of the LSE experience. Singapore TradeNet was a major systems project developed to boost the port of Singapore. Stakeholders from all over the city state's private and public sectors reached an agreement in the 1980s that the port of Singapore needed to cut costs, reduce fees and greatly speed regulatory procedures to compete for business with other Asian Tiger port cities. IT investment was identified as a critical success factor. Out of this consensus emerged a shared vision of radically streamlining trade forms and procedures with an electronic system called TradeNet (similar in concept to paperless securities trading and clearing in London). As in New York, developers used prototypes that were tested in carefully controlled circumstances and then retested with more and more participants in the trade process. Outside suppliers were hired in the context of a tightly managed project. Not only were key pieces of technology delivered on schedule and within budget, the overall program objective was achieved: turnaround times for trade documentation were reduced from a maximum of four days before, to 10 to 15 minutes after implementation of TradeNet. And Singapore did improve its profile as a preferred Asian trading center and transportation hub.

These stories — once again — prove what we said at the beginning of this book and have repeated throughout: technology in and of itself is of no value. It is the business application of technology that has the potential to deliver value. The case of the London Stock Exchange shows a learning lag that became permanent while the New York case shows how fast learning — when built into the program — can speed the arrival of business benefits.

Without proactive management of change, and business sponsor ownership of the process of managing change, the idea of managing the benefits realization process will remain a theoretical construct in your organization. The stage gates of full cycle governance will cease to have meaning. Your odds of success will only be marginally better than those of the lone gambler in a casino.

The BTOPP view of the business system, as highlighted in Figure 8-1, helps to define the change-management responsibilities of the business sponsor and the program manager. They need to give special attention to ensuring that OPP projects are well defined, fully funded and designed into the program up front.

Change is complex, and becoming increasingly so. Unlike the initiatives outlined in previous chapters, managing change is not a distinct activity that can be reduced to a series of steps. Rather, what is required is a map of the key issues and the methods for dealing with them. The key features on this map are the four critical dimensions of complexity introduced in Chapter 1: linkage, reach, people and time.

FIGURE 8-1
The BTOPP View of the Business System

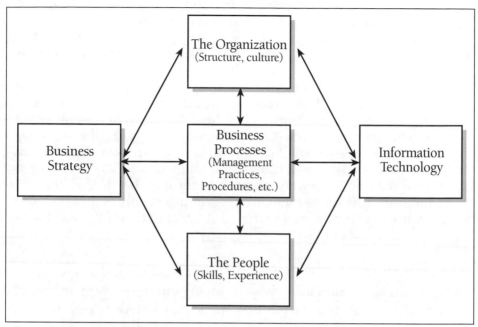

Source: Adapted from Michael Scott Morton

Results-Focused Change Programs: Managing the Four Dimensions of Complexity

The change management projects built into a blended investment program must be designed to address the four dimensions of complexity so vital to reliable benefits realization. These dimensions serve as beacons for program design and management.

- *Linkage:* Understanding how OPP projects fit into a blended investment program and what they contribute to the benefits realization process is the first step in understanding what must change.

- *Reach:* Understanding who will be impacted, and to what extent, shapes the approach to managing change within a blended investment program.

- *People:* Change is all about people. It is about how people think, manage, and act. It is about attitudes and behaviors.

- *Time:* People's ability and willingness to change are key determinants of program time frames.

First Dimension of Complexity: Linkage

The Results Chain model can be used to depict the contributions of OPP projects and where they should be built into the "paths" of a blended investment program. This ensures linkage with the accountability and measurement systems, described in Chapters 6 and 7.

Here are a series of basic steps that you can follow:

1. Use the Results Chain model to get a big picture of the why (benefits) the what (projects) and the who (accountabilities) involved in the program.
2. Define the change agenda — the key organizational, process and people issues — involved in a proposed investment program. Define the how of the transition process involved in executing the program.
3. Incorporate the OPP transition projects into the overall value case for the investment program. Ensure that the projects are fully defined, built into the benefits realization paths and properly linked to other projects.
4. Ensure that accountabilities are well defined and that the outcomes of change projects are measured.
5. Monitor and measure the progress of change projects, making adjustments as required.

Every organization's change management program will be different. Each organization will have its own particular style and method of taking these steps. In one form or another, however, all the steps are necessary to implement a benefits-focused change program.

Second Dimension of Complexity: Reach

Understanding the reach of change is crucial. Reach applies to the depth of change (What is it going to impact?) and the breadth of change (Who is it going to impact?). Change can range from fine tuning to radical transformation. It can affect a few people within the organization, or a large number of people both within and beyond the organization. The reach of change shapes the approaches chosen to manage it. This means mapping the groups and key individuals who will be impacted by change and who will play a primary role in bringing about change.

Depth of Change. Depth of change can be readily understood in terms of the evolution from automation of work through information management to business transformation. As shown in Figure 8-2, there are quite different types of change:

- *Automation applications:* These involve *work flow improvement,* and the change is largely about improving what we already do. The changes required will be largely technical ones — in competencies required to do work.

- *Information applications:* These require more change, as in the case of *process redesign.* There will still be technical change, but we are introducing new work and business processes. There will also be a requirement for structural change.

- *Transformation applications:* These involve still more change. In the case of the Knowledge Economy, with its associated *business transformations,* or even industry transformations, we will question and change the organization's raison d'être — its very purpose. In addition to the first two levels of change — technical and structural change — this will require cultural change, the most difficult change of all.

As we increase the depth of change, the potential rewards are greater, but so are the risks. We will need to clearly understand the linkages and the people issues. We will need to have an effective change management program and realistic estimates of the effort required to make the change. Understanding the depth of change will enable you to determine the difference between the current and the target state, and whether the change is relatively superficial or affects the fundamental nature of the organization.

Breadth of Change. Breadth of change refers to an integrated view of the impacts of change both on the vertical chain of command and the horizontal value chain. Understanding it helps you understand who the key players are, who will likely resist change and who can play a central role in facilitating change.

Change must be managed at three levels: enterprise, group and individual.

Enterprise: Managing change at the enterprise level deals with issues such as:

FIGURE 8-2
Depth of Change and Potential Rewards

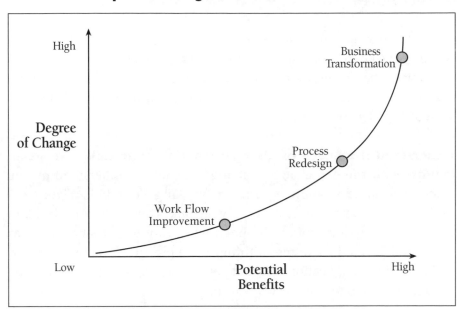

■ What other areas of the enterprise will be impacted by the change?

■ Does the proposed change fit with our current culture and values?

■ Will our current rewards structure reinforce or obstruct the change?

■ What other change is going on?

■ Does the organization have the capacity to undergo this transition at this time?

Group: Managing change at the group level (formal or informal groups, work teams) deals with issues such as:

■ Who are the stakeholders affected by this change?

■ Is there synergy between the goals and purpose of the group and the change?

■ What are the information and training needs of the affected groups?

Individual: Managing change at the individual level deals with questions individuals will have about the change:

■ Why are we doing this?

■ What will I lose?

■ What will be expected of me?

- Will I be able to contribute in a meaningful way?
- Will I succeed?

Understanding the breadth of change lets you determine whether the change has local or global impact, whether it is limited to one unit of the organization, crosses a number of units, affects the entire organization, or reaches beyond the organization to other stakeholders such as suppliers or customers.

Understand the Reach of Change: Walking Your Talk. We are all familiar with the expression "walking your talk." Understanding the reach of change is a prerequisite to walking your talk. Figure 8-3 illustrates that before you can walk your talk, you have to understand what you are talking about. It is one thing to announce that change has to happen. It is quite a different thing, and a precursor to any action, to understand the implications of what you are saying — to understand the reach of the change you are advocating.

At the thinking, or cognitive level, we become aware of a need. This often translates itself fairly rapidly into talk: "We at Acme Inc. have to make fundamental changes to our organization." All too often, the nature of those changes is not understood, and the definition of them is delegated, or more accurately abdicated. The reaction to this is often "This too will pass," and all too often, it does.

It is only when we wake up at three in the morning, reaching for the antacid, as our stomach churns with the realization of the implications of the change and the reach of what has to change, that we begin to reach understanding. This is the precursor to commitment.

The use of the Results Chain as described previously can bring you to an earlier awakening. When we have the understanding necessary to build commitment, to understand the reach of what we are committing to, then, and only then, are we ready to act. Even then, we can act only if we have the capability and the capacity to do so. Understanding the reach of change allows us to make this assessment.

Third Dimension of Complexity: People

Change is about people. Recognizing that fact, understanding how people react to change and managing the people side of change is what managing change is all about. The variety of possible people problems that can arise is enormous. Each blended investment program must be

FIGURE 8-3
The Anatomy of Change

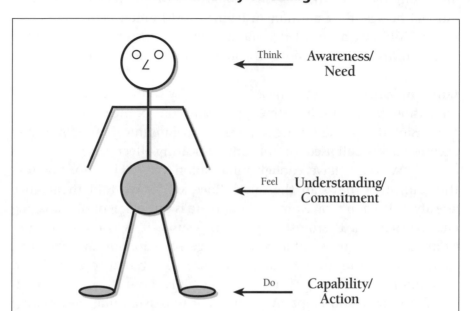

assessed for its people issues. They will not handle themselves. More accurately, they will handle themselves, but not in the way we want. When they do, we are usually sorry.

Michael Hammer has pointed out: "Coming up with the ideas is the easy part, but getting things done is the tough part. The place where these reforms are going to die is ... down in the trenches."

Resistance to change is a major issue. Some people actively seek change, but most do not, and certainly not the breadth and depth of change associated with IT-enabled business transformation. Faced with such challenges, people often have a feeling of powerlessness. There is inertia: it's easier to leave things the way they are. As John Kenneth Galbraith said, "Faced with the choice between changing one's mind and proving that there is no need to do so, almost everybody gets busy on the proof."

When people are faced with change, we are often told that we must provide an answer to the "What's in it for me?" question. While this is true, we must understand that the more common first reaction is: "What am I losing as a result of this change?" The reactions are akin to those of the grieving process: denial, anger, guilt, acceptance and finally, moving on. Too often we dismiss such reactions, either explicitly or implicitly, as emotional reactions or overreactions. Well, we were absolutely right to call the reactions emotional, but absolutely wrong in dismissing them for that reason. People are not inherently logical and rational beings; they are human beings, and human beings are emotional. Unless we acknowledge and manage these reactions, we will fail in our efforts at change and, consequently, our realization of benefits.

Communication. Communication is the key to managing the people dimension. In blended investment programs, one of the most important responsibilities of the business sponsor is communication. How many excuses have we all used for not communicating effectively?

"We don't have enough information yet." "Let's not say anything until we have all the ducks lined up." "We told them once already." "We don't have time." Yet, if there is one element of managing change that has the most impact on results, it is communication. Communication is essential to encourage participation and cooperation, to foster empowerment and accountability and to build trust. Communication is not just "telling them." It is about listening, demonstrating respect and empathy, facilitating understanding, negotiating differences and resolving conflicts.

A useful framework for communication is the concept of the four Ps of change, introduced by William Bridges in his excellent book, *Managing Transitions.*

Purpose: Why are we doing this?
Picture: What will it look like when we get there?
Plan: How will we get there?
Part: What will be my role, both in getting there,
and when we get there?

An effective communication plan can be built around these four Ps. While all four Ps are important, it is the last P — "What will be my role?" — where the greatest problems can occur. To address this P, we must ensure alignment of an individual's goals with those of the organization. We must both answer the "What's in it for me?" question and recognize what will be the perceived losses.

As seen in the case of Bank of America, Boeing SSG Supplier Management & Procurement, National Bank of Canada and a number of other real-world examples in this book, the Results Chain can also be a very effective vehicle to support communication. It can be used not only to communicate what has to change — the purpose and the picture — but how you are going to change — the plan — and what it means to individuals — their part. It can be used both to describe a program, and to communicate progress.

Whatever the techniques you choose to use, never underestimate the importance of communication. Managing communication is fundamental to any effective change process. Failure to recognize this is at the root of many failed change programs.

One specific word of caution here. One of the easiest ways to encourage resistance is to disparage the past. This immediately generates defensiveness and can lead to needless finger pointing. Most people don't maliciously do wrong things. They do the best they can with what they know and with the resources at their disposal. Criticism, implied or explicit, of those efforts serves no purpose. What it does do is undermine people's pride, confidence and self-respect, exactly the opposite of what you want to do. Rather than disparage, stress moving forward into changed circumstances, not looking back.

Reward System. The good thing about reward systems is that they work. The bad thing about them is that they work. All too often in change efforts, we overlook the reward system and the messages it sends to people. If we fail to align our reward systems with the results we want to achieve, we will not drive the behavior required to achieve those results. We must include in our reward system incentives to change, and incentives for the steady state while we are in transition. The reward system must be linked to clear and relevant measurements that are linked to outcomes and that are within the reach of an individual's accountability.

The people dimension is by far the most complex and diverse of the four dimensions because people are themselves complex and diverse. This is what makes the process of managing change so challenging, and so essential.

Fourth Dimension of Complexity: Time

Realistically assessing time frames is vital in benefits realization. Rushing will not help organizations understand complex linkage issues or have the patience to progressively commit resources to major programs using the stage gate system of full cycle governance. In our "one-minute manager" world, driven by this quarter's financial results, program trading and 15-second sound bites, we increasingly lack the will to see things through.

Our experience has been that successful change takes years, not months. Unless faced with a major crisis, organizations have a lot of inertia, and this is true particularly of successful ones. This inertia cannot be overcome overnight. Even when faced with a major crisis, not all organizations have been able to turn on a dime. Ask yourself when assessing the time dimension of change: "Are we counting on a miracle? Will this organization suddenly turn around and embrace change?"

In this regard, football coach Bill Walsh offers some interesting insights on the time it took to turn the San Francisco 49ers from also-rans into Superbowl champions in the 1980s: "My first two seasons taught me that even in defeat, you can make progress if you have the confidence, patience, a plan and a timetable.... And even though you might fail, even though it might not develop, you never panic. A lot of people bring on failure in the way they react to pressure.... The coach who has the nerve to stay with the program right up to the bitter end is the one who most often will have the best results."

The same applies to blended investment programs.

Window on the Real World: Client Stories

The Benefits Realization Approach has been applied to help organizations map and manage large-scale organizational transformation programs that pose major change challenges. The challenges described in the client stories that follow include: transformation of branch banking operations; staged implementation of a neighborhood policing system; modeling of company-wide hiring processes; and the makeover of an airline reservations system.

Although the changes were very different, once again, there was a core of common core issues. The central one was around *change bottlenecks*. They developed less around technology than around people's ability to absorb work process, cultural and organizational change. Related issues were:

- Resource scarcity
- Scarcity of managers who could deliver change and coordinate many programs
- Lack of reliable road maps to guide multiple change programs over long time frames.

In all cases, key decision makers and managers recognized that a new approach was needed.

Benefits Realization Process

Although the exact approach differed from case to case, all the clients whose stories appear here built high-level Results Chain models, based on interviews with a cross-section of senior and middle managers (in one case more than 100). Each Results Chain provided a big picture of all major change programs that was used to deal with the following issues:

- *People* issues, including the need to build training, recruitment, communication and cultural change initiatives into the overall program
- *Reach* issues where programs affected a large number of business processes and organizational units
- *Time* frames for program implementation and realization of benefits.

Results

The Results Chain model provided a map of the change programs, showing each work group and organizational unit where they fit in the big picture and what they were contributing to the change effort. Change bottlenecks were broken through a number of improvements, including:

- Better definition, sequencing, prioritization and timing of programs and major projects
- More realistic time and cost estimates
- Broader consensus through improved decision-making and program management processes.

In the case of major change programs affecting thousands of employees, the discussion and consensus building that accompanies Result Chain modeling was especially important.

Montreal Urban Community Police Service

Results Chain models were developed at multiple levels to map and organize more than 150 major change initiatives.

Neighborhood policing was on the wish list of many citizen groups, and MUC Police director Jacques Duchesneau adopted it as a model for reinventing the Montreal police force. To say the least, however, such a complex undertaking was easier said than done. Duchesneau and his colleagues recognized right off the bat that their officers couldn't just hop out of their squad cars and begin walking the beat again. In a large metropolitan police force — with more than 5000 employees, 49

215

neighborhood police stations, four operational centers and a million people to protect — there would be multiple impacts. The technology, organization and core processes of policing would all have to change from a reactive type of policing to one that supports this new approach to urban law enforcement and crime prevention.

The New York City and San Diego police departments had piloted neighborhood policing for limited time frames and in limited geographic areas. Montreal was the only major urban police department wanting to implement a force-wide program. Surveys and a strategic review by Duchesneau had indicated that radical decentralization, a return to the neighborhoods, was the best path to meet the citizens' wishes. Those wishes included a more human touch, faster response and a more visible presence in public places such as subway stations, school yards and cycling paths. Citizens were also looking for new ways to cooperate with the police to prevent serious crime, instead of just punishing criminals after the fact.

So what was involved in neighborhood policing? Duchesneau's review uncovered an array of major change programs that would be required in all areas of the force's business system. For example:

- Streamlining the chain of command from nine levels to four
- Redefining roles, responsibilities and accountabilities
- Decentralizing responsibility for daily operations while centralizing certain administrative tasks
- Re-engineering call processing
- Implementing new technology, including the life-saving emergency dispatching system
- Building customer focus into the department's culture.

Veteran police officers and administrators found that there was a lot more to do than they had initially expected. They envisaged dozens, if not hundreds, of change initiatives, which they began to design. As project overload became visible, the force turned to the Benefits Realization Approach to validate its implementation plan and assess program risks.

Results Chain models were developed at multiple levels to map and organize more than 150 major change initiatives. Neighborhood policing teams started with the targeted end results and worked backwards to create models which structured such varied initiatives as relocating to new neighborhood police stations; deploying new technologies, such as cellular phones; training officers to use bicycles and in-line skates; and implementing a new code of ethics. The Results Chain also doubled as a work plan for delivery teams.

The Police Service used the Benefits Realization Approach and the Results Chain to identify priority initiatives, clarify assumptions and assess the main risks that could arise during implementation of the program and address any lingering doubts that might be entertained by people around the table. The Results Chain model included the entire portfolio of initiatives, highlighting dependencies and potential conflicts between them. This was key to assessing risks and making prioritization decisions.

Duchesneau compares benefits realization to the dynamics of a pool game. "When you are a good player and hit one ball," he says, "it hits another one, and then bounces off another and so on. In the end, these sequences produce valuable points for the player. The [Benefits Realization] Approach gives you a moving picture of the game." By using this approach, the police service obtained a more rigorous understanding of the intricacies of the change program. It also gained a management method that Duchesneau says increased the chance of success while providing insurance against excessive risk.

In the end, benefits were harvested at many levels. With a clearer view of the complexities of implementation, the police chief and his management team were able to make much better resource commitments and prioritization decisions in a major business change program that was carried out in full view of the community.

Barclays Bank

The Results Chain clearly defined the program as what it really was — a mega-change initiative.

Branch banking is being transformed by 24-hour electronic banking, demographic shifts and changing consumer preferences. Managing the transition is a challenge. Barclays Bank, one of the major banks in the United Kingdom, decided to confront this challenge head-on with its Branch Change Program. The program included five long-term projects designed to improve credit scoring and loan approval processes, design integrated customer files, improve product penetration analysis, adjust the culture of the branch system to favor more retail selling and re-engineer business processes around these projects through better use of technology. The strategic goal was to bring branches closer to their customers and to improve customer satisfaction, while containing costs.

Barclays was well aware that implementation of the program would require major organizational, cultural, technological and people-related change. Senior management and the change teams thought they had a good overview of the initiative, and were moving to launch it, when they began to pick up on possible implementation barriers and problems. They wondered aloud: Are we asking for too much cultural change in too short a time? Are these projects interdependent? Are we being realistic about the expected benefits? What about our time frames?

"We knew something was not right," recalls Don Barratt, the senior executive responsible for the program. "The cultural changes were too great in some areas, and most of the projects were managed in silos with no interaction between them."

His team concluded that a quick reality check — by running down a list of essential questions — would not satisfy their concerns. What was required was a more comprehensive picture of the Branch Change Program. The team put implementation on hold and applied the Results Chain modeling technique to map the five projects and find linkages among them that could be used to connect the silos.

The Results Chain clearly defined the program as what it really was — a megachange initiative. It also changed management decisions and mind-sets in a number of important areas:

- Combining and sequencing projects

- Initiating new projects

- Bringing people working on different programs together to debate trade-offs, priorities and interproject linkages.

As the mapping exercise progressed, people from many parts of the organization began to share in the big picture. Building the Results Chain also helped in other important ways, Barratt says. "The most difficult element in any program of this nature is getting people to sign off on delivering the benefits. The Results Chain makes accountabilities very clear. Further, if you decide to drop a part of the Results Chain for any number of reasons, you can see clearly which benefits you will not achieve."

The Branch Change Program has delivered measurable results, and Barratt believes that benefits realization has played a critical role. He estimates that Barclays harvested 80 percent of the targeted results. Had they simply proceeded without the benefits check-up, he says, they would probably have gotten closer to 50 percent.

The Boeing Company

Management got a big picture map of the hiring process — as it was, and as it could be redesigned in the future — and of all the human resources programs that impacted hiring.

Mapping long-term change programs in large organizations is a valuable application of the Results Chain modeling technique. An ideal candidate for such mapping has been the hiring process of The Boeing Company.

This leading aircraft manufacturer recently decided to analyze its hiring process to help it achieve Vision 2016 — a corporate vision of business excellence that involved the planned transformation of many Boeing operations early in the twenty-first century. With 235 000 employees, Boeing knew that people were its most important asset. And hiring was significant in financial as well as business terms, given the scale of human resource budgets and the money invested from the beginning to the end of the hiring cycle.

Responding to Vision 2016, the human resources group began to develop a model showing how all people-related initiatives in the Vision linked to each other and to strategic business objectives of the corporation. The focus was on managing potential competition for resources among programs over many years, leveraging program interdependencies and identifying the many intermediate outcomes that would form the basis for achieving Vision 2016.

The company committed to a detailed review of the hiring process using the Benefits Realization Approach as the assessment method. A number of subprocesses were examined, including search, interviewing, recruitment and induction into the organization. Hiring was intimately linked to other major HR processes such as compensation, training, career path management and organizational change. The assessment identified a number of major issues, such as articulating the true business objectives of hiring, and involving the right groups of stakeholders in the process.

The team conducted a thoroughgoing review based on 130 interviews with a wide range of stakeholders. A comprehensive hiring Results Chain was created that included initiatives ranging from new college recruiting to the creation of Web sites, transition training for new employees and modifications to benefits packages. Boeing management got a big picture map of the hiring process — as it was, and as it could be redesigned in the future — and of all the human resources programs that impacted hiring. A good deal of management time was devoted to understanding the business benefits of changing the hiring process.

Benefits were found at many levels. The core strategic insight was that hiring — from internships through recruiting, induction and early training — is an expensive process. It should be managed as an investment in people assets rather than as an overhead expense. To earn returns on that up-front investment, it is essential to keep recruits on board. That means paying attention to career paths not only at the individual level, but also at the group and business unit levels. This insight became a guiding thread in portfolio composition decisions.

"Most organizations think in a linear pattern — using cause-and-effect thinking," says Gary Palmer, business analyst and custodian of the assessment project. "This approach gives you a multidimensional view through an understanding of the relationships between projects, people, processes and technology. It addresses complexity and defines it. There are things you just cannot simulate using modeling and simulation software. The [Benefits Realization] Approach makes it easier for you to get the big picture."

Palmer says benefits realization allowed people with different backgrounds and from different departments to develop a common vocabulary and a shared vision. Modeling all of the linkages, he says, was an education exercise for everyone involved in the process.

Qantas Airways

Merging two airline reservations systems means much more than making computers talk to each other. It means making business processes, management structures and even cultures work together.

Qantas Airways Limited is Australia's largest airline company, with 30 000 employees and annual revenues of $8 billion. After it merged a few years ago with Australian Airlines, a domestic airline company, Qantas effectively ended up with both a domestic airline division and an international one — with everything that comes with having two separate divisions: separate computer systems, procedures, business processes, management structures and even cultures. In order to reap the benefits of the acquisition, with a focus on improving productivity and customer service, Qantas had to merge the two divisions. A critical element in this was a need to integrate two reservation systems (incorporating yield management and departure control systems), which led in turn to the creation of the QUBE (Qantas Universal Business Environment) project.

Before implementing QUBE, Qantas staff who needed to book a customer on both domestic flights and international flights as part of a long-haul trip, had to deal with two reservation systems. In the words of a Qantas reservation agent, "We had to constantly move between the two reservations systems when we dealt with international travellers. Having one reservation system would allow us to look simultaneously at both domestic and international flights when customers telephone, and we could fill their requests seamlessly. Instead of considering an international traveller as two different segments (domestic and international) we wanted to view them as a single, long-haul traveller."

According to Lawrie Turner, general manager, QUBE project at Qantas, "the two reservations systems did not interact well together, there were compatibility issues and even the work processes around these systems were different. We had to address these issues to improve our customer service, reduce costs and increase efficiency — all the while maintaining uninterrupted high-level service to our customers. This simply had to happen without our customers suffering service interruption."

According to Mr. Turner, "we did not want to underestimate what had to be done to get the front-line people involved. This was not simply an IT project; this was a major business change project. Based on experience, unless you have clear accountabilities and measures for them and make those visible within the organization, results are not predictable. Our CEO was a true sponsor and champion for this critical project which enabled us to do these things."

Only after six months of in-depth analysis of the software acquired from British Airways did the scale of the work required and the cost become clear. The analysis highlighted that comprehensive testing, documentation and staff training would be required and new work processes developed. It also showed that Qantas needed to communicate its implementation strategy to staff and external stakeholders during the life of the project. According to Mr. Turner, "we saw that we had to train 10 000 people using over 100 training rooms in 65 locations worldwide. We knew that if this project failed, everybody would be blaming 'the system.'"

A rigorous business case was developed incorporating all costs. It was approved by the board, which insisted management track the benefits expected and report back to them on their achievements one year after QUBE was implemented. The organization knew the implementation would present major challenges. The reservation system is the heart of an airline company, and the company needed to perform heart surgery while it was still running. Qantas needed a way not only to merge the reservations systems, but also to merge the work processes, procedures and practices.

QUBE was implemented successfully in two phases. Full international operations and domestic reservations were transferred to QUBE in November 1996 and to domestic airports in March 1997. The system met its functional objectives. QUBE is perceived to be one of the most successful systems-related projects undertaken by Qantas. However, the true achievement for the team was to get the solution in place without interruption to customer service.

In response to the board's request to report on benefits achieved and recognizing there was significant focus on implementing QUBE, the CEO directed Turner to find a way to ensure Qantas maximized the benefits from QUBE. In response to the CEO's request, Qantas and Fujitsu Consulting (through the Fujitsu Consulting airline industry specialist business unit, Qadrant International) conducted a major study, using the Benefits Realization Approach. The study drew on the insights of staff from all areas of Qantas who were involved in the implementation of QUBE. It identified more than 300 opportunities which Qantas could pursue, based on the functions and data available from QUBE. The opportunities were assessed and ranked by the business unit responsible for their realization.

For the major opportunities, the study team used the Benefits Realization Approach to:

- Review the estimated cost and benefits of the opportunity
- Get a clearer view of all the initiatives needed by opportunity
- Prioritize the initiatives
- Get all the stakeholders on board and get their sign-off on their initiatives
- Plan all the communications-related initiatives with the employees, including a project-related newsletter and workshops
- Assign accountabilities
- Highlight what has been achieved and not achieved, to date
- Maintain focus on realizing benefits after QUBE was up and running

Qantas is now working on harvesting the longer-term benefits of QUBE, using the remainder of the ranked listing of opportunities.

According to Mr. Turner, in an increasingly competitive business world, organizations investing in large projects must consider — on top of addressing costs, risks, metrics and accountabilities — an ongoing benefits program to give them the road map needed to get the real results they are after.

Summary

Benefits and change are inseparable. In order to have an effective approach to benefits realization, you must manage change with confidence. Change management has three elements: defining the change, defining how to effect the change and managing the transition from the current state to the desired state. It's managing the transition that is toughest. With change management, "it's the soft part that's hard!"

In developing a strong change management capability, we must ensure that we fully understand:

- All the linkages involved in contributing to the desired benefits
- The reach of the change program
- The impacts of the change on all the people affected by the change.

With an understanding of these first three dimensions, we must realistically assess the resources that will be required to fully realize the benefits. This includes that most scarce resource, the fourth dimension, time. In managing change, we must also recognize that all these dimensions will themselves change during the life of blended investment programs.

What can change? Business conditions may change the priority or relevance of outcomes. Initiatives may fall behind schedule or run into other unexpected difficulties that either slow them down or bring their feasibility into question. We may not be realizing the expected contribution from an initiative. The validity of our assumptions may come into question.

We must continually monitor what is actually changing. We must track whether we are actually achieving the required changes. We must use the Results Chain to assess the impact of changes, and revise our plans based on that assessment.

As mentioned at the beginning of this chapter, management of change — proactive management of change — is a core responsibility of a business sponsor. The role must be shared with the investment portfolio managers in executive management, program managers and project managers. Without leadership, and the vision, commitment and support to drive the change that leadership must provide, change efforts are destined to fail. They are, however, equally destined to fail without good managers. Leaders are typically good at driving change, but not always as good at managing the details, the process of change. Without good management, change efforts will also fail. Good managers must have leadership skills in a special sense — leadership skills that they apply to managing the process of change.

Finally, we must recognize that change management is still in many ways more an art than a science. There are methods, techniques and tools, but these must be regarded as means to an end, not ends in themselves. Organizations, groups and individuals are all different. Change management must be adapted to recognize and manage those differences. There is no one right way to manage change. All too often, change efforts fail because we are more interested in following "the method" to the letter, than tailoring it to organizational realities. In benefits realization terms, we focus more on the change management initiative, than the changed-state outcome.

Any approach to change management must be tailored to the needs of your specific organization. You must plan the change and always be prepared to change the plan. Most of all, you must have the vision and the commitment to stay the course.

****

In Part IV, the conclusion of the book, we move to getting started on implementing the Benefits Realization Approach in your organization.

CONCLUSION

This book is designed to show how your organization can progressively learn about and implement the Benefits Realization Approach — moving from new ways of thinking through new ways of managing to action.

As explained in Part II, program and portfolio management represent major shifts in the management mind-set about information technology. Full cycle governance operationalizes the mind-set with a system for continuously monitoring performance and adjusting portfolio composition through a staged process, premised on the progressive commitment of resources.

The Benefits Realization Approach, as discussed in Part III, can only be implemented successfully when organizations meet three necessary conditions: clear and activist accountability, supported by clear and relevant measurement systems, and proactive management of change to manage the entire benefits realization process.

The next step is getting started with this ambitious program of change. Part IV presents a range of options for doing this, depending on where you are today, and how much change you are willing to undertake. We stress the importance of getting support from the top. We present a series of practical steps for getting from here to there.

As you read this chapter, remember again that this is not a mechanistic approach. No two organizations are the same. Your organization will be no exception to this rule. You need to take what you have learned so far, and your knowledge of your organization and tailor an approach that will work. In doing so, do not underestimate the extent of the change involved, and, remembering Chapter 8, proactively manage that change.

GETTING **9** STARTED

Define Your Challenge

The Benefits Realization Approach has been developed in response to a challenge. More accurately, it has been developed to deal with the multiple challenges presented by the Information Paradox and the demands of engineering IT-enabled business transformation. There are a wide range of challenges organizations can meet with greater confidence when they apply the Benefits Realization Approach. To decide how your organization should do this, it would be helpful to start by trying to define your challenge as precisely as possible.

While there is no magic formula for doing this, three common threads can be identified in the benefits realization story so far. First, the organizations that have applied the approach all faced the challenges associated with developing advanced information management applications or designing IT-enabled business transformation programs, the key features of which are reviewed in Chapter 1. They had left the automation of work era behind. Second, investment decision makers in these organizations were confronting the limitations of one-off business cases and traditional project management methods. Third, project leaders were

227

searching — consciously or instinctively — for the blended investment programs that would integrate technological change, organizational change and business process redesign within a common context.

In short, the stiff demands of the information management and business transformation eras had driven these organizations to ask one of two sets of questions (or some combination of both). Using traditional project language, they usually look something like this:

- *Project management:* How can we better design or manage this project? How can we improve the business case to sell it? How can we reduce risk and better integrate the IT side of the project with the business?

- *Project selection:* How can we deal with the overload of IT-related investment projects that are being carried out and proposed? Which ones are truly nonnegotiable, and which ones are optional? How do I pick the 10 winners out of a field of 100 ongoing and proposed projects?

The answers to the former set of questions lie in the shift from traditional project management to full-fledged program management, outlined in Chapter 3. The answers to the latter set of questions lie in the introduction of portfolio management and full cycle governance, described in Chapters 4 and 5.

Range of Solutions

Your organization's challenge will typically lie somewhere on the continuum running from a lone project that won't work to an entire grab bag of projects that are hard to select and prioritize. Defining the challenge early in the game will permit your organization to make a better choice from the range of benefits realization solutions that can be developed.

Deciding whether and how to embark on the benefits realization journey involves a measure of strategic thinking. Your decision will be based on the problems your organization faces today with regard to benefits realization, the impact these problems are having on business performance and the extent to which your organization is prepared to change to address these problems. Key executives need to be involved in discussion of these issues at the outset. What follows are a few guidelines, organized around program management, portfolio management and full cycle governance, that may be helpful in shaping the discussion agenda.

Program Management

While all programs must be tailored to a specific organization and set of projects, in general, program management solutions have been designed to meet three main types of challenge: best case, middle case and worst case.

Best Case. Executives are having trouble with the narrow scope of a one-off business case for a broadly based business transformation project. Or, perhaps, working project managers are concerned about the post-delivery risks of a major IT project they are contemplating. They are seeking help with program design before a problem occurs. In this case, the Results Chain model can be used for prevention rather than cure.

Middle Case. A major IT project or BPR initiative is bogged down, not delivering either key capabilities or the expected results. Often, the key deliverables — a software package, a high-level business process design, a new workstation — have been delivered, but there are unexpected implementation problems and resistance to change. Project managers are in the process of bolting on the required organizational, process and people (OPP) initiatives — ad hoc, after the fact. In this case, benefits realization can be used for program redesign and benefits maximization.

Worst Case. Organizations need help with runaway projects or white elephant systems that won't work. In this case, the Results Chain can be a useful device for project audit and salvage, or for starting fresh with program design.

The Benefits Realization Approach is designed essentially to find ways of increasing the return on blended investment programs. That may mean extra dollars, or increased soft benefits, including those strategic leadership positions that can rewrite industry ground rules. In the case of high-stakes business transformation programs, benefits realization can make a major contribution simply by reducing the risks.

Portfolio Management and Full Cycle Governance

Portfolio management solutions are designed for organizations worried about the value of their strategic IT investments, considered as a whole and for organizations that are troubled by too many choices and are experiencing project and change overloads. Usually, these are organizations with large installed IT bases and large potential portfolios.

To date, solutions that meet two main types of challenge have been designed: strategic case and operational case.

Strategic Case. Executives are primarily concerned with how they select major investment "projects" (programs), the vagueness of selection criteria and with the issue of business value. They feel that too many initiatives are being undertaken and are not sure which ones really produce results. They may be prepared to carry out a strategic remake of their entire business investment portfolio using enterprise-wide full cycle governance.

Operational Case. A range of players, both decision makers and doers, are concerned about how to better prioritize and sequence what is usually called "project work." There are too many change initiatives to handle all at once and a problem with resource and change bottlenecks. The project managers don't necessarily question the business value of all the change initiatives, but they urgently need to deal with practical problems of project overlaps, interdependencies and competition for scarce resources.

As can be seen from the "Window on the Real World: Client Stories" in this book, especially those in Chapters 4, 5 and 8, organizations do not usually present the challenges in the form of such simple cases. Rather, there is a mix of strategic and operational problems, as was the case with Nova Gas Transmission. These categories are starting points, then, for understanding the more complex reality of your organization.

With these words of caution in mind, it is still useful to ask: "Where does our firm fit in the broad scheme of program and portfolio management solutions? Do we want to design a single program or implement full cycle governance corporation-wide?" Answering these questions, at least on a preliminary basis, is an important first step in assessing your benefits realization needs. The next step, usually, is to identify the right executive to sponsor the initiative, formally or informally, while it gains focus.

Support from the Top

The subject matter of benefits realization is strategic, whether you are talking about the design of a business transformation program or a portfolio selection problem. To make decisions on these issues, executives need to answer the first and most strategic question of the four "ares": "Are we doing the right things?"

Implementation of benefits realization requires a major change in management style — or, as we have said, in how your people think, manage and act. This means executives must regularly answer the second "are": "Are we doing them the right way?"

Like the corporate transformation it is intended to support, benefits realization will not be accomplished easily. Senior executive support, advance planning, close attention to critical success factors and selecting the right place to begin are primary prerequisites for positive results. Determination and commitment should not be overlooked either. The Benefits Realization Approach requires considerable investments of time and money.

One of the key lessons is that the linkage and reach of both program and portfolio management are quite broad, requiring the cooperation of cross-functional management groups. All this leads to one simple conclusion: You need support from the top of your organization. Without it, you will not get very far with the Benefits Realization Approach. That means seeking the support of the most senior executive in your organization who can be recruited to the cause of benefits realization. Here are a few examples of potential candidates:

In the case of a single program, you might look for the executive who is on the hook to deliver results from a major investment but has serious doubts about the organization's ability to deliver. Another possible candidate is a visionary committed to continuing business transformation but who needs to link that vision to business results.

In the case of full cycle governance, you might look for a senior executive on the management committee responsible for major capital budgeting decisions. This could be the CFO or other executive responsible for capital budgeting analysis, for example, or even the CEO, COO or a trusted deputy.

The person chosen must understand the objectives of benefits realization, be committed to its implementation and be willing and able to take whatever actions are necessary along the way. As discussed in Chapter 8, the person providing support must be prepared to stay the course.

Practical Steps: Getting from Here to There

So far, this book has covered the general perspectives and principles that should guide your organization's approach to benefits realization. Now, let's turn to a series of five practical steps for selecting and implementing the appropriate Benefits Realization Approach to meet your organization's challenges. The steps are as follows:

- *Explore the Potential of Benefits Realization:* focusing on the challenges and a range of possible solutions.
- *Define Scope:* focusing on the choice between program and portfolio management solutions.
- *Get Organized:* creating the organizational structure of full cycle governance.
- *Manage Change:* through executive championing, communications and training.
- *Implement Benefits Realization:* through program and portfolio management, and full cycle governance.

Each of these steps is reviewed in detail below.

Explore the Potential of Benefits Realization

This is the step where you identify opportunities for benefits realization using the general principles outlined above. Your scan of opportunities should be followed by a more rigorous review of their potential business value and your organization's current situation using the four "ares" framework. It can help to prepare a written report card that can be presented to and validated with senior management. As the benefits realization concept is sold in your organization, it makes sense to recruit an executive sponsor at the same time. The exploration phase can usefully be broken into three sub-steps:

- Identify Opportunities.
- Prepare a Four "Ares" Report Card on the Current Situation.
- Recruit a Sponsor.

Each of these activities is reviewed in detail.

Identify Opportunities. Identifying opportunities requires high-level discussion of the range of challenges and benefits realization solutions reviewed above. As consideration of specific opportunities becomes more active, you can weigh the arguments for getting executive attention and endorsement. For example, a well-designed blended investment program can help structure a major initiative that will require coordinated effort across the organization such as implementation of an enterprise application package, entry into electronic commerce or embracing knowledge management. The primary selling points include: blended investments that cover all elements of the BTOPP business system; improved benefits monitoring; flexibility to adjust the program to accommodate changing conditions; progressive resource commitment; and better risk management.

Full cycle governance, implemented corporation-wide, helps extend these benefits across an entire portfolio of programs, while giving senior executives the tools and support they need to make major investment decisions.

Prepare a Four "Ares" Report Card. You can add rigor and discipline to the review of your organization's challenges by preparing a report card using the four "ares" to diagnose current problems. Questions inspired from the following list should be posed to a broad cross-section of executives, project managers, business group heads and other employees. The report card can be used to confirm or modify people's first impressions of the optimal benefits realization solution for your organization.

1   Are we doing the right things?

- Does your organization have a clear vision and strategy? Are its strategic drivers well communicated and understood throughout the organization?
- Is every initiative or project clearly linked to these strategic drivers?
- Are the outcomes and benefits expected to be delivered by initiatives and projects in your organization clear and credible?
- Are committed funds often not spent due to project delays or poor budgeting, while other potentially valuable opportunities wait in the wings?
- Are investents made in small projects at the expense of business transformation programs?

2   Are we doing them the right way?

- Do you have processes in place to ensure that the four "are's" are addressed?

- Do you have principles in place that guide all program/project decisions?
- Is there alignment/synergy between current programs/projects/initiatives?
- Are you ensuring you are able to deal with the future demands?
- Does your organization have a technology architecture?
- Are you following architectural principles and guidelines?
- Are proven technologies being used that are compliant with the corporate IT architecture?

3   Are we getting them done well?

- Are there standard processes for designing and managing projects?
- Do you have the required competencies and experience? Is success dependent on factors outside your control?
- Do you have a good track record in applying the right resources?
- Are plans validated? Is risk managed appropriately? Are there established processes in place for monitoring and control?
- What percentage of initiatives are delivered on time, within budget?
- What is the total value of project cost overruns? What is the average delay in project completion? How many projects are cancelled in midstream?

4   Are we getting the benefits?

- Is the company getting the results it expects from its programs and projects?
- Are the initiatives required to realize benefits clear, understood and achievable?
- Do all projects have a committed business sponsor?
- Are adequate and appropriate resources assigned to projects by the business areas affected?
- Are adjustments made to ensure that the effort to achieve benefits is sustained when the business environment changes?
- Are expenditures capitalized if an initiative is stopped prematurely so that value can be salvaged from the work?

- Are products maintained and supported once they have been delivered so that the business can continue to realize benefits over time?

- Are commitments to deliver benefits forgotten once the business case is approved and the investment made?

- What percentage of the expected benefits are actually achieved?

Wherever appropriate and possible, it is useful to seek quantitative data or specific examples to support the answers. The report card can then be prepared and presented to management.

Recruit a Sponsor. In the course of the exploration phase and the preparation of a report card, you will get to know the executives who support the idea of benefits realization and grasp their vision of the possible reach of the program. You can then develop a short list of possible sponsors.

If you are contemplating an initiative limited to a single program, you can recruit a business sponsor whose leadership role as owner of the program benefits is outlined in Chapters 3 and 6. A single program can be viewed as a pilot that will give the organization the opportunity to experiment and learn, with the objective of eventually applying the lessons company-wide.

If you contemplate implementing full cycle governance enterprise-wide, we have found it worthwhile to recruit a corporate sponsor. The role of this sponsor is to present and support key benefits realization concepts to senior management committees and the organization as a whole. This steward of full cycle governance must be able to communicate the vision and commitment to a new way of thinking and working. At a practical level, he or she must be in a position to ensure that the required resources are made available to implement the program.

Once the sponsor has reviewed the key opportunities and the report card, you are ready to make a preliminary presentation of the concept to a senior management committee. The presentation summarizes the four "ares" report card on the current situation, gives examples of investments that have not delivered on their initial promises and communicates the concepts and advantages of benefits realization. Other critical points to cover are:

- Best opportunities to implement a benefits realization program in your organization

- Best path to getting started (business transformation initiative, audit of a troubled project or full enterprise-wide implementation)

- Senior management commitment to proceed

- Confirmation of the appointment of an official business and/or corporate sponsor.

With support in place, it is now time to begin implementation in earnest.

Define Scope

This phase draws on the work you have already done in reviewing the best opportunities for benefits realization in your organization. As outlined above, there are two main possibilities: program management and portfolio management.

Program Management. A single blended investment program, or a small number of related ones that group high profile projects together, and ensure that they will deliver business results.

Portfolio Management. Selection and management of many programs, and implementation of portfolio management using full cycle governance.

A word of caution. All benefits realization solutions are customized — and must be — to each organization. Thus, these are not hard-and-fast choices or silver bullet formulas. Rather, they should be viewed as overlapping options that require varying degrees of commitment across the organization. For example, both implementation of an enterprise-wide application package and of full cycle governance affect the entire organization for a period of years, but it is safe to say that full cycle governance will affect more people on a more permanent basis. It may require more organizational change, though the organizational, process and people impacts of a single application package implementation should not be underestimated.

In the remainder of this chapter, we describe the main steps required for full enterprise-wide implementation of full cycle governance, as depicted in Figure 6-2 in Chapter 6, which, for reference purposes, is repeated in this chapter as Figure 9-1. Where appropriate, in the section on "Implementing Benefits Realization," we note the steps that must also be followed for the single program management option. These are indicated by the designation: (*program also*).

236

FIGURE 9-1
Structure Supporting Full Cycle Governance

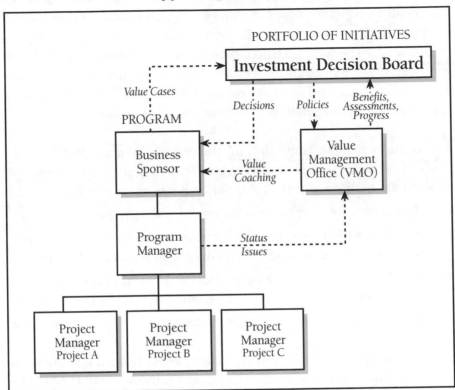

The main steps for implementing full cycle governance are: getting organized to select and monitor the portfolio; managing change to entrench new ways of thinking and working; and implementing benefits realization by creating the initial investment portfolio, based on a detailed value assessment of existing and planned projects.

Get Organized

The enterprise-wide implementation of full cycle governance requires major changes in the organization and process of investment decision making, as explained in Chapters 5 and 6. In many organizations, it makes sense to implement these changes by following three sub-steps:

■ Form the benefits realization implementation team.

■ Create the investment decision board (IDB).

■ Create the value management office (VMO).

Form the Benefits Realization Implementation Team. A team should be formed to get things started and keep the ball rolling. Its mission is to convince people to adopt the new benefits mind-set and commit to a major change in investment decision making and organization. The team is chaired by the corporate sponsor (or business sponsor). Once trained in the cornerstones of the Benefits Realization Approach, as described in this book, its first job is to define the strategy and plan for implementation. The team can then proceed to:

■ Customize benefits realization for the organization and link it to other corporate processes such as business planning, project management, budgetary control and performance measurement.

■ Define process owners for benefits realization activities.

■ Create teams with responsibility for implementation support activities, such as change management, communications and training.

■ Support the change management effort by communicating the concepts and advantages of benefits realization across the organization.

■ Measure results and report on progress to the management committee.

The benefits realization implementation team might work for several months or several years, depending on the scope of the benefits realization effort. It stays in place until the organization has embraced the new way of thinking and managing, and the machinery of full cycle governance is running smoothly. Once this has been accomplished, it should be disbanded.

Create the Investment Decision Board (IDB). Portfolio selection and management is the job of senior management. It is important for a cross-functional group of senior managers to make key investment decisions, select portfolios and monitor programs, as explained in Chapters 4 through 6. If your company has committed to implement enterprise-wide full cycle governance, a group must be established to make investment decisions. This group is the investment decision board, which will:

■ Review new investment program proposals.

■ Commit funds to the most valuable programs.

■ Monitor program expenditures and the delivery of benefits over time.

- Review active programs to check whether they are delivering benefits and, if not, redirect funding from them to other higher value programs.
- Ensure that each program is proactively managed to get the promised benefits, and to identify new emerging opportunities.

The investment decision board should be created once early implementation activities have been completed, that is, after the implementation strategy and plan have been approved, the benefits realization process has been customized and documented and essential roles defined. Board members should be provided with awareness level training on the Benefits Realization Approach. The four-P framework introduced in Chapter 8 provides a good basis for this training, conveying an understanding of why the company is doing this, what it's going to look like, how it is going to get there and what is expected from each person.

If your company decides to start with a small pilot project, creation of the IDB can wait until full corporate implementation.

The corporate sponsor is a good candidate to chair this group. Members should be as broadly representative of the business as possible, Board members will continue to fulfil their other management responsibilities and, for this reason, will require day-to-day assistance from a secretariat group: the value management office.

Create the Value Management Office (VMO). The value management office houses the experts who will support business sponsors in the design of investment programs and the preparation of value cases. At the same time, they help the IDB assess those cases. More specifically, the role of the VMO is to:

- Proactively help business sponsors identify new business opportunities and coach them on how to prepare value cases.
- Prepare its own assessment of the rigor and use of best practices in submissions to the investment decision board.
- Track individual program expenditures.
- Track the program investment portfolio.
- Monitor programs undertaken and benefits obtained, and archive all supporting benefits realization materials.

The size of the value management office will depend on the volume of active programs and new program proposals brought forward.

Comprising the VMO will be a leader and a team of value analysts who will be the champions for change at the working level. The value analysts will work with business sponsors and, in that role, be active evangelists for the new way of thinking about benefits. They will also be advocates for best practices in program definition, program valuation and value case development.

As the Benefits Realization Approach is institutionalized, and becomes "the way we do things around here," the value analysts will likely be situated in the business units, with functional reporting to the VMO leader.

Manage Change

Implementing benefits realization means entrenching a new way of thinking, managing and acting in your organization, as explained in Chapters 6 and 8. This is a long-term change process that must be architected and supported through four basic change management initiatives:

- Find senior executive champions and create a change management team.
- Plan communications initiatives.
- Design training and learning initiatives.
- Link benefits realization to other business processes.

Each of these initiatives is reviewed in detail below.

Senior Executive Champions. The temporary benefits realization implementation team, IDB and VMO are much more than formal bodies. All their members must conceive of themselves as agents, leaders and champions of change. The corporate and business sponsors play pivotal roles. Moreover, proactive change management, supported from the top, will be necessary to bring about the required transformation.

A change management team — a sub-team of the benefits realization implementation team — should be created to coordinate communication and training, and to solicit feedback from the organization. They should ensure that criticism, resistance and objections are heard and dealt with, as implementation proceeds. Communication should be open, overcoming resistance and involving employees in the change process. The change management team should adapt training to each target audience, and focus on developing the relevant competencies, where and when they are needed. The aim, as we often state it, is to provide "just enough training, and just in time."

Communications. It is vital to understand the positions of varied stakeholder groups regarding benefits realization. Based on that understanding, communications messages and channels can be adjusted to the needs of each benefits realization audience.

The first step is to identify all parties involved in or affected by the change, and determine their role in benefits realization implementation and communications. A survey should be conducted to assess their current level of awareness of benefits realization concepts and principles. Besides the management group carrying out full cycle governance, these stakeholders will include:

- Senior management
- Corporate sponsor
- Business unit heads and owners of processes that will have to change
- Doers and individuals affected by the change
- Managers who have to support the change process
- Project teams and task forces.

The information obtained from the survey should be used to define the position of the various stakeholders toward the change (opposed, neutral, proponent), and select the appropriate style and approach for communications. Stakeholders should then be grouped into target audiences, and key messages should be established for each audience, taking into account any reasons they may have for resistance to the benefits realization program. Communications with each target group should vividly describe how benefits realization will affect them, what will change and why these changes are necessary. The objective is to keep people well informed with respect to what has been done, what is going on, and what lies ahead. Again, the four-P framework provides an excellent basis for this communication. The communications team leader should be a member of the benefits realization implementation team.

Training and Learning. Benefits realization creates major learning challenges at all levels including: absorbing the concepts and principles of benefits realization; learning to use techniques like Results Chain modeling and the four "ares"; learning to use new processes such as

241

stage gating; and dealing with new organizational units like the IDB and VMO. As full cycle governance is implemented, training will be required at all levels across the organization. Tailored to each target audience, learning events should cover such subjects as:

- Concepts and principles in the chapters of this book
- Techniques for Results Chain modeling and program definition (specification of initiatives, outcomes, contributions and assumptions)
- Program and project life cycles
- Stage gate processes
- Assessment of program risks and feasibility
- Program valuation and value case preparation
- Benefits monitoring and measurement.

The training program should be developed with the learner's needs as the central focus, providing just enough training, just in time. Wherever possible, you should emphasize learning by doing.

Linking Benefits Realization and Other Business Processes. Benefits realization is not an add-on. It is integral to the way the business thinks and works. Organizations that are committed to a major corporate transformation must ensure that benefits realization is well integrated with other change initiatives, and that it forms part of the overall corporate vision. The implementation strategy and plan, the change management plan and the training plan developed for benefits realization must be aligned with other corporate change activities.

Companies can choose to adopt a results focus — making the right investments with scarce resources and ensuring that they get the promised benefits — at the same time they seek to increase quality, improve service, reduce cycle times and transform themselves into learning organizations. Benefits realization then becomes an integral part of their corporate transformation.

Implement Full Cycle Governance (or Program Management)

Once all the steps outlined above have been taken, the implementation of full cycle governance can begin. The objective at this stage is to create well-defined, well-documented programs from the current collection of work and to value them appropriately. Thoroughness and a high degree of rigor are essential. Certain steps can also be applied to the implementation of benefits realization within the scope of a single blended investment program, as indicated by the designation (programs also).

The main start-up activities, shown below, are supported by change management, communication and training and provide many opportunities for learning by doing.

- Define investment categories.
- Take inventory of current and planned programs.
- Estimate benefits (programs also).
- Validate program Results Chains and get buy-in (programs also).
- Assess and mitigate risk (programs also).
- Find a business sponsor (programs also).
- Assess program value (programs also).
- Build the investment portfolio and start benefits management.

Each of these activities is reviewed in detail below.

Define Investment Categories. Investment categories are fundamental to effective portfolio selection and management, as explained in Chapter 5. Investment categories must be defined by the investment decision board with the help of the benefits realization implementation team. The categories determine the processes that programs must pass through for valuation and selection. They can be generically described as follows (see also Chapter 4, Table 4-1, used by Nova Gas Transmission):

- Legally required programs
- Renewal of infrastructure assets, required to supply equivalent capability
- Programs to increase capacity requirements and handle business-generated increases in transaction volumes
- Programs for which funding has already been committed
- R&D programs
- Implementation of the IT architecture
- Programs to seize new business opportunities that will create measurable benefits for the organization.

Once the categories have been defined, the investment decision board must decide how to allocate capital funds to each of them, for subsequent investment.

Take Inventory of Current and Planned Programs. Grouping projects into blended investment programs is one of the core steps in implementing benefits realization, as explained in Chapters 2 and 3. In the case of a single program, the starting point is usually major IT, process redesign and other transformation projects. The next step is to group those projects with others from all areas of the BTOPP business system.

In the case of full cycle governance, all projects currently planned or under way should be inventoried and grouped into programs. This is done by the company's business units, with the help of the value management office and the benefits realization implementation team. A Results Chain is produced for each project that includes (as explained in Chapter 2):

- Intermediate and end outcomes
- Initiatives that comprise the project (the actions needed to bring about the desired outcomes)
- Contributions of identified initiatives to each outcome (linkages between initiatives and outcomes, and how they interact)
- Governing assumptions (influencing factors that are beyond the control of the project and that need to be monitored).

Once the project Results Chains are completed, they are combined to create consolidated Results Chains. Each consolidated chain should incorporate related initiatives and outcomes. Final outcomes must link directly to one or more of the company's strategic drivers. If they do not, then additional initiatives need to be defined to create this linkage. The consolidated Results Chains that are produced by this analysis represent business programs. They focus benefits realization work by:

- Identifying program elements that have a common end benefit and business sponsor
- Identifying initiatives and outcomes that will be required to realize benefits from business investments
- Determining intermediate and end outcomes that can be used as measurement points for tracking benefits realization.

Estimate Benefits (Programs Also). Order-of-magnitude estimates of benefits should now be attached to end outcomes. Rigor in quantifying them is expected as the numbers must be both reliable and credible. The following steps are recommended:

- Obtain available data on known driving variables (revenue, headcount, costs, number of system failures, volumes, customer base, total materials carrying costs etc.).
- Obtain forecasts for driving variables (these should ideally be research-based and confirmed independently).
- Obtain available data on coefficients (annual cost per employee, system failure rate, cost per transaction, carrying costs as a percentage of total purchases etc.).
- Forecast change in the coefficient value.
- If specific data is unavailable, use Delphi analysis techniques.

Validate Program Results Chains and Get Buy-in (Programs Also). Program Results Chains must be validated, and the people who will operate in the changed environment need to be involved. To identify these stakeholders and define the required level of validation, the analytical team should:

- Map areas that will be impacted by the proposed program or project.
- Identify key skills, expertise or credibility in these areas that will be important in validating program or project benefits.
- Identify individuals who might ultimately be responsible for operational areas involved in realizing the benefits.
- Identify groups with a role (e.g., validation of corporate processes and related benefits).
- Identify key ideas and the individuals or groups who may have vested interests in the outcome.

Buy-in will be key to the success of your benefits realization program. It is important to obtain commitment, and to identify natural supporters of the project who may be candidates for more active involvement in realizing benefits downstream.

Assess and Mitigate Risk (Programs Also). Risk analysis is now required for each Results Chain element, as explained in Chapters 3 and 4.

There are two questions: "How important is the contribution of this element to the ultimate outcomes? What is the level of confidence that it is achievable?" If an element is expected to contribute only marginally to these outcomes, then the second question is irrelevant. If an element contributes significantly, and it will be relatively easy to achieve, then once again no additional analysis is required. However, if the element will make a significant contribution, and confidence in achieving it is low, it needs to be examined in greater detail to accurately assess the source of risk. Contingency plans will be required, as it is these elements that represent the greatest risk to getting benefits.

Find a Business Sponsor (Programs Also). In the case of a single program implementation, a business sponsor is appointed early in the game. When full cycle governance is being implemented, this is the stage where business sponsors should be found for all the newly identified programs. As explained in Chapters 3 and 6, the business sponsor must be ready, willing and able to deliver program benefits, and be accountable for respecting time and budget constraints. Without a sponsor, a program does not exist in the eyes of the investment decision board, and it certainly will not deliver the desired business results.

Assess Program Value (Programs Also). The final step in preparing program proposals for submission to the investment decision board is to assess their value. As explained in Chapters 2 to 4, benefits realization considers several independent dimensions of value — alignment, financial worth and risk — rather than relying on a single measurement. A value assessment is required prior to each stage gate review:

- Alignment is the degree to which the program supports the company's strategic drivers, or contributes to achieving a desired future state or vision.
- Financial worth is a factor in all costs and dollar benefits, based on the most likely program outcome.
- Program risk is the degree to which the program is susceptible to loss of potential value.

Once this work is completed, a formal value case can be prepared for the investment decision board that describes the program and declares its value — backed up with detailed supporting documentation.

Build Investment Portfolio and Start Benefits Management. Value cases will be prepared for each program in the initial inventory — based on its stage of completion — as it approaches the next program or project gate. The investment portfolio will take form and grow as programs and projects come forward for review and as the investment decision board makes individual funding decisions based on their relative value.

Once a program has been added to the investment portfolio, benefits management can begin. High-level monitoring of progress against the plan ensures that significant deviations from predicted value are caught in time for corrective action. This progress monitoring does not replace program or project management; rather, it is a more global assessment of the current value status, based on output from program and project management activities.

Surviving and Thriving in a Changing World

Getting started is precisely that — just the beginning. Success in implementing benefits realization will be achieved only by experimenting and learning, experiencing the techniques first-hand and integrating lessons learned in the way your organization thinks and works.

The principles and practices of benefits realization, and the culture of a learning organization, are mutually reinforcing. Benefits realization programs will be most successful in organizations that:

- Have a big-picture view of the world
- Are prepared to experiment with new ideas and embrace risk
- Empower individuals and encourage self-directed teams
- Collect and communicate their experience
- Reward and share success.

Benefits realization is based on a big-picture view of capital investments. Decision makers need to think in terms of portfolios and programs, rather than projects. They need to understand that IT cannot stand alone, and that systems delivery projects cannot be managed in isolation from the business. Technological change, organizational change, business process redesign and learning must be blended appropriately in every program and managed together to produce the desired business results.

Benefits realization provides a way for organizations to experiment with new ideas, monitor the results and incrementally invest in change. Failures, in the form of investments that do not produce returns, are to be expected — even as the risk of failure is managed and reduced. Carefully chosen risk is considered to be an acceptable cost, as in the case of the applied R&D programs that are so central to many organizations' success in the Knowledge Economy. In such cases, risks and expected rewards are being proactively managed and kept in alignment. Risk can also be managed through portfolio diversification, which balances the riskier experiments against programs that can be counted on to deliver value.

The activist accountability built into benefits realization breaks down barriers between IT and the business and encourages teamwork across the organization, at all levels, to create new ideas and convert them into tangible value for the business. The playing field is leveled for capital investment as the organization funds the most valuable new ideas, regardless of their provenance.

Benefits realization is an open process that encourages and facilitates communication and participation at all levels. Experience is archived and reviewed to identify the factors that contribute to success, as well as failure. Processes are continually improved. Best practices are communicated through the activities of the investment decision board and the value management office, in learning events and through teamwork across the organization.

Benefits realization is focused on results, rewards and shared success. Individual and group contributions to achieving results include: initiative in proactively identifying new business opportunities; excellence in defining programs and developing value cases; on-time, on-budget delivery of projects to agreed specifications; stewardship of program and project teams in managing value; and successful harvesting of the promised benefits. These contributions should be publicly recognized.

Benefits realization offers a compass for navigating the uncharted waters of the Knowledge Economy. It supplies adaptive tools that can help organizations make the best investments in step with their changing environment. It provides instruments for decision making that can change quickly in response to corporate changes in direction — as the definition of value used to screen investments responds immediately to changes in an organization's strategic drivers, and directly links all programs to achieving them. In turbulent times, benefits realization will continually optimize the investment portfolio to maximize returns.

AFTERWORD: ENTERPRISE VALUE ... THE NEXT STEP

In the years since *The Information Paradox* was first published, the nature of enterprise value, and how to achieve it, has become a subject of much discussion. It has become increasingly evident that the failure to realize business value from investments in IT-enabled change, which initially led us to develop the Benefits Realization Approach, is simply a symptom of a wider malaise — one that presents managers with significant new challenges. The fact is, the track record for implementing *any* major change successfully is terrible. Although this track record may be more visible with IT, it also applies to any large-scale investment or change. The success rates of Business Process Re-engineering and Mergers and Acquisitions, two examples of major change, are no better than those often quoted for IT projects.

Root causes for this poor track record include:

- Failing to recognize that the leadership challenge today is one of continually implementing change ... major cultural change

- The inability to define or articulate clear and focused strategies to set the direction for change ... with a clear understanding of the value driven business outcomes that the strategies are striving to achieve

- Failure to acknowledge, surface, and come to grips with the complexity of strategy execution

- Governance processes that are woefully inadequate to manage what is, in most cases, "an uncertain journey to an uncertain destination".

Inadequate governance processes, in particular, lead to not having a clear understanding of the desired outcomes, not knowing what to measure, not surfacing and tracking assumptions, and not sensing and responding to changing circumstances in a timely or well-considered manner.

Over the last five or more years, we have worked with hundreds of organizations worldwide implementing the Benefits Realization Approach. As a result of this work, we have continued to learn. Much of our original thinking has been reinforced, and new thinking and practices have evolved.

In the first section of this Afterword, we describe how we have applied what we have learned to evolve our thinking and practices beyond benefits realization to the broader subject of Enterprise Value Management, and particularly to the linkage between enterprise value and strategy. Our approach to Enterprise Value Management includes governance frameworks and techniques to help organizations:

- Understand sources of value and develop value-focused strategies

- Define and structure comprehensive, value-based business change programs to execute business strategies

- Manage the realization of value using program-based portfolio management and a comprehensive and dynamic governance process.

In the second section, we discuss how the lessons we have learned through implementing the Benefits Realization Approach to manage investments in IT-enabled change can, and indeed must, be applied to the broader realm of Enterprise Value Management.

Moving Beyond Benefits Realization to Enterprise Value Management

The challenge of value creation is not limited to IT, nor is it an easy challenge to address. When we wrote *The Information Paradox*, we understood that value was not a simple concept. Value is complex, context specific, and dynamic. Value is indeed "in the eye of the beholder." We also recognized that value and strategy are tightly related, in that value results from the successful execution of well-chosen and focused strategies. The key word here is focus. No-one can "do it all."

Based on our experience over the last few years, we have continued to explore these topics and the relationship between them. This has led us to build on the Benefits Realization Approach to develop a new, broader, and more comprehensive approach to enterprise value — Enterprise Value Management. Our starting point was the underlying premise that IT-enabled change cannot be successful without profound, far-reaching changes to the business — changes which most companies are unable to recognize or willing to ignore.

The Business Challenge of Change

"Hope is not a method" — anon

While we have found a growing awareness of the problem of realizing value from business investments at senior levels of organizations across the world, there is still considerable denial of the extent of the problem, and little understanding of the causes. In many cases, we hear "We're doing that already," when they clearly are not or, all too often, "Well, we're no worse than anybody else." This is not exactly a great rallying cry, or one that you would expect to see on company sweatshirts or baseball caps! In many cases, there is even less willingness to undertake the significant change required to address the problem. Many organizations are just hoping that it will get better. And many are still looking for that elusive silver bullet. This could prove a costly and risky pursuit.

An approach many organizations are turning to is portfolio management, which is one of the fundamentals of benefits realization. Portfolio management is now getting a lot of press and attention. Unfortunately, much of the writing and talking about portfolio management is missing the point. The primary focus still appears to be on the technology project and the major activities of selecting and tracking these technology projects. The fundamental problem with this approach was well captured by Eric Dean, CIO of United Airlines:

> We can't measure the value of those things [IT] without measuring the use to which they are put. ROI should be based on the costs of achieving the desired change … it's not just about technology. (*Optimize* magazine, June, 2002, article discussing ROI metrics for IT.)

The fundamental building block on which portfolio management must operate is the business program. While portfolios of technology projects, applications, infrastructure, or even technology changes are of interest, that interest is primarily in the area of efficient resource utilization and cost reduction. It is only when the focus of portfolio management is the business program — and on blended investment programs, as described in Chapter 3 — that we move beyond efficiency and cost to effectiveness and business value. A leading communications service provider in the U.S. would have left most of the potential benefits of a major IT investment on the table had they not used the Benefits Realization Approach to redefine and re-scope what was an IT project into a blended business change program.

> **Key Learning:** Value does not come from technology projects. Technology only provides a capability. Value is only realized when this capability is applied and managed as part of a program of business change, including changes to business strategy, business processes, how people work, organizational structure, and technology.

Nor is selecting and tracking investments enough, even if we are working with business change programs. We need to manage their execution. While we must always "start with the end in mind", with the type of broad and innovative changes that the digital era opens up, we must learn to deal with being on that uncertain journey to an uncertain destination.

Usually, we start out with some idea of where we want to go and of how we are going to get there. However, by the time we get there, *there* won't be where we thought we were going and we won't have arrived the way we originally thought. We need to manage this journey as it evolves and changes. We need a continuous and dynamic governance process that manages the full cycle "from concept to cash", one that senses and responds to changes in the internal and external environment, and to our understanding of what is working and not working and that continually revisits our assumptions. Without such a process, the risk of ending up in the wrong place is significantly increased.

A continuous and dynamic governance process reduces the risk with investments such as enterprise resource planning, supply chain management, customer relationship management, and knowledge management. While these investments are enabled by technology, the major effort, and the major challenge, is not in implementing the technology, it is in implementing change. Enterprise Value Management is about recognizing that we are investing in change, and the management of that change. About 30 to 50 percent of the effort in major change programs is managing the process of change itself — and specifically managing the people aspects of change. Unfortunately, this is often only given cursory attention. It is not well planned and insufficient resources and time are allocated in whatever plan there is. Moreover, when schedules stretch out and budgets tighten, it is usually the first thing to go. This is not a technology problem. It is not a problem that will be fixed by focusing on IT projects in isolation. It is a business problem. If organizations are to deal with the problem, they must take a hard look at their overall governance process — from strategic planning through to program execution, including the full realization of value.

Further, if organizations are to seriously tackle the question of enterprise value with a portfolio management approach, they must recognize and apply all the fundamentals of the Benefits Realization Approach, including Program Management and Full Cycle Governance, with clear and active accountability, and clear and relevant measurement. Implementing such an approach is not about putting in place a few new forms. It is about fundamentally changing how organizations think, manage and act. It involves:

- Focusing more on business value — the desired end outcome, rather than activities
- Focusing on implementing change, not technology
- Defining comprehensive programs of business change

- Selecting investments based on the overall value to an enterprise, not to individual silos, either functional or geographic, within the enterprise

- Recognizing that the decision to select and proceed with an investment is only the beginning of an on-going governance process which includes the overall *portfolio*, the *programs* within the portfolio, and the *projects* that make up the programs

Project, Program, and Portfolio

The terms project, program, and portfolio are in wide yet inconsistent use today. In this Afterword, these terms and their relationship to business and enterprise value are defined as follows:

A *Project* is a structured set of activities concerned with delivering a defined *capability* based on an agreed schedule and budget. The capability in and of itself has no value, it is only when the capability is used as a result of a comprehensive program of change that value is realized.

A *Program* is a structured grouping of projects designed to produce clearly identified *business value*. The business value of one program will align in varying degrees to strategic objectives, may be dependent on other programs, or may potentially conflict with other programs. In order for an organization to realize the greatest value across all programs, they must be managed as a portfolio of programs.

A *Portfolio* is a suite of business programs managed to optimize overall *enterprise value*. The portfolio must be continually reviewed and managed to ensure that it is balanced to reflect strategic priorities, and that risks are mitigated and synergies exploited across programs.

To sum up, the challenge today is not implementing technology, but implementing change. The question is, how do we choose the programs of change that have the greatest potential value, and execute them such that the value is realized? At least part of the answer lies in a better understanding of the nature of value itself.

Understanding the Nature of Value

> "ROI is the buzzword of the day, yet few organizations
> understand what really drives their costs and benefits"
> — Amy Mizoras, IDC, May 7, 2002

The underlying cause of the difficulty in realizing business value lies in the increasing rapidity and complexity of change, and in the changing sources of value creation in today's business environment. Organizations today are increasingly generating value from intangible assets like brand, knowledge, improved governance processes, and re-engineered organizational structures. These intangibles provide the competitive advantage that differentiates the market leaders from the also-rans. Baruch Lev, in his work at New York University, has concluded that only 15 percent of the value of an S&P 500 company can be traced to tangible assets on the balance sheet. Paradoxically, although in many cases the dot.coms were selling intangibles, they failed miserably in managing them. This, aside from blind greed and the suspension of common sense by a large number of investors, aided and abetted by both analysts and the media, was one of the major contributors to the dot.coms being consigned to oblivion.

Intangibles have been described by Karl-Eric Sveiby as "those things that we have not yet learnt how to measure." To fully explore the concept of enterprise value, we must move our understanding of assets to include all those capabilities or resources, tangible or intangible, internal or external to an organization that the organization can influence, and understand how they interact with each other to impact the bottom line. A word of caution must be provided, however. We should not waste energy trying to precisely measure the value of intangibles. Rather, we should better understand their contribution, which together with the contribution of other assets, ultimately results in value. Basically, we should stop the quest for precision where precision does not exist, and shift to developing a better understanding of how value is created, and how we believe technology will contribute to the changes that are required to create value. In that vein, Sveiby's definition of intangibles might be modified to read, "those things whose contribution to business value we have not yet learnt to measure." In this context, organizations can often get far more value from understanding and better managing the assets that they already have than continually pursuing new assets.

Relationships, as described by Ray Mackenzie in *The Relationship-Based Enterprise*, are one example of intangible assets that represent a critically important value source to organizations. Understanding these relationships, and managing them such that mutual value is created through value-exchange-based conversations with customers, suppliers, and other stakeholders is a key competence for organizations today.

We may not be able to measure the effects of intangibles like relationships directly, but we see their effects. Like the shadows of forms in Plato's "Cave," intangibles reflect value back to the business. Actions taken to affect intangibles may be only loosely coupled to metrics, but they are still actions that we can take. The challenge is understanding and managing a value creation process, which is dynamic and complex, and is dominated by these kinds of intangible assets. Such an approach requires us to re-think the process of strategy.

Re-Thinking How We Define, Communicate, and Execute Strategy

> **"There is nothing worse than doing well that which should not be done at all."**— Peter Drucker

We must not only better understand the process of value creation, but must also be able to anchor this to an explicit, clear, and focused business strategy. Without a clearly articulated and understood strategy, it is difficult to align investment decisions with strategic direction. It is difficult, if not impossible, to decide what you will do, and also what you will *not* do. And there is a very high risk of selecting the wrong things to do.

We have heard all too often over the last few years that with business moving at "Internet speed" there is no time for strategic planning. Nothing could be more wrong-headed! While we cannot do traditional strategic planning the way we have done in the past, we should not just stop doing it. To do so would result in organizations continuing to waste large amounts of money on failed investments. We need look no farther than the dot.com graveyard, including both start-up and established bricks and mortar examples, for proof of this point. Organizations that do not have a clear strategy will miss out on significant business opportunities, and in many cases, cease to exist.

Successful Execution of Strategy is the Difference Between Winners and Losers

> **"Vision without action is hallucination"** — anon

Strategy is of no value if it is not successfully executed. Unfortunately, one of the few areas that rivals the poor track record of IT projects (or more accurately IT-enabled change) is that of strategy implementation. In a July 1, 2002, *CIO Insight* magazine article, David Norton, co-author of *The Balanced Scorecard*, quotes research conducted by CIO Insight and the Balanced Scorecard Collaborative which found that barely half of the companies adequately communicate goals to employees, only a quarter of employees have even a general understanding of the strategy, and less than 30 percent of executives believe that their budgets are strongly linked to strategy.

On many occasions, we have gone into organizations on the heels of a "big x" or strategic consultancy who have worked with the executive team to create a new multi-year strategy for the organization. It usually has a supposedly motivating theme, is packaged in glossy binders, and presented to those who were not part of its development (usually most of the organization) in Microsoft PowerPoint road shows or town hall meetings. Unfortunately, when the consultants have left, or even if they remain, those who are charged with executing the strategy (again, usually not those who were involved in its development) are left scratching their heads and wondering where to start.

The reason for this disconnect is that most strategies are both too wide in scope and too shallow in detail. The statements are often unarguable, but provide very little basis for determining what to do and what not to do. In one organization, the consultants came up with 75 focused programs of change ... an oxymoron if there ever was one. Despite our best efforts to get them to take a value-based approach to identifying those few programs that had the greatest value, and that they had the capacity to implement, they continued to roll out all 75. In the end, none were successful. The organization was so immersed in the huge change that it took its eye off running the business, and as a result the whole company failed spectacularly. It now exists only in the history books.

Many organizations today have little or no linkage between investment projects they undertake and their business strategy. Figure 1 is a simple visualization of the problem.

The consequences of this lack of linkage are evident in a number of ways:

- Business strategies are stated in "fuzzy" or motherhood terms.

- Desired business outcomes are neither clear, nor tracked.

- Results and measurements are unclear.

- Sponsorship and accountability are unclear.

- There is no context for overall governance.

- There are multiple steering committees, with little inter-program communication.

- There is a lot of "finger-pointing" between various parts of the business, particularly between the IT function and other functions.

FIGURE 1
Investment Projects Versus Business Strategy

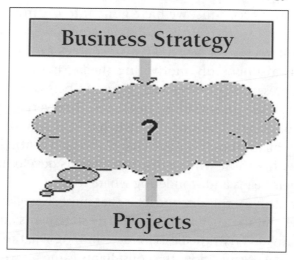

Strategy is even more important in a fast moving and uncertain business environment. What we must do to make the process of strategy more effective is to approach strategic planning and strategy execution differently — very differently. Strategy today must be value-driven and asset-based. Ultimately, business value results from the successful execution of business strategies which configure and manage all the assets of the organization to deliver the greatest possible value in line with business objectives.

Key Learning: We must take a more dynamic picture of strategy as one part of a complete value creation process — one that creates new value, uncovers latent value, and stops value leakage or erosion. Strategies should reveal the true "value levers" of an enterprise and exercise these levers to maximize the achievement of business objectives.

What's required are strategies that recognize the complexities of managing the uncertain journey to an uncertain destination that we have all embarked on at "Internet speed."

Embracing Complexity with Enterprise Value Management

"Everything should be made as simple as possible,
but not simpler" — Albert Einstein

A major cause of the failure to successfully execute strategy is that many organizations make simple or, more often, simplistic statements of strategy, and do not want to be bothered with drilling down to the complexities of implementation. However, the relationships between business change, the sources of business value, and business strategy are complex. We cannot wish complexity away by denying that it exists. For example, a client recently declined to apply the Benefits Realization Approach to a major change program that they were embarking upon. Their reaction was that the approach was too complex. They were looking for something simple. Unfortunately, in our complex world, there are few simple solutions. If we continue to exhibit "silver bullet thinking" in this way, we will continue to fail.

In another example, a large organization that we worked with was spending in excess of $US300 million to implement an enterprise resource planning system to replace a number of their current systems. Unfortunately, yet again, their focus was on implementing the technology. They did not even want to hear about the organizational changes that were required if the implementation was to deliver value. The standard response was, "You're making this more complicated than it really is!" Almost the sole desired outcome was implementation of the software on time, but not necessarily on budget. If meeting the deadline meant dropping functionality, which it frequently did, so be it. The schedule was paramount. It did not matter that little if any of the benefits specified in the original business case would be realized without major organizational change. Someone else could worry about that problem. The net result for this organization is that, if and when the software is implemented, they will have less functionality than they had with the previous systems, the software will cost more to maintain than their current systems, and the business may well suffer severe disruption, with potential regulatory or legal consequences.

> **Key Learning:** Organizations cannot continue to respond to the continuing speed and scope of change — both internally and externally — and increasing complexity with simple, or more often, simplistic solutions. Only when complexity is understood and managed can simplification occur. Recognizing, accepting, and managing this complexity is today's leadership challenge.

Enterprise Value Management helps organizations manage the complexities of the interaction of their strategies, their sources of value creation, and the ever-changing business environment in which they operate. It provides an understanding of all the sources of value, and how they interact, not as a simple chain, but as a network — a value network.

The value network moves our thinking beyond the sequential thinking of the value chain. It is based on the premise that all the assets available to an organization, tangible and intangible, internal to the organization and external to it, are potential sources of value. A further premise is that it is not the individual assets themselves, but the relationships between them, often complex relationships, that are the real sources of value. The first step in understanding the value network is to identify all these assets, then explore and map the relationships between them. From this mapping, we can identify those value levers that provide opportunities to increase value, or to reduce value erosion, as well as assets that have no potential to add value.

The Value Network

By way of illustration, let's look at one fairly common statement of strategy: "Improving customer satisfaction." At a high level, who could argue with this statement? But, if we are to turn the statement into something that has more meaning, and that can be used to provide focus in defining programs of change, and guide decisions in selecting the highest potential programs, we need to drill deeper. We need to go beyond a general statement around customer satisfaction to identify those specific value levers related to customer satisfaction. Are all customers equally important? What different classes of customer do we have? Are the same things important to all customers? What factors contribute to customer satisfaction? How satisfied do we want each class of customer to be? How satisfied can we afford them to be?

For example, in the banking sector, there are a number of different classes of customers. Some classes of customer are primarily involved in a transaction-based relationship, either over the phone, over the Internet or using ATMs. They rarely, if ever, interact with an actual bank employee. The objective of the bank in this case is to maintain an acceptable level of satisfaction while driving down the costs of service delivery. On the other hand, there are other classes of customer, often high value customers, that require a much more personal relationship. The challenge here is to identify these classes of customer, to understand what factors contribute to their satisfaction, and to focus strategy on exercising those value levers that contribute to a high level of satisfaction. This will certainly include identifying, motivating and rewarding those employees who are key to the relationship. This further involves understanding what factors contribute to these employees' satisfaction, and again focusing strategy on exercising those levers that contribute to their satisfaction.

Once we understand the relationship between specific customers and employees, we need to look at what adds value to that relationship. The employee will need to have the interpersonal and sales skills to manage the relationship. They will need knowledge about the economic environment, the customer's situation and past behavior, and the products and services available to the customer, both from their institution and from competitors. The employee might well need some leeway to customize a particular product or service for the customer, and to understand the implications of such customization on the return to the bank. There will also need to be processes that support the acquisition and sharing of this knowledge, and appropriate technology to support those processes.

With an understanding of the value network, value-focused strategies are developed to leverage the sources of value. These strategies then guide the definition of programs of value-driven change — programs that structure assets for greatest value. The realization of value is accomplished through strong program management and program-based portfolio management integrated in a comprehensive and dynamic governance process.

Value Mapping

> "Detail work is not beneath the dignity of a business leader"
> — *Execution: The Discipline of Getting Things Done*,
> **Larry Bossidy & Ram Charan**

A new technique that we have started to work with, Value Mapping, builds on the concepts of the Results Chain to bridge the gap between strategy and action. Value mapping is proving a powerful way to help executives achieve better understanding and management of the complexity of the enterprise value process. It explores the complete value network of an enterprise, including all value creating assets, both tangible and intangible, internal and external. It identifies the most important sources of value and shows how they contribute individually and collectively to the overall value creating capability of the enterprise. It drills down to the specific value levers and analyzes how they can be acted on without causing unintended damage through second- and third-level effects. In the same way that the Results Chain forces dialogue and clarity of understanding in program definition around the desired business outcomes and the full scope of effort required, Value Mapping will force more dialogue, understanding, and rigor in statements of strategy, and drill them down to statements that can be directly linked to programs of change.

The Value Mapping technique provides:

- Understanding and clarity of an organization's desired business outcomes

- Visibility of the complete value network — all the assets that the organization can use to achieve the desired outcomes

- Focusing of strategy through the definition of Strategic Drivers — those few things that the organization must excel at in order to achieve the desired outcomes

- Identification of those sources of value within the assets that offer the greatest potential contribution to the Strategic Drivers, and any constraints to their contribution

- Drilling down to specific value levers that the organization can act on to maximize the sources of value

- A comprehensive and comprehensible view of the relationships between the value levers, including identification of any conflicts, enabling clarification and further definition of executable business strategies

- A framework to understand the impact of proposed investments on the organization's value goals and strategies

- A shared vision and understanding of what is truly important to an organization in terms of how it creates value.

An example of what part of a Value Map might look like, based on the financial services example described earlier, is shown in Figure 2.

FIGURE 2
A Sample Value Map

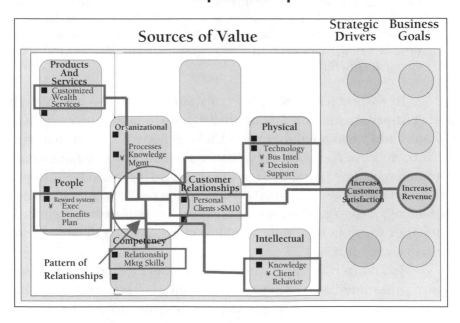

Our early work with value mapping has shown that the process of developing the value map is one that executives very quickly relate to. It helps them to "think outside the box", and "between the boxes", and quickly identify those sources of value around which they should focus their strategies and resources. The process and the resulting value maps provide a long-missing link between strategy and execution. The value levers identified in the value maps provide the "anchor" for the intermediate outcomes for the subsequent definition of business change programs using the Results Chain technique. The value map confirms the current desired destination, and defines the proposed journey. In the next section, we discuss the governance process required to manage this journey, one that must recognize that both the destination and the journey will change.

A New Approach to Governance
— Strategic Governance

"On a clear day you can see 6 months"
— Charles E. Phillips, Morgan Stanley,
Information Week Spring Conference, 2002

As David Norton, co-author of *The Balanced Scorecard*, said:

> The fact that most executive teams spend less than one hour per month discussing strategy is not an indication of poor management – it is an indication of no management. Most governance processes are built around the monthly management of budgets and operating plans. In the slow-motion Industrial Age, this was perfectly adequate. But those days are long gone. What is needed now is a new management process built specifically around strategy. (*CIO Insight*, July 10, 2002.)

In a world where the only constant is change — unceasingly more fast-paced, complex, and unpredictable — where strategy must be dynamic and where we must expect the unexpected, most current governance processes are woefully inadequate. In most organizations, planning is confused with, and too tightly linked to, the budgeting cycle and associated processes. This also all too often results in unnatural acts that are required to get the resources that someone thinks they will need when they work out what they should be doing, even though they don't yet know what that is.

Too much planning is activity-based rather than outcome-based. Few organizations have comprehensive, rigorous or consistently applied business case processes. A recent Meta Group study found that 84 percent of companies either do not do business cases for their IT projects at all, or just do them on a select few key projects. Where business cases are created, they are seldom looked at after the decision to proceed. If they are looked at, it is usually at some form of post implementation review; an event akin to an autopsy.

Organizations must evolve their processes to a governance system with the following characteristics:

- Value driven
- Enterprise-wide
- Inclusive
- Business-outcome based
- Dynamic
- Flexible

> **Key Learning:** The complexity that change entails requires a dynamic "sense and respond" governance system that recognizes that the fundamental challenge is the management of change; that clearly articulated strategies are required to direct change; and that the complexity that change entails must be both understood and managed.

Enterprise Value Management includes such a governance system — Strategic Governance (see Figure 3). Strategic Governance is an approach that continually manages the alignment between business strategy, the portfolio of programs, individual programs, the projects (both business and IT) that make up the individual programs, and enterprise architecture.

FIGURE 3
Strategic Governance

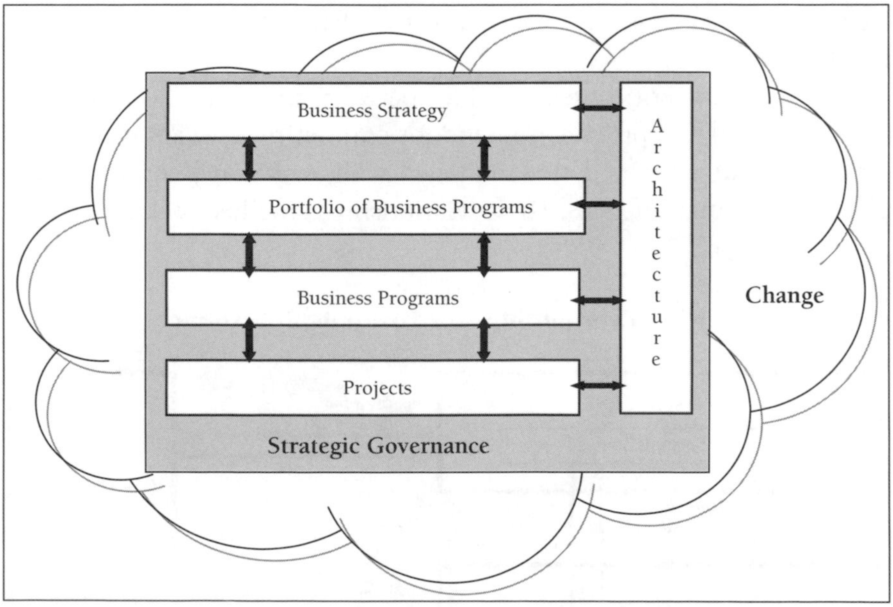

Most organizations have elements of Strategic Governance. While their effectiveness may vary, strategy and project management are well-established disciplines. Many organizations have an individual, or a group, or multiple groups responsible for strategy, although this is all too often still seen as more of an annual ritual than a process. Most organizations have some focus on project management, often having some form of Project

Management Office. Many organizations also have an architecture role, usually within the IT function. The focus is often on the technology aspects of architecture, and on the definition of those aspects, rather than the on-going management of their implementation and integration with the business. Also, an increasing number of organizations have established Program Management Offices, although in some cases these view programs as a number of related technology projects, rather than business change programs incorporating all the aspects of business, technology, organization, process, and people (BTOPP). A few organizations, particularly some of our benefits realization clients, are implementing Value Management Offices to support the value aspects of program and portfolio management. But rarely do these five critical roles come together as part of an on-going governance process, even in an annual review. Until they do, we will continue to pay a heavy price.

A word of caution: with Strategic Governance we are not suggesting that you set up five distinct offices; indeed, certainly initially, that may be the worst thing that you could do. Rather, there must be the recognition that these five roles need to exist, and to work closely and continually together.

There are critical relationships between these functions which, if managed well, will provide tremendous competitive advantage to organizations, but which, if not managed well, will have serious, if not catastrophic consequences. These relationships are illustrated in Figure 4.

FIGURE 4
Critical Relationships for Strategic Governance

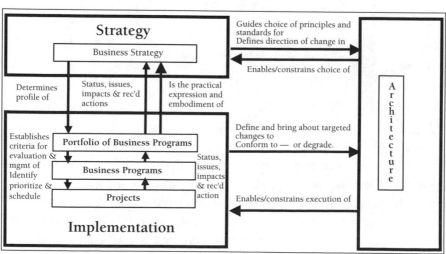

The astute reader will have noticed that, in illustrating Strategic Governance, we have allowed the dreaded "A" word to creep back in — Architecture. For many years, we have avoided using the "A" word with business audiences. It has not resonated and all too often appeared to be a sure cure for insomnia. Now, however, it is time for architecture to come out of the closet. A lack of robust and flexible architectures is at the root of many execution problems today. This deficiency, if not dealt with, will continue to be a major, and expensive obstacle to realizing enterprise value. Let's start by defining enterprise architecture.

Enterprise architecture is broad and comprehensive, not limited to technology or technical architecture. It is the architecture of the whole enterprise. It is about how the enterprise is structured. It includes every value-creating component of the enterprise, and the relationships between them. Enterprise Architecture components include business units, business processes, information, applications, technology, as well as knowledge, relationships, etc. These components are illustrated in Figure 5.

FIGURE 5
Enterprise Architecture

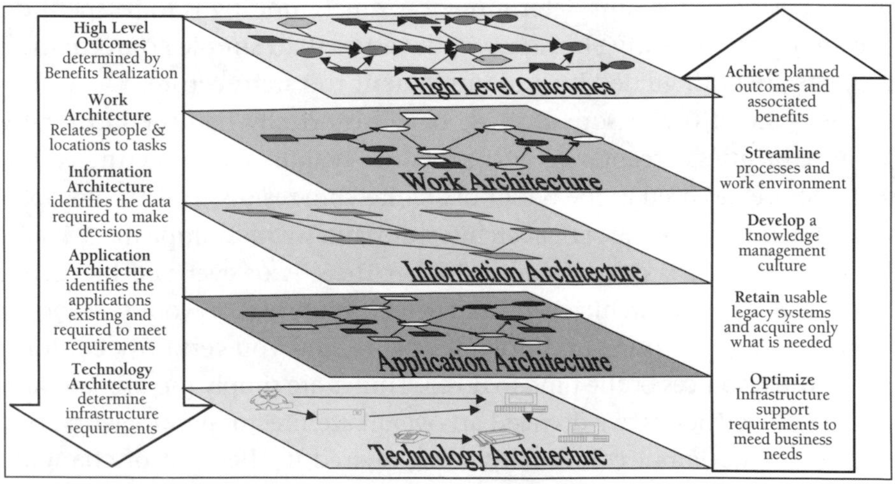

The challenge in Enterprise Architecture is to develop a structure which is both fit for purpose today and robust and flexible enough to meet tomorrow's challenges.

> **Key Learning:** Strategy, architecture, and governance are tightly linked in that the architecture must be fashioned and implemented in the light of strategy; strategy must encompass how the current architecture enables or constrains certain strategies; and governance must ensure that the two are in synch. We cannot get the strategy right without getting the necessary components of the architecture right, and vice-versa.

Enterprise Value Management provides the essential lens for getting all of this right. It provides insights into the assets we have, the relationships between them, and how we can leverage those relationships to enable enterprise strategies. Architecture is the set of rules for structuring those relationships. Business strategy defines the context for architecture, as well as the profile of the portfolio of business programs. The portfolio determines how much of the architecture is to be renovated or renewed either through wholesale change or minor refurbishment. Business programs determine how much funding is to be spent on the architecture to drive business value rather than simple conformance. Projects are both guided by and implement the architecture.

One of the reasons that we have historically had such difficulty gaining business acceptance of the business value of architecture is that architecture has been in the hands of architecture zealots. Their philosophy was, "We must have the perfect architecture, and we must implement it all." Unfortunately, it is questionable whether there is or ever will be such a thing as the perfect architecture; and even if there was, it would no longer be perfect by the time you implemented it, and you certainly couldn't afford the resources or the time to do so. Things are simply moving too fast.

Nevertheless, we do need an overall architectural framework, one that is not static but continually being revised in the light of changing requirements and changing technologies. However, the implementation of the architecture must be driven by business requirements and primarily by business value. We must move from the "big bang" implementation to a more incremental approach. At any point in time, the costs and value of implementing the architecture must be weighed against the risks of not doing so. We may not always choose to conform to the architectural blueprint, but this must be a managed decision, made with full understanding of the costs, value, and risks.

We should clarify that what we are talking about here is primarily the strategy process, and governance around the execution of that process, which is essentially the process of change. As Larry Bossidy and Ram Charan point out in *Execution: The Discipline of Getting Things Done*, the strategy process must both align and fully integrate with two other key processes — the people process, and the operations process. The people process is critical because it is people who must both execute the strategy and live with the results. The operations process is critical because ultimately change is translated into daily operations.

Differences between traditional strategic planning and Strategic Governance are summarized in Figure 6.

FIGURE 6
Traditional Strategic Planning Versus Strategic Governance

Traditional Strategic Planning	*Strategic Governance*
Industrial economy thinking	Digital economy thinking
Simplistic, cause and effect	Complex, dynamic relationships
Value Chain	Value Network
Structure (architecture) comes later	Structure (architecture) integrated with strategy
Predictable	Uncertain
An "annual" event	An on-going process
Long time frames	Short time frames
Analysis-oriented	Action-oriented
Command and control	Sense and respond
Hierarchical and imposed	Inclusive and evolving
Rigid	Flexible
Change happens	Change needs to be managed
Tightly connected to the budgeting cycle and process	De-coupled from the budgeting cycle — interacts with the budgeting process

If they are to survive, let alone prosper, organizations must continue to demonstrate that they understand how to create value, have strategies capable of delivering value both quickly and over the long term, and must have a track record of successfully executing those strategies. They must stop continually looking for "the next big thing" and better leverage what they already have. They must do the right things, do them well, and realize real and demonstrable business value. They must stop going for the "big bang" and structure change into "do-able chunks" that deliver real and measurable value in 60-day to 90-day increments. In the private sector, how well this is done plays an increasingly significant role in determining market valuation. In the public sector, the mandate, public perception, and viability of the organization may well hinge on the clarity with which its actions and investments can be tied to value.

Applying Lessons Learned to Enterprise Value Management

As we have implemented the Benefits Realization Approach in many ways with many different organizations, we have learned what factors are important to get the approach accepted, introduced and up and running — the key one being understanding the extent of the change required and managing that change. Many of these factors apply equally, if not more so to Enterprise Value Management.

- The introduction of Enterprise Value Management is itself a major change.

- It's about behavioral change – "we" thinking versus "I" thinking.

- The reward system must be aligned.

- Strong sponsorship is required.

- IT and the business must work as partners.

- Implement clear, activist accountability.

- Recognize that one size does not fit all.

- Avoid excessive bureaucracy.

- Don't fall into the analysis paralysis trap.

- Take an incremental approach.

- Pick the right place to start.

We explore these learnings in greater depth below.

The Introduction of Enterprise Value Management is Itself a Major Change

Enterprise Value Management is about identifying, focusing, defining, and managing programs of business change to drive the greatest value to the enterprise. One such program of change is the introduction of Enterprise Value Management itself. Failure to recognize this, and to manage the change, is probably the largest cause of problems that we have seen with earlier implementations of the Benefits Realization Approach. Certainly, the degree to which the change is managed will bear a direct correlation to the success of the implementation of Enterprise Value Management.

It's About Behavioral Change – "We" Thinking Versus "I" Thinking

One of the key effects of the Enterprise Value Management approach is that it provides a framework or context for dialogue — for questioning that leads to new insights — which in turn lead to changes in behavior. Three months into an implementation, a large European financial services organization found that at the executive level they were making very different decisions than they would have made before. As part of this, they were either not approving or stopping investments that they would otherwise have allowed to proceed. They were better aligning their investments with their strategic direction and, as a result, focusing their resources to realize the greatest value. This would not have occurred without some fundamental changes in behavior.

Further implications of the change from "I" thinking to "we" thinking include the following.

- *Taking the enterprise view.* Of all the changes that the Benefits Realization Approach requires, none is harder than getting executives and managers, who have in the past been blinded by individual silo views of their organization, to take the enterprise view. No approach to Enterprise Value Management will work, and organizations will continue to significantly underachieve on their portfolio of investments, until the executive and management teams learn to move beyond "I win – you lose" to "we win." This means sponsors moving beyond their initial "What do I have to do to get my proposal through this ridiculous process?" reaction to thinking about what is right for the enterprise.

- *Learning to say and accept no!* Many organizations think of portfolio management as a prioritization process. Portfolio management is about choosing where to invest and executing those investments. While prioritization is an important component of choosing, the key objective is not prioritization but selection. Selection means not only that you will decide what you will do, but also what you will *not* do. While not easy, it is much easier to decide what you will do than what you will not do. This is true both for the initial selection of an investment, and for on-going decisions regarding what investments to progress. This means sponsors accepting that when a proposed investment is not selected, it is not a failure on their part — it is just that there are investments that have greater value to the enterprise as a whole at that point in time. It means not treating the cancellation of a program as a failure, but recognizing that stopping one investment and reallocating resources to another that is of greater value to the organization is a good thing. The sponsor should not take this as a personal rebuff, nor should the executive look for someone to blame, but recognize that the governance process is working as it should.

- *Embracing shared visibility.* One of the benefits of portfolio management is that it enables, indeed forces, shared visibility of investments across the enterprise. This shared visibility is the first step to the behavioral change required to move beyond the silo view to the enterprise view. In one large telecommunications company this shared visibility alone enabled almost 30 percent of a $US70 million portfolio to be "taken off the table" and made available for higher value investments.

- *The willingness to change course.* Enterprise Value Management further requires a willingness to change course, and to accept changes in course possibly many times as we manage the uncertain journey to an uncertain destination in an ever-changing business environment. This will not be a comfortable thing for many executives to accept; but without acceptance, they will continue to steer their organizations in the wrong directions, and possibly onto the rocks of organizational oblivion.

The Reward System Must Be Aligned

Failure to take the enterprise view comes down to ego in many cases; often, unfortunately, supported by inappropriate reward mechanisms. While egos are an important part of an individual's make-up, particularly so in the case of leaders, effective ego management is an even more important attribute. Ego management may well have prevented some major corporate scandals.

A former colleague once said, "The good thing about reward systems is that they work, and the bad thing about reward systems is that they work!" Trying to change behavior, and failing to align reward systems with the desired behavior, almost guarantees failure. Reward systems must move beyond recognizing individual "hero" behavior and performance to recognizing team and collaborative partnership behavior and performance. Such recognition should be very visible, and should recognize equally, albeit differently, both positive and negative behavior. Without such visible recognition, value-limiting and even value-destroying behaviors will continue to thrive.

Strong Sponsorship is Required

There are two different aspects to sponsorship: the fundamental building block of Enterprise Value Management is the business program, and effective ownership and sponsorship are the keys to any program's success. But remember that the implementation of Enterprise Value Management is itself a major business change program. There is a significant difference between applying program management to one or more individual programs, or portfolio management to one part of the portfolio, and to institutionalizing Enterprise Value Management as part of an overall governance process. This requires sponsorship to move up and out, that is, to become higher and broader. It is at this transition point that many organizations bog down.

The ultimate responsibility and accountability for the realization of value must lie with the business. The business sponsor must be actively promoting the program, communicating why it is being undertaken, what it will look like when we get there, how we are going to get there, and what part individuals and functions will be required to play, both in getting there, and when we are there. The sponsor must promote and nurture the partnership that is so essential to success.

While the need for change can emerge bottom-up, change will not be successful without strong executive and management sponsorship. It is not enough, however, for this sponsorship to be just at the top. The "I said it therefore it is" school of leadership quite simply does not work. Sponsorship must cascade down through all levels of management.

This does not mean that you shouldn't embark on implementing Enterprise Value Management unless you have the complete support of the CEO and the whole executive team. Although ideal, this may rarely occur. It is not always or indeed often possible to turn a battleship overnight. Many organizations have started with one area of the business, or even one business change program. However, regardless of where you start, there must be strong sponsorship for the change. And, you must build on and extend that sponsorship if you are to move beyond piece-meal implementation to an enterprise-wide governance process.

IT and the Business Must Work as Partners

Historically, one of the most extreme examples of organizational silo thinking has been between the IT function and the rest of the business. Indeed, our very language, including the language of this book, perpetuates this problem. If we are to break down these barriers, which we must to realize enterprise value, the business view must come first, the functional view second. IT is just as integral a part of the business as Finance, HR, Marketing, or any other operational function. We must break the "we/they" mode of thinking and think as partners in the overall business, continually asking "What do we, as partners in the business, have to do to drive the greatest possible value for the business?"

Business owners must participate actively as "partners" in business program definition and execution. When 85 to 90 percent of the work required — the change — to realize the value of a business change program has to be undertaken by the business, that responsibility cannot be abdicated to the IT function. All affected areas of the business, including IT, must be active partners throughout the whole process of program identification, definition, evaluation, selection, implementation, and execution.

Implement Clear, Activist Accountability

Enterprise Value Management will not be successful without clear, active accountability as described in Chapter 6. This type of accountability is tied to a clear and relevant measurement system as described in Chapter 7 — and directly linked to an aligned reward system, managed through a disciplined governance process.

For accountability to be accepted and effective, organizations need to rethink their attitudes to accountability. We need to move away from the "Who do we blame when things go wrong?" view to "How can we work together to make this program successful and support the sponsor?"

Recognize that One Size Does Not Fit All

Most organizations already have some management processes in place around the prioritization, selection, and management of IT investments, even if only at the IT project level. It is better to adjust current management processes, extending them as required, than to introduce a totally new set of processes. This involves identifying what currently exists, mapping it to the Enterprise Value Management approach, changing the mandate, and possibly the membership of some groups, putting more rigor into the process, introducing new measurements, etc.

We have also found the concept of categorization of investments, introduced in Chapter 4, to be essential if portfolio management is to work effectively, and not become mired by making every single investment go through the same hoops. The reality is that different investments have different levels of freedom in allocating funds, and different levels of complexity of the logic between the proposed initiatives, and the desired outcome. Those investments where there is little choice around allocating the funds, such as, regulatory requirements, or where the linkage between the initiatives and the desired outcome is very clear, such as in the replacement of part of the technology infrastructure with new components that deliver the same or greater functionality and have lower operating costs, require a much less rigorous approach than those that are truly discretionary, or where the linkage between them and the desired outcome is unclear or complex.

Avoiding Excessive Bureaucracy

In one case the Value Management Office (VMO) sent a Value Case back to the sponsor 15 times. While the first time was reasonable, the next 14 were simply dotting the "I"s and crossing the "T"s. The purpose of any methodology is to enable a desired end result, not to slavishly follow a process every time. In the case of the Benefits Realization Approach, the purpose is to realize the greatest possible value from investments in IT-enabled change. In this context, the purpose of the VMO is not to act as the methodology police, but to support business sponsors in putting together complete and comparable Value Cases. In one financial services organization, where the VMO performed such a role, a number of business sponsors came, or were led, to the conclusion that proposed investments were not going to fly and took them off the table. As a result, unnecessary effort and management time was avoided, and resources were re-focused on what was of the greatest value to the organization.

Don't Fall into the Analysis Paralysis Trap

In one instance, a client called to complain that the tool that supports the creation of Results Chains did not support large enough models. However, the problem was not with the tool; rather there was a process problem. The trick with any process of analysis is to know when you have done enough analysis to support informed business judgment. Going beyond this point is a waste of time and, worse, delays decision-making. While it is always easier to continue to ask questions, the art of management is to know when enough is enough. Too often, on-going analysis is simply an excuse to defer or avoid making management decisions.

In a number of cases, we have worked with clients in a half-day workshop to develop a simple high-level Value Map or Results Chain. While there was clearly follow-up work required, the insights gained out of such a short high-level session significantly improved the shared understanding of the desired business outcomes, started to get everyone on the same page, and brought focus to potential strategies, candidate change programs, and the full scope of the change effort.

Take an Incremental Approach

When designing and executing programs of business change, including the implementation of the Enterprise Value Management approach, we must resist the temptation to go for the "big bang." History is replete with failures of such approaches. However, while it is unrealistic to expect that a major change can be accomplished in a few months, it is equally unrealistic to expect that we can wait two to three years to see the value of a program of change. When we are on an uncertain journey to an uncertain destination, everything will have changed in two or three years — the business environment, the technology, and the people.

The solution is to balance longer term outcomes with demonstrable short-term results. We must always keep the end in mind, but structure change into do-able chunks that deliver real and measurable value in 60-day to 90-day increments. We must communicate, build on, and learn from success. The advantages of such an approach include:

- Early realization of value

- Value realized even if the program is later cancelled

- Increased buy-in to the program

- Increased executive visibility

- Reinforcement of the power of partnership

- Early and frequent learnings that can be applied to improve future performance of the program

- A culture of success

The Enterprise Value Management approach, using Value Mapping and Results Chains, helps identify how programs can be structured to deliver incremental change and the resulting value. However, the approach will only be successful if actively managed by a Strategic Governance system, and encouraged by an aligned reward system.

Pick the Right Place to Start

Recognizing that "big bang" rarely, if ever, works, we have in almost all cases adopted the incremental approach. Generally, this takes the form of one or more pilots. Unfortunately, experience has shown that pilots all too often remain just as pilots. A more successful approach involves moving on a number of different fronts at the same time:

- Understanding where you are today, where the pain points are, and where there are opportunities for "quick wins"

- Opportunistically selecting one or two pilots to test out the approach and demonstrate success

- Implementing some basic foundational disciplines across the board, such as standardizing business cases, measurement and tracking, etc.

- Continuing to build awareness of the need to change at all levels in the organization

- Building on the increased awareness, the pilot and foundation work to extend value mapping, program management and portfolio management across the enterprise, integrating it into the overall governance processes

- Managing the implementation as a major program of change

- Communicating success

- Learning and continuing to tailor and evolve the approach to meet the specific needs and nature of your organization

The Road Forward

"Every day you make progress. Every step may be fruitful. Yet there will stretch out before you an ever-lengthening, ever-ascending, ever-improving path. You know you will never get to the end of the journey. But this, far from discouraging, only adds to the joy and glory of the climb."
— Sir Winston Churchill

With the appropriate governance structure and processes in place, the linkage that the Enterprise Value Management Approach provides will enable organizations to be responsive to inevitable and constant changes in business strategy. It will enable them to move beyond "traditional" strategic planning and management methods, which are woefully inadequate for the business environment of today and the future, to Strategic Governance. This governance process will be dynamic, and will continually manage the alignment between business strategy, the portfolio of programs, individual programs, the projects, both business and IT projects, that make up the individual programs, and the enterprise architecture.

Enterprise Value Management, building on and integrated with a Benefits Realization Approach, will provide an overall framework for Strategic Governance that will enable organizations to respond with agility to the demands of a complex, dynamic, fast-paced and constantly changing business environment — an approach that is focused on delivering business value in a world where both the destination and the journey are uncertain.

The goal of Enterprise Value Management is to provide a comprehensive framework to address the underlying causes of the value dilemma. It will force rigor in strategy definition, program definition, portfolio selection, and governance. It will integrate strategy, architecture, and action. It will provide meaningful measurements that the governance process can use to dynamically sense and respond to changing business conditions. Enterprise Value Management will be a tool that can help all organizations, large or small, private or public break the value log jam and reap the full potential of the digital era.

Adopting and implementing Enterprise Value Management, just as in the case of its genesis, the Benefits Realization Approach, is not easy. It requires vision, discipline, and the courage to stay the course. It represents a fundamental change in how we think, manage, and act. Without such change, however, we will continue to dismally under-perform. There will, as always, be a few bright stars, but most results will be mediocre at best and appalling at worse. Our organizations, the people who they serve, the people who work in them, and society as a whole deserve better. Investors and analysts will demand that we do better. We can do better. We must do better!

After meeting with organizations, their response is often "You have given us a lot to think about." While encouraging, that is not enough. The time for elegantly describing and debating the problem is over. The problem is real, and the consequences of inaction are severe. We need to move down the road to the solution. We need to move beyond thought to action — well-managed action with a clear business outcome in mind. We need to take action that increases the value that our organizations deliver to their stakeholders each and every day. There is no more important outcome!

GLOSSARY

Activist Accountability (First Necessary Condition)

Activist accountability goes beyond traditional notions of passive accountability. It includes the concept of "ownership" — meaning active, continuous involvement in managing a program and, most importantly, clear ownership of each measurable outcome and the associated benefits.

Alignment

One of three supporting measures of the four "ares" (the other two are financial worth and risk). Alignment is a measure of the fit of a planned investment direction with organizational direction, including vision, mission, goals, objectives and architectural principles.

Architecture

Description of the fundamental underlying design of the components of the business system, or of one element of the business system (e.g., technology), the relationships between them and the manner in which they support the organization's objectives.

Assumption (Fourth Core Element of Results Chain)

Condition for the realization of an outcome or of an initiative, over which the organization has no control.

Automation of Work (First IT Stage)

The automation of work tasks, such as census data calculations, check processing and payroll, yields benefits largely in the area of operational efficiency.

Balanced Scorecard

The Balanced Scorecard, developed by Robert S. Kaplan and David P. Norton, is a coherent set of performance measures organized into four categories. It includes traditional financial measures but adds customer, internal business process and learning and growth perspectives.

Benchmarking

A systematic approach to comparing an organization's performance against peers and competitors in an effort to learn the best ways of conducting business (e.g., benchmarking of quality, logistical efficiency and various other metrics).

Benefit

An outcome whose nature and value (expressed in various ways) are considered advantageous by an organization.

Benefits Realization Approach

A business oriented framework, supported by a set of processes, techniques and instruments which enables organizations to select and manage a portfolio of programs such that benefits are clearly defined, optimized and harvested.

Benefits Stream

The flow of benefits over time resulting from successful implementation and management of a business program.

Benefits Harvesting

The area of program management that focuses on the actual attainment of benefits following program commissioning.

Blended Investment Program — See Program

Business Process Re-engineering — See Re-engineering

Business Process

A set of cross-functional activities or events that result in the delivery of a specific product or service to a customer.

Business Sponsor

The individual accountable for delivering the benefits of a blended investment program to the organization.

Business System

A holistic view of business that includes strategy, business processes, organization and people, as well as technology.

Business Transformation (Third IT Stage)

Fundamental changes in an organization's mission, or raison d'être, its value chain and how it does business.

Business Case

Documentation of the rationale for making a business investment, used to support a business decision on whether to proceed or not with the investment.

Change Management

A holistic and proactive approach to managing the transition from a current to a desired organizational state, focusing specifically on the critical human or "soft" elements of change. It includes activities such as culture change (values, beliefs and attitudes), developing reward systems (measures and appropriate incentives), organizational design, stakeholder management, human resource policies and procedures, executive coaching, change leadership training, team building and communications planning and execution.

Continuous Improvement (CI)

A philosophy of ongoing betterment which originated in Japan, where it is known as *kaizen*, involving everyone in an organization on a day-to-day basis in a constant quest for continuous, incremental improvement on all fronts.

Contribution (Second Core Element of Results Chain)

The role of a component of a Results Chain in the realization of another component.

Customer Information Systems (CIS)

Systems, based on databases and/or extracts of data from different databases, that contain customer information providing a comprehensive profile of customers and their transactions with an organization. They are often used to support targeted or relationship marketing, sales and order processing and after sales support.

Data Warehouse

A database, often very large, that contains information from numerous sources in a variety of formats. Frequently used for decision support within an organization, the data warehouse also allows the organization to organize its data, coordinate updates and see relationships between information gathered from different parts of the organization.

Delphi Analysis

A method of analysis, using a technique known as the Delphi technique, where a number of individuals are asked to express their opinions, usually in response to some form of questionnaire, and to review the opinions of others, without any direct contact occurring between the individuals. The objective is to encourage open sharing of ideas without pressure to defend opinions, or excessive influence by one or more individuals. It is useful in facilitating consensus among a number of individuals or groups holding different views, and thus to support decision making.

Downsizing

The reduction in the size of a company or its labor force.

Economic Value Added (EVA)®

A technique developed by G. Bennett Stewart III, and registered by the consulting firm of Stern, Stewart, where the performance of the corporate capital base, including depreciated investments (such as training and research and development), as well as more traditional capital investments (like plant and equipment), is measured against what shareholders could earn elsewhere.

Electronic commerce (applications)

Commercial activity that takes place by means of connected computers. Electronic commerce can occur between organizations or between customers and businesses, through an on-line information service, the Internet, a BBS or electronic data interchange (EDI).

Empowerment

A philosophy which grew out of the Total Quality Management (TQM) movement, which increases the control that employees have over their own work and, as a result, enhances their sense that what they do is meaningful and contributes to their organization's performance.

Enterprise Application Packages

Enterprise application packages, also known as enterprise resource planning applications, are suites of packaged software designed to help organizations manage resources across the enterprise, and enable the integration of business processes across the supply chain, including distribution, human resources, finance, inventory management, manufacturing, procurement, project management, sales, transportation and other processes.

Executive Information Systems (EIS)

Systems designed to support senior management decision making. More advanced versions include analytical and communications capabilities to support management work.

Extranet

An extension of an Intranet using groupware technologies to share data, information and knowledge across an organization's supply chain, including suppliers and clients.

Financial Worth (Measurement)

One of three supporting measures of the four "ares" (the other two are alignment and risk), financial worth is a measure of monetary contribution, calculated using traditional accounting methods.

Four "Ares"

The four underlying questions that provide the framework for the value assessment technique.

Are 1:   Are we doing the right things?

Are 2:   Are we doing them the right way?

Are 3:   Are we getting them done well?

Are 4:   Are we getting the benefits?

Full Cycle Governance (Third Fundamental)

An integrated management system that operationalizes the concepts of program and portfolio management, distinguished by its long time frame, which supports management of the benefits realization process from the conception of projects to the harvesting of benefits — "from concept to cash."

Futzing (Futz Factor)

Term introduced by The Gartner Group to reflect the time wasted by people trying to make computers function, rather than using them to do productive work.

Information Management (Second IT Stage)

The application of IT to provide information to support improved decision making, to move decision making "closer to the customer" and to support new service and product design, yielding benefits in operational and tactical effectiveness.

Information Paradox

The phenomenon that while the unit cost of IT is decreasing, organizations continue to spend increasingly large sums of money on IT in the belief that information, and the investment in IT to provide that information, is a "good thing," despite the all too frequent reality that we cannot demonstrate a connection between investments in IT and business results.

Information Technology (IT)

A general term used to refer to all aspects of computing and communications technology, including hardware and software (both system and application software) that encompasses the creation, storage, processing, distribution and display of information for a variety of uses, including business, educational, artistic, scientific, recreational or personal.

Initiative (Third Core Element of Results Chain)

An action that contributes to one or more outcomes. It always refers to an element that can be acted upon directly.

Integration

The extent to which constituent elements of the business system (e.g., technology) are organized into a coordinated whole.

Intermediate Outcome — See Outcome

Internet

A global public network of networks based on TCP/IP communications protocols that hosts many information services including electronic mail, information publishing, electronic conferencing, file transfer protocol (FTP) and electronic commerce, which are used for the exchange of information, products and ideas.

Intranet

A private, internal implementation of the Internet using groupware technologies to share data, information and knowledge within an organization.

Investment Decision Board (IDB)

A management structure primarily accountable to manage an organization's portfolio of blended investment programs and, in doing so, manage the level of overall funding to provide the necessary balance between company-wide and specific line-of-business needs.

IT — See Information Technology

IT-enabled Business Transformation (projects)

A radical redefinition or redesign of an organization that would not be possible without the capabilities provided by IT, but which generally requires extensive changes to other elements of the business system in order for the desired transformation to occur.

JIT (Just-In-Time [Inventory Systems])

An approach to inventory control and industrial production management based on the Japanese *kanban* system which is designed to minimize inventory and increase product quality and plant productivity. Under a JIT system, workers receive materials from suppliers "just in time" for scheduled manufacturing to take place.

Knowledge Economy

An economy in which information and knowledge are the predominant economic resource — the primary ingredient of what is made, done, bought and sold — more important than raw material, and often more important than money.

Knowledge Management

The explicit and systematic capture, organization, storing, sharing and leverage of useful intellectual capital.

Knowledge Workers

People who work mainly with information and whose work is characterized by the fact that information and knowledge are both the raw material of their labor and its product.

Learning Lag

The time delay between the introduction of new technology to individuals, work groups and organizations and their learning to apply it effectively, including unlearning old ways of doing things.

Leverage

The use of an investment or resulting asset to gain a return.

Life Cycle

A series of stages that characterize the course of existence of an organizational investment (e.g., product, project, program).

Linkage (First Blind Spot)

One of four critical dimensions of complexity which constitute blind spots in traditional management mind-sets (the others being Reach, People and Time). This refers to the linkage between the expected results of an IT investment and all the other IT and business investments and intermediate outcomes required in order to realize the benefit.

Mission-Critical System

A system so vital that its failure would have catastrophic effects on an organization's ability to operate or even survive.

Modeling

Developing a simplified representation of a system or phenomenon. Such representations may be static or dynamic in which case the behavior of the system or phenomenon under different conditions can be simulated.

On-line Analytical Processing (OLAP)

A relational database system capable of processing queries more complex than those handled by standard relational databases, through multidimensional access to data (viewing the data by several different criteria), intensive calculation capability and specialized indexing techniques.

Outcome (First Core Element of Results Chain)

Change in or maintenance of the state of an element that cannot be acted upon directly. An outcome can be intermediate (contribute to another outcome) or be ultimate (the final desired state.)

Outsourcing

Organizations contracting out the ongoing management of certain internal processes to outside service providers (e.g., the running of an IS department; a data center; certain applications or business processes; or specific discrete tasks such as help desk staffing or asset, systems or network management).

People (Third Blind Spot)

One of four critical dimensions of complexity which constitute blind spots in traditional management mind-sets (the others being Linkage, Reach and Time). This refers to the number and diversity (the breadth) of people who will be impacted by a business program and the extent to which they will be impacted (the depth).

Plateaus

Plateaus represent a time-based profile of benefits. An individual plateau is a point at which an intermediate level of the anticipated benefits of a program is realized. A plateau will usually correlate to one or more intermediate outcomes.

Portfolio

A grouping of investment programs selected by management to achieve defined business results while meeting clear risk/reward standards.

Portfolio Management (Second Fundamental)

Taking a panoramic view of business needs, opportunities and investments in IT-enabled change, so as to pick and manage an optimum set of programs (the portfolio) to deliver the most value over time, while adjusting the composition of the portfolio as more knowledge is gained and in response to changes in the environment.

Proactive Management of Change (Third Necessary Condition)

Proactive management of change is an essential condition for implementing benefits realization. It is a core responsibility of the business sponsor and involves building all required change management initiatives into business programs up front and actively managing those initiatives throughout the life of the program.

Program

A structured grouping of projects designed to produce clearly identified business results.

Program Management (First Fundamental)

Management of the full program life cycle from concept to cash. It includes: definition of program scope, assessment of program value, program design, program delivery benefits harvesting and program completion.

Progressive Resource Commitment

Progressive resource commitment replaces the all-or-nothing approach toward technology investments with a pay-as-you-go method in which programs pass through a series of decision points, known as stage gates. At these points, after a decision is made to proceed, only enough funding is committed to reach the next stage gate.

Project

A group of activities concerned with delivering a defined capability based upon an agreed schedule and budget.

Project Management

Management of the full project life cycle from design to delivery. It includes: definition of project scope, project design, construction, testing and implementation.

Re-engineering

Fundamental and radical redesign of an organization's business processes to achieve performance breakthroughs.

Reach (Second Blind Spot)

One of four critical dimensions of complexity which constitute blind spots in traditional management mind-sets (the others being Linkage, People, and Time). Reach refers to the breadth of change involved in a program (how much of the organization is impacted) and the depth of change (the degree of impact of the changes required to realize the benefits of the program).

Relevant Measurement (Second Necessary Condition)

Measuring the right things, measuring things the right way and making sure that measurements guide decisions and actions.

Results Chain™

A modeling technique developed by Fujitsu Consulting that provides a graphical representation of events and conditions required to achieve a stated business outcome for a program. It has four components: outcomes, initiatives, assumptions and contributions.

ResultStation

One part of the Macroscope™, the set of deliverable-based business processes to bring about change in an organization. ResultStation™ is the critical link to making all the processes fit together by defining, evaluating and managing the change. ResultStation addresses the challenges of benefits management by providing: a comprehensive and complementary approach to investment management practices; a framework for better understanding and management of the benefits realization process; a process to enable organizations to better manage the dynamic nature of benefits identification and realization; and a framework to track the realization of benefits and adapt to the evolving context. ResultStation™ focuses on delivering business outcomes that provide the most value to an organization.

Risk (Business Risk)

Degree of probability of not realizing the benefits of a business program.

ROI (Return on Investment)

The rate of return an organization earns on an investment.

Silo (Organization)

A term, sometimes referred to as stovepipe, describing an organization structure in which individual functions operate vertically in isolation from other functions.

Silver Bullet Thinking

The naive belief that IT "solutions" come neatly packaged and stamped "benefits inside," reinforcing the idea that all you have to do is plug in the technology and, magically, benefits will flow.

Stage Gates

A stage gate is a point of time where a decision is made to commit funds to the next set of activities on a program or project, to stop the work altogether or to put a hold on execution of further work.

Supply Chain

A network of interlinked organizations including suppliers, manufacturers, distributors, retail outlets and consumers through which an organization delivers its products or services to its customers.

Time (Fourth Blind Spot)

One of four critical dimensions of complexity that constitute blind spots in traditional management mind-sets (the others being Linkage, Reach, and People). The time for the full benefits of a business program to be realized, based on understanding the previous three dimensions and recognizing that these dimensions of linkage, reach and people, will themselves change over time, further affecting the time required to realize benefits.

Total Quality Management (TQM)

A management philosophy, attributed to W. Edwards Deming, which dedicates the entire organization to a relentless pursuit of quality, which means meeting or exceeding customer expectations.

Ultimate Outcomes — See Outcomes

Value

Relative worth or importance of an investment for an organization or its key stakeholders. Its expression may take various forms, including monetary or material, substitution equivalence, subjective judgment, etc.

Value Assessment Technique

One technique that supports the Benefits Realization Approach (the other is the modeling technique, also known as Results Chain). It applies the four "ares" along the dimensions of alignment, financial worth and risk.

Value Case

Value cases replace conventional business cases in the Benefits Realization Approach to support the selection and management of programs. They are used as an ongoing operational tool to support full cycle governance.

Value Management Office (VMO)

The secretariat for the Investment Decision Board (IDB) in managing investment portfolios.

Value Chain

A technique popularized by Professor Michael Porter that defines the series of activities, grouped into primary and support activities, that an organization performs to produce and add value to its products and services.

BIBLIOGRAPHY

References

Anderson, Christopher. "Survey of Electronic Commerce: In Search of the Perfect Market," *The Economist*, May 19, 1997.

Anderton, Paula. Study Sheds New Light on IT and the CEO (by A.T. Kearney). *Computing Canada*, April 14, 1997, 23-8: 12.

Anthes, Gary H. "IRS Project Failures Cost Taxpayers $50 Billions Annually," *Computerworld*, October 14, 1996, p.1.

Arthur, W. Brian. "Increasing Returns and the New World of Business," *Harvard Business Review*, July-August, 101-109.

A.T. Kearney Inc. "The Growing Impact of Strategic Information Technology on the CEO Agenda" (Chicago World Headquarters, 1997). [On-line: http//www.atkearney.com]

Austin T. *Difficult Design Decisions in the Imperfectly Connected Real World*. Research Note; Client/Server (CS); Gartner Group, November 21, 1996.

Berg T. *The Business Value of Electronic Commerce, Part 1*. Research Note; InSide Gartner Group this Week (IGG); Gartner Group, October 4, 1995.

Berinato, Scott. "The Secret To Software Success," *CIO Magazine*, July 1, 2001.

Bernstein, Peter L. *Against the Gods: The Remarkable Story of Risk* (New York: John Wiley & Sons Inc., 1996).

Bossidy, Larry and Charan, Ram. *Execution – The Discipline of Getting Things Done* (New York: Crown Business, 2002).

Bridges, William. *Managing Transitions: Making the Most of Change* (Reading, Mass.: Addison-Wesley Publishing Company, 1991).

Brynjolfsson, Erik. "The Productivity Paradox of Information Technology: Review and Assessment," *Communications of the ACM*, December 1993, 36-12: 66-67. [On-line: http/ccs.mit.edu/CCSWP130/CCSWP130.html]

Brynjolfsson, Erik and Lorin Hitt. "Information Technology as a Factor of Production: The Role of Differences Among Firms," *Economics of Innovation and New Technology*, 1995, 3: 183-200.

Byatt, Richard. "IT and FM Outsourcing: A Perfect Fit," *Facilities Design and Management*, May 1997,16-5: 30.

Campbell-Kelly, Martin and William Aspray. *Computer: A History of the Information Machine* (New York: BasicBooks, 1996).

CIO Metrics, "U.S. IT spending will grow modestly through 2004," November 8, 2002.

Compass Analysis, "The Compass IT Strategy Census 1996." Compass Analysis Canada Ltd. (Montreal, 1996). [On-line: http://www.compass-analysis.com]

Compass Analysis, "Measuring Value in IT." Compass Analysis Canada Ltd. (Montreal, 1997). [On-line: http://www.compass-analysis.com]

Computerworld, "Executive Report: CEOs Give Credit for Today but Expect More Tomorrow," April 17, 1989, 23-16:75-78.

Computerworld "Executive Report (CEO-CFO Survey): It's Reality Time." April 29, 1991, 25-17:81-83.

Computerworld, "Management Report (CEO-CFO Survey): Squeeze Play." April 19, 1993, 27-16:86-91.

Computerworld,. "The 1995 CEO/CFO Survey: Anxious Allies." Special Report, June 12, 1995, 29-24:5-9.

Cooper, Robert G., Edgett, Scott J. and Kleinschmidt, Elko J. *Portfolio Management for New Products*, second edition (Cambridge, MA: Perseus Publishing, 2001).

Dulaney, K. *Mobile Cost of Ownership: Higher Costs for Bigger Benefits*. Research Note; Equipment Asset Management Europe (EAME); Gartner Group, December 12, 1996.

Gibbs, W. Wayt. "Taking Computers to Task," *Scientific American,* July, 1997.

Gonsalves, Antone. "Analyst Predicts IT Spending Will Be Up Slightly in 2003," *InternetWeek*, December 20, 2002.

Green, Kenny. *Software Development Projects and Their Difficulties*. Cambridge, UK: Fitzwilliam College. [On-line:http://www.fitz.cam.ac.uk/~kg201/essays/software.html]

Halberstam, David. *The Reckoning* (New York: Avon Books, 1986).

Hamblen, Matt. "FAA's IT Management Slammed," *Computerworld*, February 10, 1997, p. 14.

Hamel, Gary and C.K. Prahalad. *Competing for the Future* (Boston: Harvard Business School Press, 1993).

Hammer, Michael. "News/Trends: Now Hear This," *Fortune*, October 4, 1993, p. 18.

Hammer, Michael and James Champy. *Reengineering the Corporation* (New York: Harper Business Publishing, 1993).

Harris, Catherine L. "Information Power: How Companies Are Using New Technologies to Gain a Competitive Edge," *Business Week*, October 14, 1985, p. 108.

Hubbard, Douglas W. "Risk vs. Return," *Informationweek*, June 30, 1997, p. 637. [On-line: http://techweb.cmp.com/iw/637/37iursk.html]

Jaques, Eliott and Steven Clement. *Executive Leadership: A Practical Guide to Managing Complexity* (Cason Hall & Co. Publishers, 1991).

Kaplan, Robert S. and David P. Norton. *The Balanced Scorecard: Translating Strategy into Action (*Boston: Harvard Business School Press, 1996).

King, Julia. "IS Reins in Runaway Projects," *Computerworld*, February 24, 1997, 31-8:1.

Kurtzman, Joel. "An Interview with Paul M. Romer," *Strategy & Business*, 1997, Issue 6, 91-101.

Lacity, Mary and Vicky Sauter. *Why General Managers Need to Understand Information Systems*. Saint-Louis: University of Missouri. [On-line: http://www.umsl.edu/~lacity/whymis.html]

Laracuenta R. and M. Pinckney. *Microsoft Vies for Suite Success with Office 97*. Research Note; InSide Gartner Group This Week (IGG); Gartner Group, February, 1997.

Lehr, Bill and Frank Lichtenberg. *Computer Use and Productivity Growth in Federal Government Agencies, 1987 to 1992* (New York: Graduate School of Business, Columbia University, 1996).

Lehr, Bill and Frank Lichtenberg. *Information Technology and Its Impact on Firm-Level Productivity: Evidence from Government and Private Data Sources, 1977-1993* (New York: Graduate School of Business, Columbia University, 1997).

Licht, Georg and Dietmar Moch. *Innovation and Information Technology in Services*. Mannheim, Germany: Center for European Economic Research, May 1997). [On-line: http://www.csls.ca/conf-pap/licht4.pdf]

Lichtenberg, Frank R. "The Output of Contributions of Computer Equipment and Personnel: A Firm-Level Analysis," *Economics of Innovation and New Technology*, 1995, 3: 201-217.

Lillrank, Paul, Marko Lehtovaara, not; Sami Holopainen and Seppo Sippa. *The Impact of Information and Communication Technologies (ICT) on Business Performance*. [June 1996, On-line: http://www.interactive.hut.fi/ict-bp/]

Magee, F. *Failure Management: Get It Right the Third Time*. Gartner Group, July 25, 1996.

Markus, M. Lynne and Robert I. Benjamin. "The Magic Bullet Theory in IT-Enabled Transformation," *Sloan Management Review*, Winter, 1997, pp. 55-68.

Martin, James. "Only the Cyber-Fit Will Survive," *Datamation*, November, 1996, 42-17: 60.

McKague, Anne. "Only IS Gets Away with Such Poor Service," *Computing Canada*, October 10, 1997, 22-21: 15.

McKenzie, Ray, and Fujitsu Consulting's Center for Strategic Leadership. *The Relationship-Based Enterprise* (Toronto: McGraw-Hill Ryerson, 2001).

Newsbytes News Network. "Global IT Spending Soars-European Report," April 14, 1997.

Nulden, Urban. *Escalation in IT Projects: Can We Affort to Quit or Do We Have to Continue?* Sweden: Department of Informatics, Goteborg University. [On-line: http://www.adb.gu.se/~nulden/Research/Esca/Esca.html]

Nulden, Urban. *Failing Projects: Harder To Abandon than To Continue*. Sweden: Department of Informatics, Goteborg University. [On-line http://www.adb.gu.se/~nulden/Research/Proj/Proj.pdf]

OASIG. *The performance of Information Technology and the role of human and orga-nizational factors.* Report to the Economic and Social Research Council of UK (Version 1.0), January 1996. [On-line: ftp://ftp.shef.ac.uk/pub/uni/academic/I-M/iwp/itperf.doc]

Peltu, Malcolm. *Minimizing the Risks of ICT Failures Having Catastrophic Consequences.* IEE Colloquium on Human, Organization and Technical Challenges in the Firm of the Future (Digest #1996/050/P 6/4). London, England: The Institution of Electrical Engineers, 1996.

Pepper, Jon. "The MIS Battle for the Skies: American and United Fight for Air Supremacy with High-Stakes Investments in IT," *Informationweek,* 1991, 307: 44.

Porter, Michael E. "What is Strategy?" *Harvard Business Review,* November-December, 1996, 61-78.

Prince, C.J. "IT's elusive ROI," *Chief Executive,* April, 1997, 122: 12-13.

Rai, Arun, Patnayakuni Ravi and Patnayakuni Nainika. "Technology Investment and Business Perfomance," *Communications of the ACM,* July, 1997, 40-7: 89-97.

Rapaport, Richard. "To Build a Winning Team: An Interview with Head Coach Bill Walsh," *Harvard Business Review,* January-February, 1993, pp. 111-120.

Reimus, Byron. "The IT System That Couldn't Deliver," *Harvard Business Review,* May-June, 1997, 22-35.

Rifkin, Glenn. "CEOs give credit for today but expect more tomorrow," *Computerworld,* October 31, 1989, p.21.

Rifkin, Jeremy. *The End of Work: The Decline of the Global Labor Force and the Dawn of the Post-Market Era* (New York: Putnam Publishing Group, 1995).

Sacramento Bee, "A $115 Million Flop," March 12, 1993, B7.

San Francisco Chronicle, "London Ditches Computer," March 12, 1993, D8.

Sauer, Christopher and Philip W. Yetton. *Steps to the Future: Fresh Thinking on the Management of IT-Based Organizational Transformation* (San Francisco: Jossey-Bass Publishers, 1997).

SBT Accounting Systems. *Futz Factor Computer User Survey.* San Rafael, California: Software Business Technologies, 1997 November 17 [On-line: http://www.sbt.com/whoissbt/index.html]

Schloh, Michael. *The Denver International Airport Automated Baggage Handling System.* Computer Science Department, School of Engineering, California Polytechnic State University, 1996. [On-line: http://www.csc.calpoly.edu/~dstearns/Schloh Project/csc463.html]

SCO. *True Cost of PCs at Work: Up to Three Weeks Lost Working Time per Employee Every Year.* News Release from SCO Press Room (Santa Cruz, California, September 19, 1997). [On-line: http://www.sco.com/press/release/6651.html]

Scott Morton, Michael. *The Corporation of the 1990s: Information Technology and Organizational Transformation* (New York: Oxford University Press, 1991).

Seldes, George. *The Great Quotations* (New York: Pocket Books, 1967).

Senge, Peter M. *The Fifth Discipline* (New York: Currency Doubleday Publishers, 1990).

Stewart, B. *Enterprise Performance through IT* (Gartner Group, Gartner IT Expo, Florida, Conference Paper, 1996).

Strassmann, Paul A. "Will Big Spending on Computers Guarantee Profitability?" *Datamation,* 1997, 43-2: 75-85.

Strassmann, Paul A. *The Squandered Computer: Evaluating the Business Alignment of Information Technologies* (New Canaan, Conn.: The Information Economics Press). [On-line: http://www.strassmann.com]

Tapscott, Don. *The Digital Economy* (New York: McGraw-Hill, 1996).

U.S. Department of Transportation. *New Denver Airport: Impact of the Delayed Baggage System.* Report # GAO/RCED-95-35BR. Washington, D.C.: Bureau of Transportation Statistics, 1994.

U.S. Department of Transportation. *Report to the Honorable Frank R. Wolf, Chairman Subcommittee on Transportation and Related Agencies, Committee on Appropriations, House of Representatives (Concerning FAA Aviation Acquisition and the Advanced Automation System Project).* Report # GAO/RCED-96-159. Washington, D.C.: United States General Accounting Office, 1996.

Violino, Bob. "Return on Investment," *Informationweek,* June 30, 1997, 637: 36-44.

Willcocks, Leslie and Catherine Griffiths. "Predicting Risk of Failure in Large-Scale Information Technology Projects," *Technological Forecasting and Social Change,* 1994, 47: 205-228.

Woodall, Pam. "Survey of the World Economy: The Hitchhiker's Guide to Cybernomics," *The Economist,* September 28, 1996.

Zuboff, Shoshana. *In the Age of the Smart Machine: The Future of Work and Power* (New York: Basic Books, 1988).

Supplementary Readings

Beck, Nuala. *Shifting Gears: Thriving in the New Economy* (Toronto: Harper Perennial, 1993).

Betts, Mitch. "Drop That Mouse! The Boss is Coming!" *Computerworld,* January 23, 1995, pp. 29-34.

Davenport, T.H. *Process Innovation: Reengineering Work Through Information Technology* (Boston: Harvard Business School Press, 1993).

David, Paul A. "The Dynamo and the Computer: An Historical Perspective on the Modern Productivity Paradox," *American Economic Review,* May, 1990, 80-2: 355-361.

Griliches, Zvi. "Productivity, R&D and the Data Constraint," *American Economic Review,* March 1994, 84-1: 1-23.

Information Society Project Office. *Information Technologies, Productivity and Employment,* Report to the Directorate General III; European Commission. [On-line: http://www.ispo.cec.be/infosoc/promo/pubs/ prodemo.html]

Jorgensen, Dale W. and Kevin Stiroh. "Computers and Growth," *Economics of Innovation and New Technology,* December, 1994, 295-316.

Keen, Peter G. *Shaping the Future: Business Design through Information Technology,* (Boston: Harvard Business School Press, 1991).

Lafleur, Brenda and Peter Lok. *Jobs in the Knowledge-Based Economy: Information Technology and the Impact on Employment* (Ottawa: The Conference Board of Canada, 1997).

Nakamura, Leonard I. *Is US Economic Performance Really that Bad?* (Federal Reserve Bank of Philadelphia Research Working Paper No. 95/21, October, 1995).

Tapscott, Don and Art Caston. *Paradigm Shift: The New Promise of Information Technology* (New York: McGraw-Hill, 1993).

Van Ark, Bart, Erik Monnikhof and Nanno Mulder. *Productivity and Innovation in Services: An International Comparison Perspective.* Conference on Service Sector Productivity and the Productivity Paradox. (Ottawa: Centre for the Study of Living Standards, April 11-12, 1997).

Weber State University. *Measurements for Information Technology* (Ogden, Utah: Department of Information Systems & Technologies, 1996). [On-line: http://www.weber.edu/IST/ITFM/measure.html]

INDEX

Accountability 86, 87, 140, 150, 157-78, 183, 185, 186, 190, 194, 199, 202, 207

Activist accountability 2, 35, 41, 45, 51, 63, 154, 175, 225, 248, 253

Alberta Pool 32-34

Alignment 41, 52, 76, 101, 113, 115, 129, 151, 168, 181, 188, 197, 234, 246, 248, 253

Amazon.com 19, 29

Ares. *See* Four ares.

Assessing program value 71, 75-76, 101, 115

Assumptions 48, 49, 50, 55, 92, 93, 123, 242, 253

Austin, T. (Gartner) 10,

Automation of work 1, 7, 13, 15-16, 20, 25, 27, 30, 34, 51, 63, 66, 75, 129, 149, 180, 208, 227, 253

Ayres, Rand 33, 34

Balanced Scorecard 76, 80, 179, 182, 186, 189, 195, 196, 253

Bank of America 98-99, 212

Barclays Bank 217-18

Barratt, Don 218

Benefits
  harvesting 139, 151-52, 153, 175, 193, 248, 254
  mind-set 38, 46
  plateau 89-90, 259
  Realization Approach 1, 2, 31, 33-34, 35, 37-62, 68, 69, 70, 74, 77, 78, 81, 85, 91, 96, 97-98, 99, 100, 102, 106, 109, 123, 128, 138, 139, 142, 151, 154, 155-56, 169, 170, 173, 175, 176, 177, 178, 179, 181, 182-83, 185, 188, 189, 193, 194, 195, 196, 197, 198, 199, 201, 202, 203, 205, 213, 214, 215, 216-17, 219-20, 221, 222, 225, 227, 228, 229, 231, 232, 235, 236, 238, 239, 240, 241, 242, 244, 245, 247, 248, 249, 250, 251, 252, 254

Benjamin, Robert I. 21

Berg, T. 73

Bezos, Jeff 29

Blended investment programs 2, 42, 43-44, 45, 50, 55, 61, 71, 77, 79, 84, 86, 94, 95-96, 102, 105, 107, 109-110, 117, 129, 138, 143, 148-49, 151, 165, 167, 175, 176, 181, 183, 187, 190, 192, 198, 202, 206, 207, 210, 212, 214, 223, 228, 229, 233, 236, 243, 244, 250, 251

Boeing Company, The 109, 123, 124, 127-28, 212, 218-20, 254, 259

BPR. *See* Business Process Re-engineering.

Bridges, William 212

BTOPP business system 72-74, 75, 78, 80-81, 94, 95, 101, 105, 108, 148, 149, 182, 183, 193, 205, 206, 233, 244

Business cases 20, 21-22, 26, 31, 32, 50, 78, 88, 106, 108, 112, 130, 132, 135, 227, 251, 254

Business process re-engineering (BPR) 21, 40, 55, 56, 74, 95-96, 125, 127, 161, 171, 181, 182, 187, 188, 195, 254, 260

Business sponsors 41, 86-87, 101-2, 119, 136, 138, 142, 143, 150, 156, 159, 162-63, 166, 167, 169-71, 172, 173, 174, 175, 176, 177, 178, 197, 202-3, 205, 212, 223, 231, 232, 234, 235-36, 237, 238, 239, 240, 241, 243, 244, 246, 254

Business transformation 1, 14, 18-19, 21, 22, 26, 27, 28, 30, 34, 35, 37, 54, 62, 63, 66, 75, 94, 100, 106, 129, 131, 149, 153, 158, 175, 177, 187, 190, 208, 209, 228, 229, 230, 231, 233, 236, 254

Change management. *See* Proactive management of change.

CIS. *See* Customer information systems.

Clement, Stephen D. 159, 163, 171

Client stories 30-32, 54, 58-59, 94, 109, 123, 151, 175, 196, 214,

Client stories (cont'd) 230-34, 38, 54, 56-61, 74, 75, 94, 109, 151-53, 166, 230
Alberta Pool 32-34
Bank of America 98-99, 212
Barclays Bank 217-18
Boeing Company, The 109, 123, 124, 127-28, 212, 218-20, 254, 259
Ericsson 38, 56-57, 74
Montreal Urban Community Police Service 215-17
National Bank of Canada 59-60, 212
Nova Gas Transmission (NGT) 52, 103-4, 106-7, 109, 112, 115, 123, 124-27, 131, 142-43, 148, 151-53, 166, 175-76, 196-98, 230, 243
Oregon Department of Transportation (ODOT) 47, 48, 109, 123, 124-27
Qantas Airways 220-22
Quebec Workers Compensation Board 60-61
Royale Belge 95-96
SaskTel 99-100
Sollac 57-58
SUNCORP-Metway 74-75, 96-98
Competing for the Future 19
Computerworld 8, 12
Concept to cash 39, 42, 44, 101, 132, 177, 198
Conditions. *See* Necessary conditions.
Continuous improvement 182, 195, 196, 255
Contribution 48, 49, 50, 55, 123, 242, 255
Coote, Bob 152
Core components of program management 70-93, 94, 101, 115, 161, 177, 236-37
Core elements of benefits realization 48, 49, 50, 55
Corniou, Jean-Pierre 58
Corporation in the 1990s, The 4, 72
Critical dimensions. *See* dimensions of complexity.
Customer information system (CIS) 67, 84-85, 88, 92, 114, 255

Defining program scope 70, 71-75, 77, 80-81, 94, 101, 161, 177, 236-37
Delphi analysis 115, 255
Denver International Airport 12
Design to delivery 39, 132
Designing and managing programs 71, 77-93, 101
Dimensions of complexity 23-28, 34, 48, 72-73, 77, 78, 79, 81, 83, 84, 87-91, 94, 104, 134, 139, 141, 155, 180, 182, 183, 186, 193, 198, 199, 205, 206, 207-14, 223
Doyle, Bevan 70
Duchesneau, Jacques 215-17

Economic Value Added (EVA) 8, 76, 255
Economist, The 5
Edison, Thomas A. 6
Education Department of Western Australia 69-70
EIS. *See* executive information systems
Electronic commerce 6, 18, 28, 51, 120, 233, 255
Enterprise application packages 30, 33, 87, 89, 103, 137, 233, 236, 256
Ericsson 38, 56-57, 74
EVA. *See* Economic Value Added.
Executive Leadership 159, 163

Fifth Discipline, The 35, 161
Financial worth 76, 101, 113-14, 115, 117-19, 181, 197, 246, 256
Forslund, Patrick 57
Four "ares", the 52, 35, 51-53, 75-76, 101, 112, 113, 114-18, 129, 133, 136, 149-50, 169, 181, 197, 231, 232, 233-35, 241, 256
Four Ps 212, 239, 241
Fee-for all 2, 30, 43, 105, 129, 251
Full cycle governance 2, 35, 40, 41, 42, 44-45, 46, 62, 63, 64, 130, 131-54, 155, 158, 163, 165, 166, 175, 176, 177, 178, 179, 181, 182, 186, 195, 196, 198, 199, 203, 205, 213, 225, 228, 229-30, 231, 232, 233, 235, 236, 237, 238, 241, 242, 256
Fundamentals 2, 35, 40, 42-45, 63-155
Futzing 10, 256

Galbraith, John Kenneth 211
Gartner group reports 4, 10, 73
Gibbs, Wayt 5

Hamel, Gary 19
Hammer, Michael 211
Harris Research 10
Hawthorne, Edward 98
Holser, Michael 128
Houle, Jean 61
Huet, Eric 95

Information management 1, 14, 16-
    17, 20, 63, 66, 75, 94, 129, 149,
    208, 228, 256
Initiative 48, 49, 50, 55, 94, 123, 188,
    199, 203, 205, 223, 224, 230, 233,
    234, 242, 244, 257
Investment decision board (IDB) 135,
    150-51, 152, 155, 165-68, 169, 170,
    171, 174, 178, 196, 197, 198, 237,
    238-39, 240, 242, 243, 246, 247,
    248, 257
Ismael, Candace 128
IT-enabled business transformation
    21, 22, 26, 28, 35, 54, 62, 106, 131,
    153, 158, 177, 186, 211, 249, 250,
    251, 252, 257

Jaques, Elliott 159, 163, 171
Just-in-time (JIT) 18, 33, 257

Kaplan, Robert S. 76, 80, 179, 182,
    186, 195, 253
Kearney, A. T. reports 8
Kettering, Charles F. 203
King, Julia 12
Knowledge economy 1, 10, 21, 28-29,
    3o, 34, 35, 37, 51, 91, 154, 165,
    190, 208, 248, 250, 257
Knowledge workers 10, 34, 258

Learning lags 5, 6, 20, 34, 63, 89, 90,
    106-7, 205, 258
Linkage 23, 27-28, 34, 77, 78, 81, 83,
    84, 94, 104, 134, 139, 141, 155,
    182, 183, 186, 193, 198, 199, 205,
    206, 207, 208, 213, 223, 258
London Stock Exchange/Taurus 12,
    203-4, 205
Lulay, Tom 125

Managing Transitions 212
Markus, M. Lynne 21
Maynard, Luc 56, 74
McCurry, Kelly 100
McNaught, Bruce 153, 175-76, 198
McRae, Jay 125
Measurement. *See* Relevant measure-
    ment.
MEDIC 190-92
Mind-set 1, 20, 23, 34, 37, 53, 55, 63,
    71, 106-7, 109, 133, 154, 158, 177,
    225, 238, 250
Montreal Urban Community Police
    Service 215-17

National Bank of Canada 59-60, 212
Necessary conditions 2, 35, 41, 45-46,
    63, 154, 155-224, 253
New York Stock Exchange 204, 205
Norton, David P. 76, 80, 179, 182,
    186, 195, 253
Nova Gas Transmission (NGT) 52,
    103-4, 106-7, 109, 112, 115, 123,
    131, 142-43, 148, 151-53, 166, 175-
    76, 196-98, 230, 243

Oregon Department of Transportation
    (ODOT) 47, 48, 109, 123, 124-27
Outcomes 48, 49, 50, 55, 92, 94, 123,
    140, 182, 183, 184, 185, 186, 187,
    188, 189, 191-92, 193, 198, 207,
    223, 224, 233, 242, 244, 258
Ownership 41, 45, 46, 86, 87, 142,
    159, 162, 167, 177, 202, 205, 235

Palmer, Gary 219-20
People 24-25, 27-28, 34, 72-73, 78,
    79, 83, 84, 87-88, 104, 134, 139,
    141, 155, 183, 186, 199, 205, 206,
    210-13, 207, 208, 215, 223, 259
Piette, André 60
Plateau. *See* Benefits plateau.
Porter, Michael 149
Portfolio management 2, 35, 40, 41,
    42, 43-44, 62, 63, 64, 102, 103-130,
    132, 145-49, 151, 153, 155, 158,
    163, 165, 167, 181, 198, 199, 203,
    223, 225, 228, 229-30, 231, 232,
    233, 237, 236, 238, 243, 247, 248,
    250, 251, 259
Prahalad, C. K. 18

Proactive management of change 2, 35, 41, 46, 53, 63, 119-20, 130, 139, 140, 154, 156, 199, 201-24, 225, 239, 248, 259

Program management 2, 35, 40, 41, 42-43, 44, 51, 62, 63, 64, 65-102, 130, 132, 139, 144, 155, 158, 166, 168, 171-73, 174, 177, 178, 181, 197, 198, 199, 203, 205, 223, 225, 228, 229, 231, 232, 234, 235, 236, 237, 238, 239, 240, 242-47, 245, 246, 247, 248, 251, 259

Progressive resource commitment (stage gates) 2, 44, 64, 130, 133, 136-45, 153-54, 163, 225-26, 233, 259

Project management 2, 22, 39, 41, 66-69, 71, 131, 132, 135, 138, 144, 145, 154, 158, 168, 172-74, 193, 203, 223, 227, 228, 229, 230, 233, 234, 237, 242, 245, 247, 259

Qantas Airways 220-22
Quebec Workers Compensation Board 60-61

Reach 23, 27-28, 34, 79, 83, 84, 104, 134, 141, 155, 183, 186, 199, 205, 206, 207-10, 215, 223, 260

Relevant measurement 2, 35, 41, 45, 51, 63, 140, 154, 155, 179-99, 225, 242, 260

Results Chain 34, 35, 47-51, 53, 55, 59, 60, 61, 68, 74, 77, 78, 80, 81, 82, 83, 84, 87, 88-89, 90, 92, 94, 95-96, 97, 98, 99, 100, 110, 114, 120, 123, 124, 125, 127, 128, 129, 139, 140, 143, 147, 155, 161, 167, 170, 171, 175, 177, 181, 183-86, 187, 188, 189, 190, 191, 193, 195, 196, 197, 198, 202, 207, 210, 212, 215, 216, 217, 218, 219, 223, 229, 241, 242, 243, 244, 245, 251, 260

Risk 76, 78, 101, 110, 114-19, 129-30, 142, 151, 168, 181, 197, 234, 246, 248, 250, 260

Royale Belge 95-96
Runaway projects 11, 229, 251

Salow, Robert 4
SaskTel 99-100

SBT Accounting Systems 10
Scientific American 5
Scope. *See* Defining program scope.
Scott Morton, Michael 4, 6, 7, 13, 72, 206
Senge, Peter 35, 161
Seven plus one key conditions of activist accountability 158, 160-65, 170, 177
Silver bullet thinking 21, 22, 30, 34, 35, 37, 50, 53, 54, 66, 134, 158, 204, 236, 260
Singapore TradeNet 204-5
Singleton, Neil 75, 97
Sloan, Alfred 203
Sloan *Management Review* 21
Sollac 57-58
Squandered Computer, The 4
Stage gates 2, 44, 64, 130, 133, 136-45, 153-54, 158, 178, 181, 198, 203, 205, 242, 260
Stages of IT evolution 1, 13-20, 21, 22, 25, 26, 27, 28, 30, 34, 35, 37, 51, 54, 62, 63, 66, 75, 94, 100, 106, 129, 131, 149, 153, 158, 175, 177, 180, 187, 190, 208, 209, 227, 228, 229, 230, 231, 233, 236, 253, 254
Standish Group (reports) 12
Stewart, B. (Gartner) 4
Stoffles, Adrian 69
Stout, Kathy 99
Strassmann, Paul A. 4, 8, 9
SUNCORP-Metway 74-75, 96-98

Taurus. *See* London Stock Exchange/Taurus.
Three necessary conditions. *See* Necessary Conditions.
Three fundamentals. *See* Fundamentals.
Three core components of program management. *See* Core components.
Time 26, 27-28, 34, 78, 79, 84, 88-91, 104, 134, 141, 155, 180, 183, 186, 199, 205, 206, 213-14, 215, 223, 261
Total Quality Management (TQM) 182, 188, 195, 196, 255, 261
TradeNet. *See* Singapore TradeNet.
Traynor, Dave 100

Truman, Harry S. 157
Turner, Lawrie 220-22

Value
    assessment 1, 14, 16-17, 20, 35, 46,
        50, 52, 51-53, 63-64, 66, 71, 75-
        76, 94, 101, 112, 113, 114-18,
        129, 133, 136, 149-50, 169, 181,
        197, 208, 228, 231, 232, 233-35,
        241, 256, 261
    cases 110, 112-17, 129, 130, 133,
        135, 136, 141, 153, 167, 172,
        177, 181, 199, 207, 237, 239,
        240, 246, 247, 248, 251, 261

    management office (VMO) 135,
        150-51, 152, 155, 165-66, 168-
        69, 172, 174, 178, 195, 237,
        239-40, 242, 244, 248, 261

Walsh, Bill 214
Whitehead, Tom 106-7, 151-52, 197,
    198
Woodall, Pam 5

Zuboff, Shoshana 12